SKILLS, WAGES,
and
PRODUCTIVITY
in the Service Sector

edited by
THIERRY NOYELLE

**Conservation of Human Resources
Studies in the New Economy**

WESTVIEW PRESS

Skills, Wages, and Productivity in the Service Sector

Conservation of Human Resources
Studies in the New Economy

Skills, Wages, and Productivity in the Service Sector, edited by Thierry Noyelle

Does Job Training Work? The Clients Speak Out, Eli Ginzberg, Terry Williams, and Anna Dutka

New York's Financial Markets: The Challenges of Globalization, edited by Thierry Noyelle

Immigrant and Native Workers: Contrasts and Competition, Thomas R. Bailey

Beyond Industrial Dualism: Market and Job Segmentation in the New Economy, Thierry Noyelle

Computerization and the Transformation of Employment: Government, Hospitals, and Universities, Thomas M. Stanback, Jr.

Technology and Employment: Concepts and Clarifications, Eli Ginzberg, Thierry Noyelle, and Thomas M. Stanback, Jr.

Skills, Wages, and Productivity in the Service Sector

EDITED BY

Thierry Noyelle

WESTVIEW PRESS

BOULDER • SAN FRANCISCO • OXFORD

Conservation of Human Resources Studies in the New Economy

This Westview softcover edition is printed on acid-free paper and bound in library-quality, coated covers that carry the highest rating of the National Association of State Textbook Administrators, in consultation with the Association of American Publishers and the Book Manufacturers' Institute.

Published in 1990 in the United States of America by Westview Press, Inc., 5500 Central Avenue, Boulder, Colorado 80301, and in the United Kingdom by Westview Press, 36 Lonsdale Road, Summertown, Oxford OX2 7EW

Library of Congress Cataloging-in-Publication Data
Skills, wages, and productivity in the service sector / edited by
  Thierry Noyelle.
    p. cm.—(Conservation of Human Resources studies in the new
economy)
  Includes bibliographical references and index.
  ISBN 0-8133-1078-4
  1. Service industries—United States—Labor productivity.
2. Wages—Service industries—United States. 3. Service industries
workers—United States. I. Noyelle, Thierry J. II. Series.
HD9981.5.S54 1990
331.11'8—dc20   90-12397
                                                          CIP

Printed and bound in the United States of America

The paper used in this publication meets the requirements
of the American National Standard for Permanence of Paper
for Printed Library Materials Z39.48-1984.

10   9   8   7   6   5   4   3   2   1

Contents

List of Tables   vii
Acknowledgments   xi

1   Overview, *Thierry Noyelle*   1

2   Emerging Patterns of Work, *Susan Christopherson*   11

3   Shifts in Employment, Occupational Structure, and Educational Attainment, *Eileen Appelbaum and Peter Albin*   31

4   A Special Focus on Employment Growth in Business Services and Retail Trade, *Robert Bednarzik*   67

5   The Changing Face of Retailing, *Thomas M. Stanback, Jr.*   80

6   Business Services: Accounting, Management Consulting, and Computer Software, *Thierry Noyelle*   122

7   Adult Education and Training Markets, *Nevzer Stacey and Duc-Le To*   160

8   Productivity in Services: A Valid Measure of Economic Performance? *Thomas M. Stanback, Jr., and Thierry Noyelle*   187

9   Toward a New Labor Market Segmentation, *Thierry Noyelle*   212

10   Conclusion, *Thierry Noyelle*   225

About the Contributors   233
Index   234

Tables

2.1   Age and Gender Composition of the Part-Time
       Work Force, 1987   14

2.2   Percentage Distribution of Workers in All
       Industries and in the Temporary Help Industry by
       Selected Characteristics, May 1985   18

2.3   Self-Employed as a Percentage of the Labor Force
       by Gender, 1975 and 1985   19

2.4   Self-Employed as a Percentage of the Labor Force
       by Gender and Race, 1985   20

3.1   Percentage Distribution of Employed Civilians by
       Industry and Gender, 1987   35

3.2   Percentage Distribution of Gross Domestic Product
       by Industry, 1973, 1979, and 1987   35

3.3   Average Annual Rates of Growth of Gross Domestic
       Product by Industry, 1973–1979 and 1979–1987   36

3.4   Percentage Distribution of Employment
       and Employment Growth by Industry, 1973,
       1979, and 1987   37

3.5   Median Annual Earnings of Wage and Salary
       Workers, 1986   40

3.6   Labor Force Characteristics by Sector, 1987   42

3.7   Labor Force Characteristics by Industry, 1973   47

3.8   Labor Force Characteristics by Industry, 1987   48

3.9   Earnings of Wage and Salary Workers, 1987   49

3.10   Occupational Distribution of Employment by
       Industry, 1987   53

3.11   Occupational Characteristics, 1987   55

3.12   Occupational Characteristics by Gender, 1987   57

3.13   Percentage Distribution of the Educational
       Attainment of the U.S. Labor Force, 1973
       and 1987   58

3.14   Increase in Employment of College Graduates,
       1973–1987   61

3.15   Ratio of Industry Share of College Graduates to
       Industry Share of Total Employment, 1973, 1979,
       and 1987   62
       APPENDIX: Census Codes of Industries Listed in the Tables 66

4.1   Number and Percentage Distribution of Jobs by
       Major Industry, 1987, and Net Changes, 1986–1987   68
4.2   Number of U.S. Jobs by Detailed Industry, 1973,
       1979, and 1987   70
4.3   Number and Percentage Distribution of Jobs in
       Business Services, 1987, and Net Changes,
       1973–1987   73
4.4   Number of Jobs in U.S. Business Services
       Industry, 1973, 1979, 1982, and 1987   75
4.5   Number and Percentage Distribution of Jobs in
       Retail Trade, 1987, and Net Changes, 1973–1987   76
4.6   Number of Jobs in U.S. Retail Industry, 1973,
       1979, and 1987   77

5.1   Sales and Annual Sales Growth of Selected
       Publicly Held Retailers, 1987 and 1978–1987   82
5.2   Percentage of Employment Held by Women and
       Minorities, Three Retailers   117

6.1   Employment Growth in Business and Related Services,
       1970–1986   124
6.2   Annual Receipts of Business and Related Services,
       1980–1986   124
6.3   Worldwide and U.S. Revenues of Accounting,
       Management Consulting, and Software, 1983–1987   128
6.4   Eight Largest Accounting Firms Worldwide, 1988   129
6.5   Twenty Largest Management Consulting Firms, 1987   130
6.6   The Top Fifteen Software Companies, 1985, 1986   131
6.7   The Top Fifteen Service Companies, 1985, 1986   131

7.1   Number and Percentage Distribution of
       Occurrences of Training by Type and Source of
       Training and by Occupation, 1983   162
7.2   Number and Percentage Distribution of
       Occurrences of School Training by Type and
       Source of Training and by Occupation, 1983   164

7.3   Number and Percentage Distribution of Adult
       Education Courses Provided by Educational
       Institutions and Nonschool Providers by Type
       and Job-Related Status, 1978 and 1984   166

7.4   Number of Institutions and Participants Engaged
       in Postsecondary Education, Various Years,
       1978–1987   168

7.5   Female/Male Training Participation Ratio by
       Education, Race, Occupation, and Industry, 1981   179

8.1   Average Annual Rates of Change in GDP per Worker
       in Seven OECD Countries: Agriculture, Industry,
       and Services, 1960–1985, 1979–1985   188

8.2   Methods for Estimating Constant Dollar Gross
       Product Originating in Goods-Producing Sectors
       and Selected Services   191

8.3   Bureau of Economic Analysis Methods of
       Estimation of Real Gross Product Originating in
       Service Industries   192

8.4   Methods Used to Obtain Value-Added at Constant
       Prices for Market Services   194

8.5   Selected Indices of Output per Employee,
       Compensation per Employee, and Capital
       Consumption to Labor Compensation in the
       United States, Japan, and Germany, 1975, 1980, 1985   198

8.6   A Simple Hypothetical Model Comparing U.S. and
       European Growth   206

Acknowledgments

This book is based on a report prepared for the Center for Educational Research and Innovation of the Organization for Economic Cooperation and Development as part of a multicountry program of research on skill changes and skill formation in the service sectors.

The bulk of the research presented in this book was financed by a grant from the International Labor Affairs Bureau and the Women's Bureau of the U.S. Department of Labor. In addition, Thomas Stanback's research on the retailing sector benefited from supplemental funding from the Centre d'Etudes et de Recherches sur l'Emploi et les Qualifications (France); my chapter on business services was financed by the National Center on Education and Employment, Teachers College, Columbia University, under a grant from the Office of Educational Research and Improvement of the U.S. Department of Education; and my chapter on labor market segmentation was prepared under funding from the Ford Foundation. The chapters by Nevzer Stacey and Duc-Le To and by Robert Bednarzik were prepared as part of the authors' ongoing research for the U.S. departments of education and labor. We are grateful to each of these institutions for their support and belief in the importance of and need for the research presented here.

The usual disclaimer applies. Statements, findings, conclusions, and recommendations presented in the book are solely those of the authors and do not represent the official views of the agencies or organizations named above.

Thierry Noyelle

1

Overview

Thierry Noyelle

Increasing competition, the rise of the services, and the rapid diffusion of computerized technologies are developments that have each contributed to a profound transformation in the nature of work, the demand for skills, and the structure of labor markets in the United States. In this book, eight labor market economists and educational analysts look at the implications of this transformation for skills, wage distribution, and productivity. The authors suggest that a new "human economy" is now taking shape, one that is remarkably different from that of the postwar decades.

Consider only a few of the findings that are presented in this book. Once numerically dominant, adult white male workers have become a minority in the U.S. work force, although one that, admittedly, retains enormous control over certain labor market outcomes. Labor market bonds between employers and employees that once favored lifetime attachments have loosened dramatically for large segments of the labor force. Paralleling these two developments, wage distribution is changing, productivity growth in the services appears to be stagnating, and educational preparation and lifelong training are taking on an importance unequaled in the past, for both individuals and firms.

Much of the research presented in this book confirms findings by others showing that the need for the up-skilling of the labor force has become one of the most critical challenges facing the U.S. economy if it is to retain its competitiveness and sustain its growth through the 1990s and beyond. And, as is suggested by the study of retailing presented in Chapter 5, these are challenges not only for the firms and workers in the high-skilled sectors of the economy but also for those in sectors often viewed, perhaps too simplistically, as "low-skilled."

The fact that the ongoing skill transformation and the new needs for skill preparation are occurring within a labor market context that is

1

profoundly different from that of the recent past presents the U.S. economy not only with new opportunities but also with new risks, especially in addressing the nagging issues of inequality among different groups of workers.

As shown by several of the contributors to this book, the record of improvement of women and minority workers relative to white men during the 1980s remains mixed. By some measures, women and minority groups have continued to improve their position in terms of educational attainment and occupational achievement during the 1980s. Yet, wage differentials between white men and these two groups remain very large, even for those employed in similar occupations. In addition, the record of access to firm-based training by certain groups of workers may be questionable.

Indeed, by some measures, wage disparities would appear to have widened during the 1980s. There is also, if only anecdotal, evidence that large firms, which in the past may have been willing to assist certain groups of workers with remedial training, are shying away from such practice, perhaps because increased competition makes it increasingly difficult for them to recover the costs of such investment. Likewise, there is some evidence suggesting that the hiring and promotional practices of large firms in some of the newer service sectors in regard to women and minority workers continue to trail behind those in older sectors. Finally, there is evidence suggesting that, while women and minority workers may be catching up with white men in terms of formal educational preparation, at times doing even better than white men do, firm-based training practices remain biased toward white men, at least in the aggregate. How much this development results from the fact that firms differentiate increasingly between "core" and "contingent" workers— with women and minority workers often dominant among the latter— remains unclear, however. For that matter, the evidence presented in several of the following chapters is, at times, contradictory.

Nowhere in this report do the authors propose a definitive assessment of these trends and their possible long-range implications for the economy. This is so in part because many of the developments underway are not clear-cut and because hard data are typically lacking to venture a more sure-footed reading of current trends. Yet everyone would agree that the ongoing restructuring of labor markets will likely force us to recast our equal employment opportunity (EEO) policy, if such a policy is to be effective in the 1990s. In this respect, if access to training is increasingly central to determining current and future employment opportunities and if access to firm-based or firm-sponsored training is unequal, one could envision an EEO policy for the 1990s that places a more direct focus on training than in the past. The EEO policy put in place in the 1970s aimed to entice, and, if necessary, force companies to bring the gender and race composition of their occupational distribution in line with the composition of the aggregate labor market. The new policy, which would complement, though obviously not abrogate, the old policy, could demand that firms keep a record of their training expenditures, show how their training dollars are distributed among gender and race groups, and improve their practices if the distribution of their training dollars proves uneven.

Clearly, addressing these and other labor market issues in the 1990s will not be trivial. But our willingness to do so will say much as to whether as a society we are willing to confront and, ultimately, resolve some of the disturbing developments that may have accompanied the shift to the new economy.

In Chapter 2, Susan Christopherson examines some of the factors that have given rise to new work patterns, new employment relationships, and new labor market groups in the U.S. economy in recent years. These new groups—often called "contingent workers"—include many who are employed part-time, as self-employed workers, as leased workers, by temporary work agencies, or as high-turnover, full-time employees. For all, a common characteristic is the often highly ad hoc and temporary nature of their implicit "work contract" with employers.

Christopherson stipulates that several major factors have contributed to the rise of these new labor market groups. On the labor demand side, there has been a growing pressure on firms to control costs and a parallel pressure on them to achieve and retain greater flexibility in mix of skills, both of which are a result of increasing competition. On the supply side, there has been a dramatic transformation of the labor supply, including a phenomenal rise in the labor force participation of women and a reconfiguration of the youth labor supply. In the process of analyzing these factors, Christopherson tries to move beyond a strand of analysis which, more often than not, has tended to oversimplify the reasons for the shift toward a more "flexible" U.S. labor force, by focusing excessively on the need for controlling labor costs.

Christopherson is careful to point out that the rise of contingent employment is not unique to the service sectors but is pervasive throughout the economy. She also is careful to stress that some of the patterns of contingent employment that emerged during the 1980s or earlier, under conditions of widespread labor surpluses, are likely to be transformed in the 1990s as the U.S. economy shifts to an era characterized by an aging labor force and recurring labor shortages. Nevertheless, she presents an equally convincing case that, contrary to the views developed by some economists, the restructuring of the labor market around contingent labor is not simply a cyclical development but a structural phenomenon that is likely to stay with us.

In Chapter 3, Eileen Appelbaum and Peter Albin present an extensive analysis of changes in employment characteristics over the last two decades based on data from the *Current Population Survey* (CPS). The wealth of their empirical findings makes it difficult to do justice to their chapter in just a few sentences. Nevertheless, a few key points can be highlighted.

Noting their dissatisfaction with both "postindustrial society" and "deindustrialization" theories of the transformation of the U.S. economy, Appelbaum and Albin propose to analyze recent changes by means of a taxonomy that cuts across the goods and service sectors, rather than between the two sectors. Their taxonomy, which is based on their earlier research for the Office of Technology Assessment of the U.S. Congress, establishes a distinction between sectors with high "information and knowledge" intensity. Using CPS data, the authors note important differences in occupational distribution and educational requirements between the information and knowledge intensive sectors and the other sectors within both goods-producing and service industries. Furthermore, they note that while information and knowledge services have generated more than 9 million new jobs since 1973 and absorbed more than 5.7 million college-educated workers, typically at earnings that compare favorably with those in the older manufacturing sectors, the other services have added 11.2 million jobs over the same time period. However, 7.7 million of these jobs have been in sectors in which median earnings of full-time workers in 1986 were one-third or less below the median for the older manufacturing sectors, and in which the proportion of part-time jobs ranged from 25 to 40 percent of employment. In addition, the shift in employment growth toward the non-information and knowledge intensive service sectors is one that has accelerated during the 1980s, partly because in contrast to the 1970s, the older manufacturing sectors have been net losers, not net gainers of jobs in recent years.

The authors' opinion is that such a shift has resulted in increasing the economic dualism of the U.S economy. In concluding, Appelbaum and Albin venture to ask what the long-term impact on the U.S. economy might be if an expansion of a technologically progressive, high-wage, information and knowledge service sector and a low-wage sector occur simultaneously. To quote from their chapter:

> The key role of mass production manufacturing in fueling rapid economic growth in the 25 years following the end of World War II, by providing for the rise in real wages and the spread of mass consumption, is well established. However, the period since 1979 suggests the feasibility of

robust employment growth and rapid economic expansion in the presence
of rising income inequality. Low wages in the other services keep the
costs of these labor-intensive activities from rising too rapidly relative to
the costs of the outputs of the technologically progressive sectors. Meanwhile, high wages among a significant proportion of workers in information
and knowledge intensive sectors, especially male workers, mean that there
will continue to be consumers with sufficient discretionary income to
purchase these services. . . . It remains to be seen, however, whether such
a pattern of employment growth can be sustained or whether increases
in income inequality will undermine economic growth via the saturation
of markets for mass-produced items and the slow diffusion of technologically
sophisticated consumer goods and services.[1]

An alternative scenario for the 1990s, one that is not suggested by
the authors but one that can legitimately proposed within the framework
of their analysis, is that rising labor shortages will eventually push up
wage levels and capital intensity in the non-information and knowledge
intensive service sectors and undo some of the dualistic developments
of the 1980s.

The short chapter by Robert Bednarzik helps establish the transition
between the chapters by Christopherson and Appelbaum and Albin,
mostly macroeconomic in their approach, and the mostly microeconomic
and human resource-oriented chapters by Thomas Stanback and myself,
on retailing and business services, respectively. Focusing on recent
employment growth in retail trade and business services, Bednarzik
reminds us that, even within those very rapidly growing sectors of the
economy, much variations can be found at the detailed level—be it in
terms of sheer growth or in terms the share of employment held by
women.

For example, despite high rates of growth during the last two decades
throughout much of the retail trade sector, subsectors such as department
stores, car dealerships, variety stores, gasoline service stations, men's
and boys' clothing stores, and others have experienced slow growth or
even decline, suggesting a maturation and transformation of their markets.
In terms of the share of employment held by women, Bednarzik's data
for the retail sector suggest that even though more women than men
are employed in the sector, such subsectors as lumber yards, hardware
stores, car dealerships, auto part supplies, gasoline stations, household
appliance stores, and radio, television, and music stores, remain male
dominated. In computer software and data processing services, one of
the fastest growing subsectors of the business service sector, Bednarzik's
data suggest a disturbingly small but steady decline in the share of
employment held by women.

In Chapter 5, Thomas Stanback takes a sweeping look at the U.S. retailing sector as it enters a new decade. Stanback's research is based on in-depth analyses of ten retailers—six of which are presented in some detail in his chapter—complemented by examinations of public information and interviews with investment analysts. Stanback's findings are striking both by the depth of the transformation that he uncovers in the sector and by the extent to which such a transformation puts pressure on skills and skill preparation, including at the lowest occupational echelons.

Despite large differences among the firms studied either in terms of size, merchandising objectives, or sales strategies, Stanback notes remarkable similarities in the extent to which firms are altering the responsibilities of their middle- and upper-level management and are seeking to increase the skills of their store personnel.

At the lowest echelons, the widespread new emphasis on customer service means a more careful selection of new employees, more extensive training in product knowledge (ranging from assisting customers in mixing garments and colors according to current fashion, to answering food preparation queries in supermarkets), and more extensive training in service behaviors (ranging from dress codes, to training in the handling of difficult customers and crisis situations). Along with this new emphasis is the insistence that everyone be trained—be they part-time or full-time employees, long-standing or short-term employees, skilled clerks or baggers. One disturbing trend is that, as large firms in the sector become more demanding in terms of whom they hire and employ, the role that large organizations once played in providing remedial training for the least skilled may vanish as competitive pressure makes it increasingly difficult for firms to write off or pass along to consumers the costs of that investment.

In the middle echelons, Stanback observes a rise in management's responsibilities in promoting the new human resource objectives of the firm and in feeding back to top management pertinent information such as pricing and merchandising policies of competitors and the changing tastes of customers.

Further up the hierarchy, Stanback observes that merchandising and buying functions have become both increasingly more complex—partly due to the multiplication of available products—and more centralized, as firms increasingly need to project a unique, well-focused image across many geographical markets.

In Chapter 6, I take a look at changes in skill needs in three subsectors of business services: accounting, management consulting, and computer software. I too describe sectors that are under extensive transformation, with profound implications for skills, skill preparation, and, more broadly speaking, human resource management. I first show how three sectors that were once quite separate from one another have increasingly come to overlap. Then I show how this growing overlap of sectors has brought together firms with very different skill needs, very different traditions of skill preparation, and very different labor markets, leading at times to clashes in corporate culture.

One finding from my research is that the relatively high degree of openness of the human resource systems of business service firms toward the external labor market (high rates of job-hopping), rather than being dysfunctional, is actually one element of their stability. For it is one of the ways in which certain skill needs are fulfilled, one of the ways in which skill preparation is achieved, and one of the ways in which new market opportunities are opened up. Another major finding is that in contrast to other sectors of the economy which worry about the quality of secondary and early postsecondary education, business service employers who hire principally, if not exclusively, at a four-year or more college level, are only remotely concerned by the travails of secondary education. What they are most concerned with, however, is the strengthening of their firm-based training as it is the basis for the development and diffusion of their firm-specific products and technologies.

Both Stanback's and my chapters underscore the growing need for a better educated and better trained work force, a topic directly addressed by Nevzer Stacey and Duc-Le To in their chapter. In Chapter 7, the two authors survey what is known about adult participation in educational and training programs. They look at the issues, first, from the point of view of the providers of training and, next, from the point of view of the trainees themselves. In their typology of educational and training providers, Stacey and To propose a distinction among school-based, work-based, and community-based providers. School-based providers include adult basic and secondary education programs, four-year colleges and universities, two-year colleges, postsecondary noncollegiate providers, and correspondence schools. Work-based providers include private employers, trade unions, professional associations and consulting firms, public sector agencies, and the military. Community-based providers include a variety of organizations ranging from churches to youth organizations and civic associations, some of which played or continue to play an important role in the delivery of CETA and JEPTA programs, the two largest federal training programs during the 1970s and 1980s.

Very little data are available to measure, let alone compare, levels of service offered by the respective providers. Based on data from a special Bureau of Labor Statistics (BLS) survey, the authors are able to report that work-based providers in 1983 accounted for 55 percent of training occurrences (training events as defined by interviewees) for the purpose of *qualification training* (training needed to acquire current job) and school-based providers accounted for 40 percent of such training occurrences. This compared to 60 percent versus 29 percent, respectively, for *skill-improvement training* (training needed to improve current job skills). Furthermore, based on 1978 and 1984 data collected by the Department of Education, the authors point to a recent shift in where adults obtain adult education courses, away from secondary schools, two-year and four-year colleges and universities mostly toward employers and, possibly, new providers such as specialized training firms.[2]

Turning to other findings from the 1983 BLS survey, the authors point to several developments in the distribution of educational and training opportunities among different groups of trainees. One finding is that adult women and minority groups have improved their access to *qualification training* relative to white men, and at times may even be doing better than white men. Another finding is that women and minority groups continue to lag behind white men in terms of their access to *skill improvement training*. If it is true that training opportunities for adult workers are shifting simultaneously toward relatively more employer-provided training and relatively more skill improvement training, then the latter finding is a disturbing one for women and minority workers.

In Chapter 8, Thomas Stanback and I tackle one of the most contentious current debates among economists, namely, how to explain the large employment growth in the service sectors of the U.S. economy during the 1970s and 1980s.

A widely held explanation is that the origins of rapid employment growth in service sectors must be found in their low productivity. In the United States, the theory has been most cogently articulated by economist William Baumol but follows those developed earlier by Clark, Fisher, and Fuchs.[3] The theory stresses that the growing size of services relative to goods is explainable principally in terms of a productivity differential between the goods-producing and the service sectors. This theory has numerous disciples not only in the United States but also in Western Europe where a number of economists have suggested that the reason for the recent slow employment growth in the services in Europe when compared to the United States, is that European service employers have invested more in new technology in their service sectors than have U.S. employers, and, thus, have boosted European productivity faster than their U.S. counterparts.

In the chapter, we review both measurement and conceptual difficulties associated with service productivity as it is currently used both in the United States and OECD-member countries. Our findings are startling. In the case of the United States, official productivity measures are meaningless for over 60 percent of the service sector. As for the alleged

differences in measured productivity between the United States and
other OECD-member countries, they owe principally to differences in
methods of measurement.

We also review available data on capital consumption in the service
sector of the United States and other OECD-member countries. As is
the case with productivity measurement, we conclude that the quality
of available statistical evidence is much too weak to arrive at any strong
conclusion. One conclusion from these two reviews of the evidence,
however, is that the empirical foundation for the "low-productivity
growth" theory as proposed by Baumol is extremely weak, casting serious
doubts on the theory.

This leads us to propose an alternative theory to help explain recent
employment growth in the U.S. economy. Our theory emphasizes the
importance of demand growth and stresses that while the existence of
productivity differentials is possible, they are not necessary to explain
recent employment growth in the services. Instead factors such as rapid
product and market transformation, changes in input-output linkages,
the rising importance of foreign trade and global specialization, and
other factors that have contributed to transforming and boosting service
demand are at least as important in explaining employment growth in
the services.

Finally, in Chapter 9, I return to some of the themes of the opening
chapters and suggest that the transformations examined in this book
are part of a fundamental restructuring of postwar labor markets, not
simply marginal responses or adjustments to changing economic conditions. As in the case of the previous chapter, this chapter is based
on earlier work, namely on a paper that I prepared several years ago
for a symposium held at the University of Lille. I have made limited
changes to the original paper for purposes of its inclusion in this volume
simply because I felt that it had held up reasonably well to the test of
time. My analysis of structural changes underlying recent labor market
transformations is consistent with that proposed by Christopherson in
Chapter 2 and leads me to suggest that labor markets are being reorganized
around three major segments: a segment of "core" workers, a segment
of "skilled contingent workers," and a segment of "low-skilled contingent
workers." I then show how this new labor market segmentation differs
from the postwar "dual labor market" segmentation theory described a
number of years ago by Piore, Doeringer, and others,[4] suggesting, in
particular, that its roots are increasingly less in differences in size of
firms, but increasingly more in occupational differences.

Based on findings from case studies, I suggest that this new segmentation results in differentials in access to internal mobility opportunities, and also, if only by inference, to certain kinds of firm-based

training. However, I also point out that for many in the skilled contingent worker segment additional education and training is not necessarily inconsistent with high rates of mobility via the external labor market.

As for low-skilled contingent workers, I suggest that their fate lies in part in the direction to be taken by future labor market transformations. If the aggregate trends uncovered by Appelbaum and Albin continue well into the 1990s, there is little to suggest that the position of low-skilled contingent workers will improve in the near future. However, if the microcosmic developments uncovered by Stanback in his chapter become widespread, one might be cautiously optimistic and project that the position of these weakest actors in the labor market may improve markedly and that firms may actually play a major role in their up-skilling.

These are only a few of the key issues raised in the eight core chapters of this book. But they should provide the reader with some sense of direction as he or she progresses through the book. Also, my efforts at weaving together in this overview the many themes addressed in the eight chapters is not intended to gloss over the differences of opinion or interpretation that may exist among the authors. In the last chapter, I return to some of the commonalities as well as differences of opinion among authors, if only to stress the limits of what is known about the labor and skills implications of the transformation of the service sectors.

Notes

1. E. Appelbaum and P. Albin, Chapter 3 of this volume, p. 64.

2. The concept of an adult education course is more restrictive than the concept of a training occurrence as used in the *Current Population Survey* since it does not include many less formal training events such as on-the-job training.

3. W.J. Baumol, "Macroeconomics of Unbalanced Growth," *American Economic Review* (June 1967); C. Clark, *The Condition of Economic Progress* (London: Macmillan, 1940); A.G. Fisher, *The Clash of Progress and Security* (London: Kelley, 1935); and V.R. Fuchs, *The Service Economy* (New York, NY: Columbia University Press, 1968).

4. P. Doeringer and M.J. Piore, *Internal Labor Markets and Manpower Analysis* (Lexington, MA: D.C. Heath/Lexington Books, 1971).

2

Emerging Patterns of Work

Susan Christopherson

The repercussions of the current transformation of the U.S economy go far beyond a decline in manufacturing jobs and an increase in service employment. What is changing in the United States is not just the number of jobs and their sectoral distribution but the way in which work is organized and distributed. In other words, we are witnessing a qualitative transformation of work, not just quantitative shifts within established employment patterns. One of the most important dimensions of this transformation is a redistribution of work time within the work force and an increase in the number of workers whose work time can be adjusted to short-term changes in the demand for a product or service. These workers are often described as a contingent or peripheral work force, but this simple categorization does not capture significant differences within this work force. Part-time workers, for example, frequently work on permanent, if short-hour, contracts. Self-employed independent contractors may be external to the firm but earn very high wages. And while the form of employment, such as part-time work, may be long established, the composition of the part-time work force has changed over time.

Two questions are frequently raised about the emerging patterns of work in the United States. The first is whether employment trends toward a more flexible work force represent a structural change in labor demand or merely a cyclical fluctuation. The second question concerns the origins of the new employment patterns. Among the explanations that have been proposed are: changing labor supply conditions, including an increase in the portion of the work force desiring shorter hours of work; employer requirements for more flexible staffing patterns; or employer desires to reduce labor costs. Evidence on changes in patterns of work over time relative to business cycle fluctuations indicates that the first question can be answered with a firm yes. Answers to the second question are more complicated, involving social and political as well as economic variables.

In this chapter, some significant emerging employment patterns are described and related to changes in the organization of production and the increasing service orientation of the U.S. economy. I then consider whether the flexible character of the U.S. work force is exceptional or could be replicated in other industrialized countries.

Emerging Patterns of Work

From 1973 to 1979, 12.5 million jobs were added to the U.S. economy. Another 14.5 million jobs were added in the 1980s. Nearly one-quarter of these jobs were part-time and approximately 66 percent were filled by women. Per capita work hours were 14 percent higher in 1986 than in 1965, while hours worked per working age adult (between the ages of 16 and 65) declined 4 percent during the same period. In general, higher gross national product per capita has been achieved by adding more people to the work force.[1]

With respect to the overall supply of labor, several trends are evident. First, more U.S. teenagers are entering the service sector work force and at increasingly younger ages.[2] Labor force participation rates of women also have dramatically increased. The most recent data show that 66 percent of U.S. women currently hold jobs or are actively seeking them. Among college graduates, this figure is 81 percent. At the same time, the percentage of older men (aged 55–64) in the work force declined from 90 percent in 1950 to 50 percent in 1987. The racial mix of the U.S. work force also is changing. The Bureau of Labor Statistics predicts that a majority of the people entering the labor force during the next decade will be black, Hispanic, and Asian.[3]

Another indication of the redistribution of work in the U.S. work force is evidence showing a decreasing unemployment rate among the employed population but a continuing hard core population of "discouraged workers," people who say they want work but are not seeking jobs or who work less than half the year and earn under $10,000. This group is estimated at between 10 million and 20 million people and excludes the majority of nonworkers who remain out of the work force for reasons of health, education, or retirement.[4] Although the U.S. unemployment rate has fallen from 9.5 percent in 1983 to approximately 5 percent in 1989, this statistic measures only the status of those who are actively in the work force. Despite apparent labor shortages and a declining unemployment rate, the number of discouraged workers has remained sizable and stable since the recession of the early 1980s.

Within the employed work force, patterns of work and the distribution of work time are also changing. The 40-hour workweek is becoming less common in the United States with considerable growth in both longer and shorter workweeks. For example, the number of women working more than 49 hours per week increased 50 percent between May 1979 and May 1985.[5] The year-to-year variation in work hours is also increasing. The average year-to-year change in work hours during the 1970s was nearly 320 hours. Variation in work hours ranged from 280 hours per year for white women workers to 350 hours for black workers.[6] Thus, fewer adult Americans hold stable full-time jobs and receive pay for 40-hour workweeks. Within these general patterns of work reorganization in the United States, two trends stand out: an increase in the variability of working hours and an increase in flexible jobs, including part-time jobs, temporary work, and self-employment.

Part-Time Jobs

One out of every six U.S. jobs, or about 20 million, is a part-time job. This yearly average figure understates the dimensions of the part-time work experience, however, for a much larger proportion of the work force is employed part-time at some point during the year. In 1985, for example, the number of people who worked part-time for a portion of the year was double that of the annual average number of part-time workers.[7] Part-time jobs are not only a sizable portion of total employment, they are growing faster than full-time jobs. Of the 10 million jobs created since 1980, one-quarter have been part-time. There are two categories of part-time workers—those who work part-time by choice and those who work part-time because full-time work is not available to them. A growing portion of the part-time work force, 5.6 million, are involuntary part-time workers compared to 13.5 million voluntary part-time workers.

The U.S. Bureau of Labor Statistics defines part-time workers as people who work one to 34 hours per week, except for usually full-time workers who are working fewer hours for noneconomic reasons, such as holidays. Part-time workers are classified as involuntary or working part-time for economic reasons if they answer the question, "Why are you working fewer than 35 hours a week?" with the following responses: slack work, material shortages or repairs, starting or ending a job during the week, or inability to find full-time work. Part-time workers are classified as voluntary if they answer the same question with any reason other than those used to identify involuntary part-time workers. The reasons for "voluntary" part-time work may include inability to find work at a sufficient wage to pay for child care or lack of transportation. The

Table 2.1   Age and Gender Composition of the Part-Time Work Force, 1987

Group	Percentage of Labor Force	Part-Time Employment as a Percentage of Group
All 16–21	10.9	46.0
Women 22–44	27.7	22.9
Women 45–64	11.0	24.1
Men 22–64	48.0	6.8
All 65+	2.4	52.4
Total	100.0	18.4

Source: C. Tilly, "Short Hours, Short Shrift, Understanding Part-Time Employment." Unpublished research paper (Washington, DC: Economic Policy Institute, 1988).

limitations on the definition of what constitutes involuntary part-time work suggest that at least a portion of the voluntary part-time work force might prefer full-time jobs if their personal economic situations were different.

In examining statistics on part-time jobs and part-time workers in the United States, it is important to recognize that the most frequently used source of information on short-hour work is the *Current Population Survey* (CPS) which is a survey of individuals and households regarding their total weekly work hours and not a count of jobs. This method undercounts part-time jobs since a growing portion of the work force works full-time but at two or more jobs. About one-fifth of workers holding part-time jobs are multiple jobholders.[8] This trend toward multiple job holding is not surprising since part-time workers make up 65 percent of those U.S. workers working at or below the minimum wage.[9]

Since the 1950s, part-time work has shown two trends: a secular increase over time and a tendency to fluctuate more with respect to the business cycle. Part-time work has increased very slowly as a portion of the total work force (from 16 percent in the 1950s to 19 percent in 1989). This long-term secular trend has been substantiated by studies which separate cyclical and secular trends.[10] Research on the retail sector—the employer of the majority of part-time workers—suggests, however, that the use of part-time workers may be waning as employers face a labor shortage in exactly those labor force segments which, up to now, have made up the bulk of the part-time work force, women and youth (Table 2.1).[11] Employers appear to be implementing strategies, such as more self-service, to make them less dependent on labor, including part-time labor.[12] This gradual trend is supported by evidence that the rate of growth in voluntary part-time employment began to slow by 1980 and that of involuntary part-time employment began to increase.

Of the 2.9 percent increase in part-time employment between 1969 and 1987, 2.4 percent is attributable to growth in involuntary part-time work.[13]

The increased cyclical sensitivity of the part-time work force is attributable to the larger portion of this work force which is involuntary. Bednarzik's analysis of this work force shows different cyclical sensitivities even within the involuntary part-time work force. Slack work tends to follow the output cycle, while inability to find a full-time job follows the employment cycle.[14] In apparent divergence from the historical pattern in which involuntary part-time work grew during periods of recession and declined during periods of recovery, involuntary part-time employment has risen steadily since the mid-1970s though it still exhibits cyclical fluctuations.

Involuntary part-time work differs from voluntary part-time work in its occupational profile and sectoral distribution. Fifty-one percent of the part-time workers in goods-producing industries are involuntary in comparison with service industries where less than 25 percent are involuntary.[15] Involuntary part-time work has increased in every occupational group but is still concentrated in blue-collar occupations.

Again, research on the retail sector indicates some convergence in the way part-time workers are used in the manufacturing and retail industries. Voluntary part-time workers historically have provided employers with a certain degree of flexibility not only because their working hours could be altered in response to seasonal, weekly, or daily demand but also because of their high turnover rates and interchangeable skills. With a labor supply shortage, retail employers appear to be altering the working hours of full-time employees in order to achieve flexibility, thus increasing the number of involuntary part-time workers. This pattern is much closer to that in manufacturing.[16]

Temporary Work

Temporary Help Services. Although part-time jobs still dominate the flexible labor market, other forms of flexible employment are expanding more rapidly, particularly temporary work. In the temporary industry close to one million workers are employed as temporaries at any one given time but, more significantly, perhaps as many as six million people work as temporaries at some time during any given year. Average annual employment in the industry increased from 340,000 in 1978 to 944,000 in 1987. The temporary supply industry is growing at three times the growth rate of service industries and eight times the rate of all non-agricultural industries.[17] Between 1989 and 1995, the temporary help industry is projected to grow 5 percent annually in comparison with a 1.3 percent growth rate for all industries.

The role of the temporary industry and the temporary employee has changed over time. As the temporary agency becomes more established as a labor market intermediary, more firms are restructuring work to use a permanent temporary labor force to do certain jobs. Rather than a part-time phenomenon, temporary workers are more frequently employed on long assignments, for weeks and even months.[18] The head of a law firm continuously using temporary workers exemplified this trend in stating, "We concluded we were better off maintaining a staff for minimal demand. We can satisfy short-term increases with temporary help. It's more cost effective and better management." And, according to the president of a major temporary agency, "Our business has changed from a replacement and fill-in service to an effective tool for managing labor costs."[19]

Temporary work contracts can take a number of forms including a short-term job; a long-term job with no employment security, lower pay, or no benefits; or a structured internal temporary worker pool (most common in large public institutions, such as universities and hospitals). Recruitment and hiring of these temporary workers are carried out independently of the hiring of permanent personnel. The temporary industry, in fact, employs only a small portion of temporary workers. The largest portion are "direct hires," employed as on-call workers in large firms and, more and more frequently, in local, state, and federal government agencies. The U.S. federal government is one of the largest employers of temporary workers, and under revised regulations can hire "temps" for up to four years without providing benefits or job security. Approximately 300,000 workers in the executive branch, including the postal service, are currently employed as temporary workers. Among the private firms with their own "in-house" temporary labor services are Standard Oil, Hunt-Wesson, Beatrice Foods, Hewlett Packard, and Atlantic Richfield (ARCO).

The actual number of temporary jobs is difficult to determine because employers are not required to provide information on their work force in terms of employment contract. Employers in the United States can usually terminate employees at will, since employment contracts are rare and there usually is no legal difference between temporary and "permanent" employment. To be clearly distinctive, a temporary work force would have to be employed under specific conditions, for example at lower hourly wages or without benefits. They would also be hired with the explicit (rather than implicit) understanding that their job tenure will be limited. Because, as of yet, no public agency collecting statistics on the work force distinguishes among workers on these bases, we cannot estimate how much labor turnover is a function of loss of jobs by workers who anticipated continuous employment and how much is attributable to a change in the employment contract for a portion of the work force. Available information is largely anecdotal or based on surveys of firms.[20] Among the few firm surveys which shed light on this phenomenon, a Bureau of National Affairs survey of 442 firms indicates that 90 percent use short-term hires. The data in this survey allowed Abraham to calculate that the use of workers on explicit temporary job contracts is probably twice as large as that represented in the temporary industry.[21]

One reason to hire temporary workers directly, rather than through a temporary industry agency, is cost. A majority of employers of short-term hires and on-call workers indicates that these workers receive lower hourly wages than permanent workers in the same types of jobs. In contrast, the hourly costs of temporary help service workers hired indirectly from an agency are higher than for permanent workers.[22]

Who makes up the temporary work force? Temporary workers are similar to the part-time work force—they tend to be young and female. The best available information on the characteristics of this work force is from the May 1985 *Current Population Survey*, and is summarized in Table 2.2. It indicates that 64 percent of temporary workers are women and that one out of three is between 16 and 24 years of age. Blacks also are overrepresented in the temporary work force, constituting 20 percent of the temporary work force compared with 10 percent of the work force across all industries.

Occupationally, 52 percent of temporary help service workers, that is workers employed in the industry rather than direct hires, are employed in technical, sales, and administrative support occupations, mostly in clerical occupations. The concentration of clerical workers is 2½ times their concentration in all industries. Sixty-six percent of these workers work full-time. The second largest group, operators, fabricators, and laborers, are more likely to be men, more likely to be black, and more likely to be part-time workers.[23]

Within the industry, non-office temporary help appears to be growing faster than the clerical component of the industry. Agencies specializing in non-office temporary help accounted for only one-third of total temporary help service employment in 1972 but for 45 percent of the total by 1982.[24]

Employee Leasing. Employee leasing is, in many ways, a spin-off of temporary help. However, unlike temporary help, employee leasing is more likely to occur in small rather than large firms and to encompass a much larger portion of the firm's labor force. The leasing company performs all the functions of an employer including hiring, firing, and salary reviews. This form of contingent labor has expanded, at least in part, because of tax law provisions that encourage small businesses, such as professional offices, to transfer employees to external employers.

Table 2.2 Percentage Distribution of Workers in All Industries and in the Temporary Help Industry (THS) by Selected Characteristics, May 1985

Characteristic	Percentage Distribution	
	All Industries	THS Industry
Age		
16 to 24	20.1	32.7
25 to 54	67.4	57.6
55 and over	12.5	9.7
Total, 16 and over	100.0	100.0
Sex and race		
Men	55.0	35.8
Women	45.0	64.2
White	86.9	75.4
Black	10.4	20.2
White		
Men	55.7	33.2
Women	44.3	66.8
Black		
Men	49.4	48.9
Women	50.6	51.1
Occupation		
Managerial and professional specialty	24.0	11.0
Technical, sales, and administrative support	31.6	52.1
Administrative support, including clerical	17.3	43.3
Service occupations	13.7	10.8
Precision production, craft and repair	12.1	4.6
Operators, fabricators, and laborers	16.6	16.9
Farming, forestry, and fishing	2.1	4.4

Source: W. Howe, "Temporary Help Workers: Who They Are, What Jobs They Hold," *Monthly Labor Review* (November 1986): 45–47.

Employee leasing is, at present, a limited but growing phenomenon. The most recent estimate of the size of the leased employee work force in the United States was 200,000 workers.[25]

Self-Employed Independent Contractors

There are a series of definitional questions that must be dealt with before interpreting how the expansion of self-employment is related to new patterns of work. Public data provide different if complementary information on this category of work. The *Current Population Survey* (CPS), the major source of information on the self-employed, defines these workers as sole proprietors and partners of unincorporated businesses. This definition undercounts the actual number of self-employed

Table 2.3   Self-Employed as a Percentage of the Labor Force by Gender, 1975 and 1985

	Men (%)	Women (%)
1975		
Unincorporated	7.57	2.70
Incorporated	3.01	0.53
1985		
Unincorporated	7.57	3.56
Incorporated	4.42	1.13

Source: D. Evans and L. Leighton, *Self-Employment Selection and Earnings Over the Life Cycle.* Report prepared for the Office of Advocacy (Washington, DC: Small Business Administration, December 1987).

workers because those workers who identify themselves as owning a controlling interest in an incorporated business (irrespective of whether the incorporated enterprise has any employees) are identified as wage and salary workers and employees of the corporation. Wage and salary workers who own a side business are also excluded from the CPS count of the self-employed. The *Survey of Income and Program Participation* (SIPP) provides additional data on the self-employed, particularly on the number of hours worked by business owners, and on multiple businesses.[26] Both surveys yield similar distributions of employment. Approximately 7.5 percent of the employed in the United States are self-employed in unincorporated businesses and an additional 2.6 percent operate incorporated businesses. Side businesses (in addition to full-time employment) are operated by between 2 and 3 percent of the work force. The SIPP data indicate that 13.5 million nonagricultural businesses existed in 1983, 700,000 more than the 12.8 million business owners. So, over 4 percent of the business owners owned more than one business.

The role of self-employment in the U.S. economy is one indication of the structural shifts in the economy over the past 15 to 18 years. Self-employment declined steadily between 1950 and 1970, led by losses in retail trade. Self-employment in agriculture has always been high but continues to decline (from 67 percent of all full-time equivalent employment in 1950 to 50.1 percent in 1986). Despite continuing declines in certain sectors, such as agriculture where self-employment has been the predominant employment form, self-employment began to grow after 1970, primarily in new sectors. In addition to services, self-employment has grown in manufacturing and in transportation, presumably because of the deregulation of the trucking industry.

As with other emerging forms of employment, there are significant differences in the self-employed work force by gender and race (Tables 2.3 and 2.4). For example, among business owners more women than men were sole proprietors (70 percent compared to 60 percent). More

Table 2.4   Self-Employed as a Percentage of the Labor Force by Gender and Race, 1985

	Unincorporated	Incorporated	Total
Men			
White	8.4	4.3	12.7
Black	2.9	0.8	3.7
Other races	8.5	4.1	12.6
Total	8.0	4.1	12.1
Women			
White	3.8	1.1	4.9
Black	1.3	0.1	1.4
Other races	4.7	1.5	6.2
Total	3.5	1.0	4.5

Source: D. Evans and L. Leighton, Self-Employment Selection and Earnings Over the Life Cycle. Report prepared for the Office of Advocacy (Washington, DC: Small Business Administration, December 1987).

men than women own side businesses (17 percent compared to 15 percent) and more women than men own casual businesses. Casual businesses are defined in terms of total earnings ($1,224 average in 1983), but 37 percent of casual business owners reported working full-time at them. As a consequence of this distribution, self-employed women had annualized earnings of $3,767 in 1983 while annualized earnings for men were $13,520 (higher than the $12,079 earned by female paid employees).[27] According to the 1987 CPS, the median earnings for male self-employed incorporated workers were $35,114 and for female, $16,669. For unincorporated self-employed workers, the medians are $17,942 for men and $7,930 for women.[28] Despite these differentials, women constitute the fastest growing portion of the self-employed work force. Between 1979 and 1983, the number of unincorporated self-employed women increased five times faster than men and more than three times faster than wage and salary women. More than 9 percent of working women own a business in the United States. In contrast with women, minorities are not increasing in the category of business owners or the self-employed. In 1983, only 3.1 percent of employed blacks owned businesses and only 5.9 percent were self-employed.

Two important conclusions can be drawn from an analysis of these emerging patterns of work distribution in the United States. First, there is substantial evidence that flexible forms of work have increased over time, irrespective of business cycle fluctuations. Second, these types of work are differentially distributed among segments of the work force. Women, youth, and minorities tend to be concentrated in the lower wage and lower skilled categories of flexible work while white males tend to dominate the higher wage, higher skilled categories, such as self-employed workers in professional services. This suggests that the new patterns of work may affect segments of the work force differently with respect to job training, benefits, and occupational mobility.[29] The next two sections look at labor demand and labor supply to explore why labor deployment patterns are changing in the United States.

The Emergence of a New Market for Service Products

As the United States has become an economy dominated by service employment, the ways in which we define and distinguish among service activities have become more varied and sophisticated. Services are now distinguished with respect to their relationship to manufacturing, their employment profiles, and, more recently, with respect to their information intensity.[30] There also is a growing awareness that the expansion in services and the form service employment has taken are not attributable to a single cause but originate in a set of processes, some of which are specific to the United States.

The expansion of business services can be traced to the global division of labor that began to emerge in the 1950s. Globalization and the location of financial services and the corporate headquarters of transnational firms in the United States have been a major stimulus to the expansion and evolution of these branches of activities in the domestic economy.[31] Also because the growth of business services is closely linked to the transformation of manufacturing and more generally to the expansion of markets, business services have expanded in much the same way, if not to the same extent, in many industrialized countries.

The transformation of consumer and social services has somewhat different origins. As more women have entered the wage work force, services formerly provided in the home, such as child care, food preparation, and care of the elderly, are being "commodified." These services, now increasingly provided by national (and international) firms, are becoming standardized as economies of scale are achieved. Fast-food companies are the major model for this transformation.

Finally, services formerly provided in the public sector, such as nursing care, building maintenance, security, and transportation, are being transferred to the private sector. This cost-driven policy not only is transforming public sector employment but is expanding the market for commodified service "products."

Production Organization and Labor Demand

An analysis of the organization of production within and among service-providing firms demonstrates some significant differences between services and manufacturing and among service sectors. Service firms, as a whole, operate through more establishments than do goods-producing firms, regardless of the employment size of firms. In firms with 500 or more employees, service firms average 37 establishments per enterprise in comparison with 17 establishments per manufacturing enterprise.[32] The average size of a service establishment is 11 employees compared to 60 in the average manufacturing establishment.[33] And, while employment grew 34 percent in very small service firms (1–19 employees) between 1976 and 1984, employment in very large firms (more than 500 employees) grew 27 percent during the same period. In health care, the growth rate in the very large firm category was 56 percent.[34]

A 1989 study by the Federal Reserve Bank of Chicago as well as industry case studies provide evidence for a new wave of vertical integration.[35] According to the *Chicago Fed Letter*, employment at retail firms with over 500 employees increased 16 percent between 1984 and 1986 compared to an increase of only 2 percent at retail firms with fewer than 100 employees. In business services, employment growth in large firms accelerated between 1984 and 1986. In health services, a period of small firm growth between 1982 and 1984 appears to have ended in the late 1980s as large health care firms, primarily hospitals, found ways other than vertical disintegration to control costs. In short, the emerging production pattern in services in the United States is that of a large firm made up of a large number of establishments. An example of this trend is Beverly Enterprises, a nursing home chain. This company, which employs 116,000 people (more than Chrysler Corporation at 115,000), deploys its labor in 1,200 different locations. Another example is the highly successful Wal-Mart Corporation which has 1,400 retail establishments throughout the United States.

In common with manufacturing, service industries dominated by large firms have complex labor demand profiles. But service industries also differ along two dimensions which do not appear to be as significant in manufacturing. The first is the degree and intensity of public or client contact. The second is a difference related to the range and nature of skills required, encompassing generalized social skills as well as firm-specific and professional skills. Many clerical jobs in financial services, for example, have little or no public contact and use general rather than firm-specific skills. Bank tellers, in contrast, have firm-specific skills. Employers have a number of options in meeting their needs for a work force with social as well as task-specific skills. They can implement organizational and technological methods to use a segment of employees more intensively and to generally decrease dependence on labor. On the other hand, they can use the work time of many workers and match that work time to changes in demand for the service.

Until quite recently, service industry employers, recognizing the sizable labor supply, favored the second alternative, in particular, using voluntary part-time workers. But changes in the labor supply and an imperative to rationalize service production and distribution now appear to be encouraging a trend toward the first alternative. This involves strategies such as increasing self-service and more involuntary part-time work and overtime (allocating the work time of a smaller set of workers rather than the work time of a larger set). Workers on temporary job contracts are significant under both sets of conditions but may be used in different ways. If employers are not particularly interested in reducing dependence on labor, the employment of temporary workers may serve as a screening device for long-term employment. In a situation of "stretch out," the more intensive use of already employed workers, temporary workers may be used more strategically, for example, during seasonal peaks in demand.

While large firms reallocate work time and jobs in order to achieve scale economies and provide service at lower cost, small firms continue to play an important part in the U.S. service economy. Small firms are particularly significant at either end of the skill and cost spectrum of service provision.

Independent contractors, for example, are an important source of high skilled professional workers for industries needing short-term specialized services. Independent contractors are prevalent in electronics, chemicals, and business services, and among a set of professional occupations, including graphic design, engineering, technical writing, systems analysis, and programming. These occupations have some common characteristics that make them amenable to independent contracting. They are highly skilled, but their skills are not industry specific. They can move across industry boundaries with relative ease. At the same time, they frequently work on projects that are nonroutine and carried out within a definite time frame. They increase their employment opportunities by concentrating in industrial regions such as the Santa Clara Valley in California or Route 128 in Boston.

Independent contracting is also used as a method to obtain workers without paying benefits, thus saving not only benefit costs but bookkeeping costs. This type of contracting, also subject to abuse of working conditions and "off-the-books" payment, is typified by homework in electronics and apparel but more recently has been growing among clerical workers.[36]

Another major group of small firms is characterized by the ephemeral nature of their production activities. Industries in this category include those such as publishing, advertising, and entertainment which utilize highly skilled labor and those such as apparel or electronics which use low-skilled labor to complete one-time orders through "fly-by-night" sweat shops. These firms often are not enduring entities but project-oriented, organized to last only for the duration of a particular production project. This type of production requires a highly localized labor force. The need for firm- or industry-specific knowledge is low while the need for highly personal or specialized skills (in advertising, publishing, entertainment) or connection with a combined social-economic network is very high. These are the ultimately flexible firms in which a group of people are brought together to produce only one component or product.

Labor Supply Conditions

One reason for the increase in flexible work forms in the United States in the 1970s was labor supply conditions. The U.S. labor force grew 3 percent per year during the early 1970s as the baby boom generation entered the work force. Women in the United States not only entered the work force in increasing numbers during this period but, in a break with previous patterns, began staying in the work force in larger numbers after having children. In the mid–1980s, two-thirds of women with young children (aged 6–17) were in the work force. This is double the number in the 1950s.[37] Female labor force participation overall rose from 38.6 percent in 1966 to 53.0 percent in 1986. Increasing female labor force participation in the United States is at least indirectly linked to the decline in male earnings. Real mean earnings for men aged 20–24 fell 26 percent between 1973 and 1986. What magnified the impact of increased female labor force participation is that many of the new service jobs require generalized rather than specific skills. And, as jobs have become more similar across industries and across regions, they can draw from a relatively homogeneous and better educated female labor pool.

The other group that moved into the work force in large numbers was youth. As the number of older teenagers extending their education increased, many delayed entry into the full-time work force and constituted a sizable and generally over-qualified work force for flexible jobs. This situation is changing now as the pool of older teenagers shrinks and employers hire younger and younger workers to fill part-time jobs. Ironically, though it is acknowledged that young teenagers are increasingly employed, there are no statistics on their participation rates because the U.S. Department of Labor removed 14 and 15 year olds from the labor force statistics in 1967.

Many of these changes in U.S. labor utilization and labor supply conditions are regionally specific with employers seeking new sources of labor, including both young teenagers and retired people, in those areas where labor force participation rates for women have historically been high and where unemployment rates are below the national average. Teenage work force participation is also very high in areas such as Washington, D.C., and Boston where housing costs are extremely high. This has led some observers to speculate that teenage employment is filling gaps in family incomes.[38] As such, it is part of a general trend in the United States to increase the number of hours worked in response to a 3.5 percent decrease in real hourly wages since 1979.

There is some evidence that the trend toward flexible patterns of work will abate or at least change with the predicted labor shortage in the U.S. economy in the next ten years. Although the percentage decline in young people entering the work force between 1980 and 2000 will be much less severe in the United States than in many Western European countries—9 percent in the United States versus 42 percent in West Germany and 19 percent in Britain—it will still have an impact.

Firms have a range of alternatives open to them in responding to the labor shortage. Some firms will likely attempt to decrease their reliance on labor. As a result, we are likely to see more new service activities become automated or self-service.[39] For other firms, there will be a strong incentive to import immigrant service workers to fill the gap at the low end of the wage scale particularly in major urban service economies such as Los Angeles and New York.

Current economic analyses of the depth of labor shortages and their potential upward effects on wages tend to support the idea that they will affect a fairly narrow segment of occupations and industries. Although there are indications that there will be some wage increases at the bottom end of the spectrum, there appears to be a surplus of workers willing to take jobs at between $8.00 to $10.00 per hour (1988 dollars). Since labor shortages are also geographically concentrated, their effects on current employment patterns, including flexible patterns of work, are unclear.

Exceptional American Flexibility?

On virtually every measure, the U.S. work force stands out as being more "flexible," that is more responsive to changes in supply and demand in the market, than its counterparts in other industrialized countries. Labor turnover, as measured in the percentage of jobholders who hold jobs for two or fewer years, is higher in the United States than in 13 other industrialized countries with which it was compared in an OECD study. Wage flexibility as measured in the dispersal of wages within sectors is also greater in the United States than in industrialized countries generally.[40] And, although the United States has a lower percentage of workers in part-time jobs than the United Kingdom or Sweden, the share of total labor input (in terms of hours) by part-time workers is higher in the United States. And, while part-time work is increasing faster in other industrialized countries, the United States is unique with respect to the multiple forms and extent of flexibility that characterize its work force.

Many reasons are offered for these tendencies in the U.S. economy, including lower productivity in services and increased female labor force participation. One of the most common explanations is that the growth in the demand for flexible labor arises from recent short-term business cycles, which have increased inter-firm competition. In order to remain competitive, firms must circumvent the regulatory structures in national economies that inhibit rapid adjustment in the quality and quantity of labor. A more flexible work force reduces what is perceived as unproductive work time. In addition to direct wage savings, the increase in labor flexibility and in new patterns of work reduces non-wage labor costs. Firms gain from eliminating pay for time not worked during sick leave, vacations, and holidays. In addition, employers avoid other costly obligations, such as severance pay, job training costs, and, in the case of temporary workers, recruitment costs. Thus, the growth of forms of work, such as part-time and temporary work, which fall outside the employment security system, are explained as a response to structural rigidities which prevent the labor market from "clearing."[41] These rigidities are, in turn, associated with high employment.

There is, obviously, a basic contradiction in this explanation. The proportion of flexible workers in an economy cannot be seen both as a measure of its capability to adjust speedily (as in the case of the United States) and as a measure of its inflexibility. If one accepts the argument that structural rigidities produce more part-time and temporary jobs, then the case of the United States is an anomaly. The United States has by far the least "rigid" employment security system and the largest flexible work force. It is, in reality, the very lack of employee protection and bargaining power, particularly among women and minority workers and particularly in services, that has enabled U.S. employers to utilize workers flexibly. In sum, U.S. labor flexibility has its roots in both industrial relations as practiced in the country and in changes in labor demand.[42]

The flexible U.S. "solution" to increasing global competition appears to derive from a particular set of conditions. First, U.S. labor demand is growing in services and in particular sectors, such as health, retail, and business services. In this respect, its labor demand is distinct from countries such as Germany or Japan which still have a sizable portion of the work force employed in manufacturing. Second, the United States has a heterogeneous labor force that is segmented by occupation and industry. The history of the use of immigrant labor has produced labor relations contracts which, although contradictory in some respects, are impersonal rather than based on familial or regional loyalties and has encouraged the design of jobs in order to separate labor power from the personal characteristics of the work force. In contrast with societies where flexibility is being achieved through relations which entail personal obligation, labor flexibility in the United States is a matter of changing the content of an already impersonal work contract. For the employer, the separation between labor power and labor supply is increased by selectively using employee time.

The heterogeneity of the U.S. work force also explains why European solutions to unemployment, such as work-sharing, have never been plausible in the U.S. context except, for a short period of time, within the male manufacturing work force.

The largest component of the flexible labor force in the United States, women workers, also differs considerably from their counterparts in other industrialized countries. They have higher average levels of educational attainment and the lowest rate of predictability in natality patterns of any industrialized country. For a variety of complex reasons that have emerged from changes in the family as well as in the production system, U.S. women are now expected to be lifetime wage earners. Women in many other industrialized countries continue to follow a pattern of wage work only before and after child-rearing.

Thus, with respect to both demand for and supply of flexible labor, the United States is characterized by conditions which set it apart from other industrialized countries.

Conclusion

In looking at the flexibility alternative it is important to recognize that despite the apparent and quantifiable short-term cost savings obtained through changing work organization and redistributing work to use a flexible work force, there are significant costs. Some are borne by the flexible worker, for example, in the form of income insecurity, increased job search costs, and self-financing of benefits. Some are borne by regular employees, particularly middle-level management and service employees whose working hours have increased partially as a consequence of increased supervisory responsibilities and extension of tasks. Others are borne by the firm in the form of poor performance and high rates of job turnover. Finally, there are societal costs.

Because the United States has only minimal social welfare provisions and no national health care insurance, the public sector must absorb the additional costs associated with a large uninsured population, currently 37 million individuals. In addition, there is concern that the quality of the labor force will suffer if education and job training are sacrificed to immediate earnings.

Notes ·

1. U.S. Office of Technology Assessment (OTA), "Technology and the American Economic Transition" (Washington, DC: OTA, 1988).

2. F. Joselow, "Why Business Turns to Teenagers," *New York Times*, Business Section, 26 March 1989, pp. 1, 6.

3. R. Kutscher, "Projections 2000—Overview and Implications of the Projections to 2000," *Monthly Labor Review* (September 1987).

4. L. Uchitelle, "America's Army of Non-Workers," *New York Times*, Business Section, 27 September 1987, p. 1.

5. S. Smith, "Growing Diversity of Work Schedules," *Monthly Labor Review* (November 1986); and OTA (n. 1).

6. G. Duncan, "Years of Poverty, Years of Plenty" (Ann Arbor, MI: Survey Research Center, University of Michigan, 1984).

7. C. Tilly, "Short Hours, Short Shrift, Understanding Part-time Employment" (Unpublished research paper, Economic Policy Institute, Washington, DC, 1988).

8. J. Stinson, "Moonlighting by Women Jumped to Record Highs," *Monthly Labor Review* (November 1986): 22–25.

9. E. Mellor and S. Haugen, "Hourly Paid Workers: Who They Are and What They Earn," *Monthly Labor Review* (February 1986): 20–26.

10. B. Ichnowski and A. Preston 1985, "New Trends in Part-time Employment," *Proceedings*, 38th Annual Meeting of the Industrial Relations Research Association, 1985; and R. Ehrenberg, P. Rosenberg, and J. Li, "Part-time Employment in the United States" (Paper delivered at a conference on "Employment, Unemployment and Hours of Work," Berlin, Germany, September 1986).

11. In the 1940s, men who worked part-time outnumbered women who worked part-time because of the concentration of part-time work in primary sector industries. See C. Leon and R. Bednarzik, "A Profile of Women on Part-time Schedules," *Monthly Labor Review* (October 1978): 3–12; and D. Morse, *The Peripheral Worker* (New York, NY: Columbia University Press, 1969). Approximately 24 percent of the contemporary agricultural work force works part-time, but the total number of agricultural workers has diminished since the 1950s. As women entered the work force in the 1960s, however, the voluntary part-time work force increased substantially in trade and services.

12. S. Christopherson, T. Noyelle, and B. Redfield, "Labor Demand in the Changing Retail Sector" (Report to the Employment and Training Administration, U.S. Department of Labor, Washington, DC, 1989).

13. Tilly (n. 7).

14. R. Bednarzik, "Short Workweeks During Economic Downturns," *Monthly Labor Review* (June 1983): 3–11; and R. Bednarzik, "Involuntary Part-time Work: A Cyclical Analysis," *Monthly Labor Review* (September 1975): 12–18.

15. Tilly (n. 7).

16. Christopherson, Noyelle, and Redfield (n. 12).

17. F. Carre, "Temporary and Contingent Employment in the Eighties, Review of the Evidence" (Unpublished report prepared for the Economic Policy Institute, Washington, DC, 1988).

18. T. Plewes, "Understanding the data on part-time and temporary employment" (Paper presented at a conference on "Women and the Contingent Workforce," sponsored by the U.S. Department of Labor, Women's Bureau, February 1987).

19. S. Oates, "Temporary Employment Industry Booming," *San Francisco Chronicle*, Section F, 7 August 1985, p. 6.

20. Bureau of National Affairs (BNA), "The Changing Workplace: New Directions in Staffing and Scheduling" (Washington, DC: BNA, 1986); D. Mayall and K. Nelson, "The Temporary Help Supply Service and the Temporary Labor Market" (Report Submitted to the Office of Research and Development, Employment and Training Administration, U.S. Department of Labor, Washington, DC, 1982); and Uchitelle (n. 4).

21. K. Abraham, "Flexible Staffing Arrangements and Employers' Short Term Adjustment Strategies," *National Bureau of Economic Research Working Paper* 2619 (1988) Cambridge.

22. BNA (n. 20).

23. Plewes (n. 18); and Carre (n. 17).

24. Abraham (n. 21).

25. J. Day, "Rent-a-Staff: A New Lease on Work?" *Across the Board* 25(7):54–58.

26. S. Haber, E. Lamas, and J. Lichtenstein, "On their Own: The Self-Employed and Others in Private Business," *Monthly Labor Review* (May 1987): 17–23.

27. Haber, Lamas, and Lichtenstein (n. 26).

28. E. Appelbaum and P. Albin, Chapter 3 of this volume.

29. S. Christopherson, "Workforce Flexibility: Implications for Women Workers," Institute for Social Science Research, University of California Los Angeles, Working Papers in the Social Sciences, 1987–88, Volume 3, Number 2.

30. Appelbaum and Albin, Chapter 3 of this volume.

31. T. Noyelle and T. Stanback, *The Economic Transformation of American Cities* (Totowa, NJ: Rowman & Allenheld, 1984).

32. Small Business Admininstration (SBA), *The State of Small Business: A Report of the President* (Washington, DC: GPO, 1987), p. 300.

33. M. Granovetter, "Small Is Bountiful: Labor Markets and Establishment Size," *American Sociological Review* 49(1984): 323–334.

34. SBA (n. 32), p. 301.

35. Federal Reserve Bank of Chicago, *Chicago Fed Letter* (March 1989); Christopherson, Noyelle, and Redfield; and S. Christopherson and M. Storper, "Industrial Politics and Flexible Production: The Motion Picture Industry," *Industrial and Labor Relations Review* (April 1989).

36. K. Christensen, *Women and Home-based Work: The Unspoken Contract* (New York, NY: Henry Holt & Co., 1988).

37. OTA (n. 1).

38. Joselow (n. 2).

39. J. I. Gershuny and I. Miles, *The New Service Economy: The Transformation of Employment in Industrial Societies* (London: Frances Pinter, 1983).

40. Organization for Economic Cooperation and Development (OECD), "Flexibility in the Labour Market, A Technical Report" (Paris: OECD, 1986), p. 51.

41. OECD (n. 40), p. 112.

42. Christopherson (n. 29).

3

Shifts in Employment, Occupational Structure, and Educational Attainment

Eileen Appelbaum and Peter Albin

The success of the U.S. economy in generating large numbers of new jobs after 1973, when compared to Western Europe where aggregate employment has stagnated, is widely known. Between 1973 and 1987, the U.S. economy added 27 million jobs, 14.5 million after 1979. Most of these new jobs have been in the service sectors. As a result, service sector employment, which in 1973 accounted for 62 percent of all U.S. jobs, increased to 67 percent of total employment (63 percent of total output) by 1987.

In analyzing employment growth in the United States, however, the simple distinction between manufacturing and service industries is insufficient. Service industries are quite diverse; some are capital-intensive, make extensive use of computer, information, and control technologies, and are important inputs into the production of other goods and services. The growth of these service industries has important implications for economic development, trade, the growth of wages, and the employment of skilled workers. By comparison, other service industries exhibit the low productivity growth traditionally associated with services. Employment growth in these service industries depends on either or both government subsidies or the availability of a low-wage labor force in order to overcome what has been termed, "the cost disease of stagnant services," the increase of costs in stagnant activities relative to those in which productivity growth is high. As we demonstrate in this chapter, these sharply contrasting characteristics of service industries mean that occupational and employment characteristics of jobs in these industries also differ sharply. One implication is that the impact on the economy of the accelerating shift to service employment will differ sharply depending on where within the service sectors new employment is located. Elsewhere we have proposed a taxonomy of firms and industries into broad sectors, on the basis of "information and knowledge intensity."[1] Information and knowledge intensity is a multidimensional property of firms and industries, reflecting the nature of the output produced, the extent of computer rationalization of the production process, and the organizational adaptation to information and computation technologies. Data limitations make it impossible for us to implement a completely new classification scheme for the U.S. economy based on the information and knowledge industry as defined above. Nevertheless, to the extent possible, we find it useful to regroup conventionally defined manufacturing and service industries into subsectors that partly reflect information and knowledge intensity.[2]

In our taxonomy, we measure computer rationalization in an industry by its investment in electronic computing equipment and by its employment of workers in computer-related occupations. As for the nature of the output, we adopt Machlup's proposal, developed further by Porat, that all industries, which produce information machines, which transform, communicate or transport information, or which sell information services, be included in the information sector of the economy.[3] In addition to private industries which engage in market transactions of information goods and services, included are public education, public research and development, the postal service, and public administration. Because of the lack of appropriate data, we are unable to capture the dimension of organizational adaptation to information and computation technologies in our taxonomy.

The resulting sectoral division of industries seems quite reasonable. (See the Appendix at the end of this chapter for a detailed description of our taxonomy.) In the industrial sector, "information and knowledge manufacturing" includes electronic computing equipment; office and accounting machines; radio, TV, and communication equipment; professional and photographic equipment; scientific and controlling instruments; and printing, publishing, and allied industries. "Other industries" encompasses construction; other durable goods and nondurable goods manufacturing; and transportation and public utilities. In the service sector, "information and knowledge services" consists of education; professional services; business services except janitorial services and detective and protective services; communications; finance, insurance, and real estate; and public administration. "Other services" includes hospitals; other health services; social welfare services; personal and recreation services; private household services; eating and drinking places and hotels; vehicle sales; retail trade; wholesale trade; automobile service and repair; and guard, cleaning, and repair services. The remaining industries—agriculture, forestry, fisheries, and mining—are classified as "extractive industries."

It is generally recognized that the skill requirements of firms depend on the nature of the firm's output, the technology employed—particularly computer and information technologies, and the organization of the firm—especially work organization and industrial relations. Not surprisingly then, the sectoral division of industries utilized in this chapter helps to clarify shifting employment, occupational, and educational attainment patterns.

A principal finding of our research is that there are important differences in occupational distribution and educational requirements between the information and knowledge intensive sectors and other sectors within both manufacturing and services. We conclude from this that evocations of a "post-industrial" society miss the point by combining all service industries into a single sector and stressing the distinctions between services and goods, rather than by taking note of the informational distinction that cuts across these industries. But the "deindustrialization" thesis—namely, that the decline of employment in manufacturing industries implies, principally, a shift to a low-wage, low-productivity growth economy—also misses the point.

What emerges from our analysis is that the shift to employment in service industries has resulted in increasing the economic dualism in the U.S. economy. The differences between information and knowledge services and "other services" are stark. Thus, some services, such as communications, have experienced rapid productivity growth. Likewise, in wholesale trade and financial services, capital-labor ratios are rising. Information and knowledge services have generated more than 9 million additional jobs since 1973 and absorbed more than 5.7 million college-educated workers at earnings that compare favorably with those in the "other industry" sector. Over the same time period, however, the "other service" sector has added 11.2 million jobs, 7.7 million of them in sectors in which median earnings of full-time workers in 1986 were one-third or less below the median for the industrial sector, and in which the proportion of part-time jobs ranges from 25 to 40 percent of employment.

There are major economic costs associated with this kind of employment growth. At the time of this writing, the U.S. employment rate was down to its 1978 level, but the proportion of the U.S. population living in poverty had risen. Over the last decade, the number of poor people has increased by nearly 10 million. Average hourly real wages have been stagnant in the United States since 1973. And a recent report from the Census Bureau shows that income inequality increased over the last 20 years.[4] Many of these costs have been borne by women.

There are also important, unanswered questions about the sustainability of this type of employment growth. What are the implications of an increasingly two-tier economy for consumption patterns? How will this affect the role of the United States as a major market for mass-produced goods and services? What are the future implications of growth in low-wage jobs and the increase in the poverty population for motivation and access to higher education? And how will this affect the labor skills available to information and knowledge intensive industries? What will be the effect of these developments on the shift back to manufacturing that will be necessary if the United States is to control its trade deficit? Will the United States become an attractive location for the low-wage assembly operations of foreign multinationals? How would this affect U.S. economic development? Many of these questions are beyond the scope of this chapter, which is limited to examining recent developments in employment, occupational structure, and educational attainment. Nevertheless, they serve to warn us that current developments are not benign. To focus simply on the magnitude of recent employment growth, without recognizing the economic and social costs associated with it, would be a mistake. Likewise, it would be wrong to project recent employment trends blindly into the future.

This chapter examines recent employment trends using unpublished data from the *Current Population Survey* (CPS) for March 1973, 1979, and 1987. The CPS is a monthly survey of 60,000 representative households that is conducted by the U.S. Census Bureau on behalf of the U.S. Department of Labor, Bureau of Labor Statistics (BLS). Based on population weights, BLS extrapolates and reports these data for the population as a whole. Nineteen-seventy-three and 1979 were chosen because they are peak years in the U.S. business cycle; 1987, because it is the most recent year of the current expansion for which data are available.

Trends in Employment and Output Growth by Industry

Table 3.1 summarizes employment data for March 1987 utilizing our information-knowledge based sectoral division of industries. About 33 percent of all employment in the United States is in goods-producing industries and intermediate activities. Information and knowledge manufacturing accounts for only 3.2 percent of total employment; other industry, for 26.5 percent. Of the men, 45.4 percent hold jobs in the goods-producing industries; of the women, only 18.4 percent. The remaining 67 percent of total employment is in service-producing industries. Information and knowledge services account for 27.7 percent of all jobs— 22.9 percent of jobs held by men and 33.5 percent of jobs held by women. Other services account for 39.0 percent of all jobs—31.6 percent

Table 3.1 Percentage Distribution of Employed Civilians by Industry and Gender, 1987

| | | Percentage Distribution of Employment by | | | | | |
| | Number | Industry | | | Gender | | |
Industry	(millions)	Total	Men	Women	Total	Men	Women
Extractive	3.96	3.6	5.3	1.5	100.0	81.3	18.7
Information-knowledge manufacturing	3.56	3.2	3.5	2.9	100.0	59.3	40.7
Other industry	29.07	26.5	36.6	14.0	100.0	76.1	23.9
Information-knowledge services	30.40	27.7	22.9	33.5	100.0	45.5	54.5
Other services	42.86	39.0	31.6	48.0	100.0	44.5	55.5
All industries	109.85	100.0	100.0	100.0	100.0	55.0	45.0

Source: U.S. Department of Commerce, Bureau of the Census, *Current Population Survey* (March 1987).

of jobs held by men and 48.1 percent of those held by women. Thus, nearly 82 percent of women hold jobs in service-producing industries compared with about 55 percent of men.

Output and employment trends for 1973–1987 are reported in Tables 3.2, 3.3, and Table 3.4. Output data presented in Tables 3.2 and 3.3 are from the National Income and Product Accounts of the United States compiled by the Bureau of Economic Analysis (BEA). Working from published data, we have rearranged the industries to conform, insofar as possible, with our sectoral divisions. The output measure is real (or deflated) gross domestic product. An imputed value for the services of owner-occupied and rental housing is included by BEA in the value of the output of the real estate industry, though this differs in kind from the services provided by the rest of the financial services industry and

Table 3.2 Percentage Distribution of Gross Domestic Product by Industry, 1973, 1979, and 1987

Industry	1973	1979	1987
Extractive industries	7.5	6.5	5.6
Information-knowledge manufacturing	3.4	3.8	3.9
Other industry	32.7	30.9	28.9
Information-knowledge services	32.8	34.4	35.5
Information-knowledge services minus housing[a]	25.6	27.0	27.9
Other services	23.6	24.3	26.1
Gross Domestic Product[b] (in billions of 1982 dollars)	2,726.6	3,146.9	3,824.3

[a]Except imputed housing costs.

[b]Measured as the sum of gross product by industry (without corrections for statistical discrepancies or discrepancies that arise as a result of measuring GDP as the sum of incomes).

Source: Author's calculations. Derived from U.S. Department of Commerce, Bureau of Economic Analysis, *National Income and Product Accounts of the United States, 1929–1982* (Washington, DC: GPO, 1986); and *Survey of Current Business* (July 1988).

Table 3.3   Average Annual Rates of Growth of Gross Domestic Product by Industry, 1973-1979 and 1979-1987

Industry	1973-1979	1979-1987
Extractive industries	0.2	0.4
Information-knowledge manufacturing	4.4	2.8
Other industry	1.4	1.6
Information-knowledge services	3.2	2.8
Information-knowledge services minus housing[a]	3.3	2.9
Other services	2.9	3.4
Gross Domestic Product	2.4	2.5

[a]Except imputed housing costs.

Source: Author's calculations. Derived from U.S. Department of Commerce, Bureau of Economic Analysis, National Income and Product Accounts of the United States, 1929-1982 (Washington, DC: GPO, 1986); and Survey of Current Business (July 1988).

results in very few jobs. We report the output of the information and knowledge services sector with and without imputed housing services.

Output since 1973 has grown most slowly in the other industry sector, with a compound average annual rate of growth of 1.4 percent between 1973 and 1979, rising slightly to 1.6 percent between 1979 and 1987. The small information and knowledge (IK) manufacturing sector was the most rapidly growing sector of the economy between 1973 and 1979, with an average annual growth rate of 4.4 percent. This rate was substantially higher than the growth rate for information and knowledge services (3.2 percent) or for other services (2.9 percent). During the 1979 to 1987 period, however, the rate of output growth in I-K manufacturing fell to 2.8 percent per year—a rate equal to that of I-K services, which also slowed. Both of these growth rates were substantially below the growth of output in other services, which accelerated to a 3.4 percent annual rate, with much of the increase coming from wholesale and retail trade. As a result of these differences in growth rates, I-K manufacturing increased slightly its share of output between 1973 and 1987, from 3.4 to 3.9 percent; the share of other industries declined sharply, from 32.7 to 28.9 percent; and the shares of both service sectors increased substantially: I-K services from 25.6 to 27.9 percent and other services from 23.6 to 26.1 percent.

Turning to employment trends (Table 3.4), we note that the rate of employment growth slowed substantially during the 1980s, declining from the 2.4 percent annual rate of growth during 1973-1979 to 1.8 percent during 1979-1987. The declines were sharpest in the industrial sectors where even I-K manufacturing recorded a slowdown from 3.0 percent annual growth in the earlier period to just 1.1 percent in the later one. Employment growth in both I-K services and other services

Table 3.4 Percentage Distribution of Employment and Employment Growth by Industry, 1973, 1979, and 1987

Industry	Percentage Distribution of Total Employment			Average Annual Rate of Employment Growth		Percentage Distribution of Employment Growth	
	1973	1979	1987	1973-1979	1979-1987	1973-1979	1979-1987
Extractive	4.0	4.7	3.6	0.0	0.3	-0.1	0.7
Information-knowledge manufacturing	3.4	3.3	3.2	3.0	1.1	4.2	2.1
Other industry	30.6	32.6	26.5	1.3	0.0	17.1	-0.6
Construction	6.1	6.1	6.2	2.1	2.2	5.5	7.4
Nondurable manufacturing	7.2	8.6	6.0	-0.5	-0.6	-1.8	-2.3
Durable manufacturing	12.3	12.7	9.4	1.8	-1.5	9.4	-9.5
Transportation, public utilities	5.0	5.2	4.9	1.9	1.3	4.1	3.7
Information-knowledge services	25.2	23.6	27.7	3.5	3.0	35.8	44.2
Education	8.7	8.6	8.4	2.7	1.4	9.8	6.6
Professional services	2.3	1.7	2.6	7.4	3.5	6.1	4.8
Communications	2.1	2.2	2.1	1.2	1.7	1.1	1.9
Finance, insurance, real estate	6.0	5.3	6.7	4.5	3.3	10.5	11.6
Business services	1.6	1.3	3.1	5.6	10.9	3.4	13.4
Public administration	4.5	4.4	4.7	2.6	2.3	4.9	5.9
Other services	36.8	35.9	39.0	2.8	2.5	43.0	53.6
Hospitals	4.0	3.8	4.0	3.6	1.5	5.9	3.4
Other health	3.1	2.6	3.7	5.0	4.1	6.0	7.7
Social welfare	2.3	1.8	2.8	6.3	4.5	5.3	6.3
Personal and recreation	2.8	2.8	3.0	2.4	2.6	2.8	4.2
Private household help	1.4	1.9	1.0	-3.2	-1.9	-2.3	-1.3
Eating, drinking/hotels	5.0	4.2	5.8	5.4	3.7	10.2	11.3
Vehicle sales	2.2	2.5	2.0	0.3	0.3	0.3	0.4
Retail trade	10.0	10.3	10.0	1.9	1.8	8.0	10.3
Wholesale trade	3.9	4.0	4.1	1.7	2.4	2.8	5.4
Auto services, repair	1.0	0.9	1.2	4.9	4.0	1.9	2.4
Guard/cleaning/repair	1.2	1.1	1.5	4.2	4.8	2.0	3.5
Total	100.0	100.0	100.0	2.4	1.8	100.0	100.0

Source: U.S. Department of Commerce, Current Population Survey (March 1987, March 1979, and March 1987).

37

also slowed somewhat in the most recent period but remained above the economy-wide growth rate. As a result, the employment share of service industries increased. By 1987, nearly 28 percent of all jobs were in I-K services and another 39 percent were in other services.

Examining employment growth by detailed industry, only three sectors experienced net declines between 1973 and 1987—the small private household services industry (domestic servants) and the two branches of manufacturing (other than information and knowledge manufacturing, nondurable goods, and durable goods). The loss of manufacturing jobs occurred primarily in the later period, 1979–1987. Job gains in durable goods manufacturing and in information-knowledge manufacturing between 1973 and 1979 resulted in actual increases in manufacturing employment during that period. At the other end of the spectrum, the sector with the largest share of new job growth over the entire period was finance, insurance, and real estate. This sector accounted for 11.1 percent of new jobs added during the entire period, and 11.6 percent of jobs added between 1979 and 1987. Business services, eating and drinking places, and motels also experienced explosive employment growth. Business services, which accounted for only 1.3 percent of total employment in 1979, contributed 13.4 percent of new jobs between 1979 and 1987. As a result, their share of total employment increased to 3.1 percent in 1987. Employment growth in eating and drinking places and motels over this time period was nearly as dramatic. The industry accounted for 4.2 percent of total employment in 1979 but accounted for 11.3 percent of new jobs in the last eight years. Over the entire period, 1973–1987, job growth in restaurants and motels was actually stronger than job growth in business services—10.8 percent compared to 8.7 percent of all new jobs, respectively. The other large gainer of net new jobs was retail trade, 10.3 percent of new jobs between 1979 and 1987, up from 8.0 percent in the 1973–1979 period.

On the whole, the average annual rate of employment growth in information and knowledge services was considerably more rapid than in other services, although the larger size of the other service sector resulted in a larger share of new jobs being created in that sector. Between 1973 and 1979, other services contributed 43.0 percent of new jobs, compared with 35.8 percent for information and knowledge services. And between 1979 and 1987, other services contributed more than half of total U.S. employment growth, 53.6 percent, compared with 44.2 percent for information and knowledge services.

Job creation in information-knowledge services can be attributed to the role of these services as inputs into the production of other goods and services. But what explains the large employment growth in other services? We would argue that low wages are a big part of the explanation.

In industries where low wages prevail, low wages slow the rationalization of work and the diffusion of computer-based technologies, whose rationale for adoption is often that they are labor saving. As a result, such industries can be expected to experience slow productivity gains. We note that productivity growth in what we have termed other services is slower in the United States than in most Western European countries, and slower today than in earlier periods.[5] Sufficiently low wages in these industries serve to offset the rising labor costs that would otherwise be associated with slow productivity growth and thus make possible the continued expansion of employment. Nearly two-fifths (37.0 percent) of new job growth between 1979 and 1987 was in sectors included in the other service grouping in which median earnings of full-time, year-round wage and salary workers in 1986 were below $15,500. This is $7,000 less than the $22,555 median earnings of all full-time workers employed in the other industry grouping and almost $9,000 less than the $24,507 median earnings of full-time workers employed in durable goods manufacturing, the very sector in which most of the job losses during this period took place (see Table 3.5).

In descending order of net new job creation, the industries in which job creation was high and wages were low were: restaurants and hotels, 11.3 percent of new jobs, median earnings of $11,515; retail trade, 10.3 percent of new jobs, median earnings of $15,514; health services other than hospitals, 7.7 percent of new jobs, median earnings of $14,837; personal and recreation services, 4.2 percent of new jobs, median earnings of $14,546; and janitorial, protective, and repair services, 3.5 percent of new jobs, median earnings of $15,233. In total, these industries created more than 5.3 million additional jobs over this time period. This 37 percent share of new jobs created between 1979 and 1987 represented a substantial increase over the earlier 1973–1979 period when these industries contributed 29 percent of all new employment.

In contrast, the share of additional jobs generated by the better paid publicly provided or publicly subsidized services—public administration, education, hospitals, and other social welfare services—declined between the earlier and later periods. These sectors accounted for 26 percent of jobs created between 1973 and 1979, nearly as large a share as the low-wage industries. But their share of new job growth between 1979 and 1987 fell to 22 percent while the share of the other sectors included in the other service grouping increased to 37 percent (see Table 3.4). In absolute terms, public administration, education, hospitals, and other social welfare services added 3.2 million jobs between 1979 and 1987. The slowdown in average annual employment growth rates in the sectors between 1973–1979 and 1979–1987 was sharpest in education and hospitals. In education, the average growth rate fell by half, from 2.7 percent

Table 3.5   Median Annual Earnings of Wage and Salary Workers (in dollars),[a] 1986

Industry	Both Genders	Men	Women
Extractive	18,282	18,824	16,441
Information-knowledge manufacturing	24,828	29,784	18,656
Other industry	22,555	25,578	15,656
Construction	21,221	22,141	16,323
Nondurable manufacturing	20,450	25,593	14,118
Durable manufacturing	24,507	26,938	17,355
Transportation, public utilities	26,258	28,553	18,982
Information-knowledge services	23,033	28,828	18,886
Education	22,269	26,873	20,184
Professional services	25,864	35,166	19,348
Communications	28,111	30,397	24,904
Finance, insurance, real estate	19,637	29,879	16,773
Business services	21,733	29,296	18,455
Public administration	23,748	27,586	18,316
Other services	17,772	21,479	14,379
Hospitals	20,127	23,889	19,083
Other health	14,837	22,647	14,170
Social welfare	16,274	20,278	14,515
Personal and recreation	14,546	18,396	11,910
Private household help	7,394	11,640	7,067
Eating, drinking/hotels	11,515	14,098	10,075
Vehicle sales	18,583	19,715	13,463
Retail trade	15,514	20,074	12,298
Wholesale trade	21,961	24,861	17,005
Auto services, repair	16,234	16,622	15,001
Guard/cleaning/repair	15,233	16,103	11,806
All industries	20,662	25,274	16,464

[a]Full-time, year-round employees. Excludes self-employed incorporated, who are counted as employees in published statistics.

Source: Author's calculations based on unpublished data from the U.S. Department of Commerce, *Current Population Survey* (1986).

a year to 1.4 percent. In hospitals, the decline was even greater, from 3.6 percent to 1.5 percent. More modest declines were registered in public administration, from 2.6 percent a year to 2.3 percent, and in other social welfare services, from 6.3 percent to 4.5 percent (see Table 3.4).

Demographic changes provide a partial explanation for slower growth in education (the last of the baby-boomers graduated from high school in 1979) but not for the slowdown in employment growth in the other three sectors. If anything, increases in the number of older Americans should have increased demand for hospital services, and the increase in single-parent households should have raised the demand for other social welfare services. A large part of the explanation for slower growth lies in a sharp decrease in the federal commitment to social programs and government services from the Carter to the Reagan administrations. Hospitals, in particular, were hit hard by the institution of a new federal payment plan for elderly or indigent patients that effectively reduced the federal subsidy for hospital care. In turn, this translated into more stringent employment policies even before the payment plan went into effect.[6] Other health services was less affected by these changes because indirect subsidies via Medicare and Medicaid are much lower than for hospitals. In addition, specialized facilities (e.g., psychiatric centers and orthopedic centers) were explicitly excluded from the new reimbursement plan; and reimbursement of short procedures units were not much affected by the changes. There was, as a result, some shifting of employment from hospitals to other health services.

To conclude, employment growth slowed after 1979 through the entire economy but most significantly in manufacturing, including information and knowledge manufacturing, and in publicly provided or publicly subsidized educational and hospital services. Together, these sectors, in which median 1986 earnings of full-time, year-round employees varied from $20,127 to $24,828, provided 27.5 percent of the new jobs between 1973 and 1979 but less than 1 percent between 1979 and 1987. Employment growth in the latter period was divided between the remaining information-knowledge and the remaining industries in the other services sector. Median full-time earnings in information-knowledge services were $23,033; median full-time earnings in other services were $17,772, but, as observed above, most of the jobs added in this sector were in industries paying $15,500 or less.

Labor Force Characteristics

In this section, we turn to a discussion of the gender and racial characteristics of the workers employed in each sector of the U.S. economy. There are, as might be expected, important distinctions between service industries and goods-producing industries, especially in their employment of women workers. But there are also important differences within each major sector, between employment in information and knowledge intensive activities and employment in other activities.

Labor Force Characteristics by Major Sector in 1987

Table 3.6 summarizes labor force characteristics by major sector in 1987. Service industries are major employers of women, and about 55

Table 3.6 Labor Force Characteristics by Sector, 1987

Characteristic	All	Extractive	Information-Knowledge Manufacturing	Other Industry	Information-Knowledge Services	Other Services
Total employment (in thousands)	109,854	3,964	3,561	29,071	30,395	42,862
Percentage of total	100.0	3.6	3.2	26.5	27.7	39.0
Percent						
Female	45.0	18.7	40.7	23.9	54.5	55.5
Male	55.0	81.3	59.3	76.1	45.5	44.5
Black[a]	9.8	3.5	7.2	10.4	9.8	10.1
White[a]	87.2	94.2	89.2	87.0	87.4	86.6
With college degree	22.9	12.4	29.9	13.6	40.3	17.1
Men	24.7	12.1	35.7	14.6	48.0	20.4
Women	20.6	13.6	21.2	10.3	33.9	14.5
With some college	20.5	14.4	22.2	17.3	22.7	21.6
Young (16–24)	17.4	17.2	14.4	12.9	12.7	24.2
Prime (25–54)	69.5	62.4	73.8	74.0	74.4	63.4
Older (55+)	13.0	20.4	11.9	13.1	12.9	12.4
Full-time	81.8	81.3	91.2	93.6	83.5	71.9
Part-time	18.1	18.7	8.8	6.4	16.5	28.1
Wage and salary	91.3	60.9	97.9	93.5	94.1	90.0
Unemployment rate						
Total	6.3	8.8	6.1	9.5	3.3	6.3
Men	6.8	9.5	5.3	9.5	3.2	6.3
Women	5.7	5.5	7.1	9.4	3.3	6.2

Median annual earnings[b] (in dollars)

Wage and salary						
Total	20,662	18,282	24,828	22,555	23,033	17,772
Men	25,274	18,824	29,784	25,578	28,828	21,479
Women	16,464	16,441	18,656	15,656	18,886	14,379
Self-employed incorporated						
Total	30,672	20,554	32,337	32,253	39,802	29,108
Men	35,114	23,424	40,547	34,444	41,637	32,526
Women	16,699	10,593	12,013	19,273	22,638	16,212
Self-employed unincorporated						
Total	15,386	7,725	15,193	18,157	26,068	14,567
Men	17,942	8,153	21,297	18,616	30,366	18,852
Women	7,930	6,338	10,949	11,860	14,911	7,137
Median hourly earnings[b] (in dollars)						
Usually full-time	7.24	6.67	8.43	8.08	7.85	6.25
Usually part-time	4.24	4.33	5.01	5.27	5.06	4.04

[a]Blacks and whites do not sum to 100 percent because other minorities are not shown.
[b]For year-round, full-time workers. Transportation and public utilities are included in wage and earnings data for "other services" and not in "other industry." As a result, median earnings in "other services" are overstated.

Source: Author's calculations based on unpublished data from the U.S. Department of Commerce, *Current Population Survey* (March 1987).

percent of the work force in both I-K and other services is female compared with 41 percent in I-K manufacturing and only 24 percent in other industry.

Most of the part-time jobs are found in service industries. Just over 28 percent of workers in other services and 16 percent of workers in I-K services work part-time. The proportion of part-time employment in I-K manufacturing, however, is about 9 percent and in other industry only 6 percent.

Perhaps because of its extensive part-time employment, the other service sector also provides employment for a large proportion of young workers. About one-quarter of the workers in this sector are between the ages of 16 and 24, though less than 10 percent are teenagers (younger than 20 years old). Excluding extractive industries, the proportion of teens employed in each of the other sectors is below 3 percent. Workers above the age of 55 make up 12 to 13 percent of employment in the nonextractive industries.

Blacks are 9.8 percent of employed workers in the United States and 10 percent of the work force in both service sectors and in other industry. Blacks are underrepresented in I-K manufacturing, however, where they make up only 7 percent of the work force.

Despite these similarities, there are major differences between the characteristics of jobs in information and knowledge intensive sectors and other sectors. I-K services and I-K manufacturing employ a much higher proportion of college-educated workers than the other sectors. Educational attainment, as measured by the median number of school years completed, is highest in I-K services, where the median is 14.5 years, followed by I-K manufacturing, where the median is 13.4 years. Median education in the extractive industries, other industries, and other services varies from 12.4 to 12.7 years (not shown in Table 3.6).

The differences among sectors is even more dramatic when the proportion of employees with college degrees is compared. The proportion of workers with a college degree is 40.3 percent and 29.9 percent, respectively, in I-K services and I-K manufacturing. This is substantially higher than in the rest of the economy, where employment of workers with four or more years of college varies from 17.1 percent in other services to 13.6 percent in other industry and 12.4 percent in the extractive industries. The proportion of workers with postgraduate education employed in I-K services is twice that in any other sector— nearly 20 percent, compared with 9 percent of employees in I-K manufacturing, 6 percent in other services, and 4 percent in both other industry and the extractive industries (not shown in Table 3.6). An additional 20 percent of the work force in both information and knowledge sectors—services and manufacturing—has a bachelor's degree. Finally, counting all workers who have completed at least one year of college, 63 percent of those employed in I-K services have attended college. This contrasts sharply with the other services sector in which more than 60 percent of the work force have never attended college (see Table 3.6).

If we distinguish on the basis of gender, we find that about 38 percent of female workers and 48 percent of male workers in information and knowledge services have a college degree, compared with only 15 percent of female workers and 20 percent of male workers in other services. Similarly, about 36 percent of men and 21 percent of women in information-knowledge manufacturing have college degrees, compared with 15 percent of men and 10 percent of women in other industry.

Unemployment rates also differ by sector. The overall unemployment rate for workers with previous work experience in March 1987 was 6.3 percent, 6.8 percent for men and 5.7 percent for women. The lower unemployment rate for women is due to their disproportionate representation in industries in which unemployment is lower, and not to lower unemployment rates for women within industries. Unemployment rates are lowest in information and knowledge services, where they are about 3.3 percent for both men and women.

Self-employment is lower in the information and knowledge sectors. Only 6 percent of employment in information-knowledge services is self-employment compared with 10 percent in other services; and only 2 percent in information-knowledge manufacturing compared with almost 7 percent in other industry.

Finally, median earnings—whether self-employment or wage and salary—are substantially higher in the two information and knowledge sectors than in the corresponding service and industry sectors. Comparing only year-round, full-time workers, median earnings of wage and salary workers are lowest in other services. For men, median earnings in this sector are $21,479 compared with $28,828 in I-K services; in other industries, they are $25,578 compared with $29,784 in I-K manufacturing. For women, median earnings in other services are only $14,379 compared with $18,886 in I-K services; in other industries, they are $15,656 compared with $18,656 in I-K manufacturing. Thus, women in the information and knowledge sectors do better than women in other sectors, but they earn substantially less on average than men in the industries in which they are employed. In the two service sectors, mean earnings of women are about 67 percent of those of men, while in the industrial sectors they are about 62 percent of those of men (see Table 3.6).

Earnings of self-employed workers employed year-round and full-time follow a similar pattern, except that self-employed women fare worst in the I-K manufacturing sector. The relatively high earnings of self-employed incorporated workers in other services is due to the inclusion of doctors and dentists offices, nursing homes, freestanding surgical units, social workers, and so on in this sector. Unincorporated self-employed workers include free-lance workers of all kinds. Median earnings for male self-employed incorporated workers is $35,114 and for female, $16,699. For unincorporated self-employed workers the medians are $17,942 for men and $7,930 for women.

Finally, for hourly waged workers, it is possible to compare median hourly wages of full-time and part-time workers. As shown in Table 3.6, part-time workers in the other service sector are the lowest paid, at $4.04 an hour; full-time workers in information-knowledge manufacturing are the highest paid, earning $8.43 an hour. Hourly earnings of full-time workers are $8.08 in other industries. These are before-tax hourly earnings, and do not include the value of fringe benefits which are generally lower for, and often unavailable to, part-time workers.

Labor Force Characteristics by Detailed Sectors

In this section we turn to an examination of labor force characteristics by detailed sectors.

Part-Time Employment. Part-time employment increased steadily between 1973 and 1987, from 16.6 percent of total employment in 1973, to 17.4 percent in 1979, and 18.2 percent in 1987 (Tables 3.7 and 3.8). Part-time employment is heavily concentrated in other services, accounting for 28 percent of all jobs in 1987, compared with 16.5 percent in information and knowledge services. Part-time work is especially prevalent in retail trade (34 percent of workers) and restaurants and hotels (40 percent).

In general, part-time employment has expanded in line with the expansion of other services, where 63 percent of all part-time jobs are found. However, the rate of expansion of part-time jobs among other services has slowed in recent years. Between 1973 and 1979, 32 percent of all jobs added in other services were part-time jobs; between 1979 and 1987, this proportion dropped to 26 percent. Even in retail trade and restaurants and hotels the proportion of new jobs filled on a part-time basis, while still high, was substantially lower than before 1979. In information-knowledge services, the proportion of new jobs filled on a part-time basis fell from 21 percent between 1973 and 1979 to 14 percent between 1979 and 1987. Part-time employment in this sector rose from 16.3 percent of all jobs in 1973 to 17.1 percent in 1979 before falling back to 16.5 percent in 1987.

Part-time job growth in hospitals fell precipitously during the 1980s as hospital services and employment were restructured following the change in federal payment for hospital care of the elderly and the

Table 3.7   Labor Force Characteristics by Industry, 1973

| | Percentage | | | |
Industry	College Graduate	Part-Time	Women	Black
Extractive	6.3	17.5	15.0	5.3
Information-knowledge manufacturing	15.5	8.4	36.1	5.9
Other industry	6.9	5.2	21.0	9.9
Construction	5.2	7.4	5.7	7.7
Nondurable manufacturing	7.4	4.2	38.1	11.8
Durable manufacturing	7.3	3.1	20.0	9.0
Transportation, public utilities	7.1	9.4	13.4	11.8
Information-knowledge services	33.4	16.3	49.7	9.1
Education	55.9	26.3	63.7	10.8
Professional services	47.4	14.5	35.2	3.7
Communications	6.7	6.6	35.8	12.7
Finance, insurance, real estate	19.0	11.9	51.3	6.2
Business services	18.7	22.4	52.0	4.6
Public administration	19.6	6.1	32.6	11.2
Other services	10.3	27.8	50.4	10.3
Hospitals	14.5	14.5	76.3	18.3
Other health	26.8	26.2	72.0	8.7
Social welfare	34.2	24.5	51.0	12.8
Personal and recreation	6.5	35.3	58.4	9.8
Private household help	1.8	65.8	91.3	38.0
Eating, drinking/hotels	2.8	40.1	59.3	9.8
Vehicle sales	4.8	17.6	12.0	5.6
Retail trade	7.0	32.1	49.2	6.0
Wholesale trade	14.3	7.3	21.8	5.3
Auto services, repair	2.0	12.9	9.7	8.0
Guard/cleaning/repair	4.9	22.8	16.9	10.5
All industries	14.6	16.6	38.5	9.5

Source: U.S. Department of Commerce, *Current Population Survey* (March 1973).

indigent. Part-time workers in hospitals, who are the highest paid of all part-time workers, were especially hard hit as hospitals adjusted to the anticipated reduction in federal payments. Some of the responsibility for care of the poor and the old was shifted to nursing homes and to other social welfare services, both of which increased their use of part-time workers after 1979. Hourly wages in these industries in 1987 ($5.54 and $4.22 an hour, respectively) were well below the $8.77 an hour paid by hospitals (see Table 3.9).

Part-time employment is highly concentrated in just a few sectors and, within those sectors, in just a few occupations. Three sectors, restaurants and hotels, retail trade, and education, provided less than

Table 3.8   Labor Force Characteristics by Industry, 1987

Industry	Percentage				
	Union Member	College Graduate	Part-Time	Women	Black
Extractive	9.0	12.4	18.7	18.7	3.5
Information-knowledge manufacturing	10.5	29.9	8.8	40.7	7.2
Other industry	27.0	13.6	5.7	23.9	10.4
Construction	23.2	8.6	9.6	8.4	7.2
Nondurable manufacturing	23.4	14.3	4.9	40.8	14.6
Durable manufacturing	27.4	15.7	3.6	25.1	8.8
Transportation, public utilities	34.3	15.1	9.6	20.8	12.4
Information-knowledge services	20.9	40.3	16.5	54.5	9.8
Education	31.6	57.1	27.3	65.3	10.7
Professional services	2.2	55.3	12.3	44.5	3.5
Communications	48.9	19.3	5.5	39.5	13.8
Finance, insurance, real estate	3.0	29.0	12.4	59.7	8.3
Business services	3.1	35.4	20.6	53.0	8.7
Public administration	30.0	30.7	7.6	41.2	13.2
Other services	8.4	17.1	28.1	55.5	10.1
Hospitals	15.9	32.7	16.4	77.5	15.0
Other health	7.8	31.6	24.9	77.4	10.5
Social welfare	8.1	33.6	31.6	69.1	13.2
Personal and recreation	8.2	14.2	31.8	60.3	8.6
Private household help	0.2	2.6	65.7	88.2	23.5
Eating, drinking/hotels	3.8	7.5	39.9	56.8	11.4
Vehicle sales	2.6	8.7	12.4	18.8	5.2
Retail trade	10.4	11.9	34.2	56.0	7.8
Wholesale trade	8.2	21.1	8.7	28.8	5.8
Auto services, repair	4.1	3.9	13.3	14.5	6.5
Guard/cleaning/repair	10.5	7.8	25.7	29.7	14.8
All industries	17.1	22.9	18.2	45.0	9.8

Source: U.S. Department of Commerce, *Current Population Survey* (March 1987).

25 percent of all jobs in the economy in 1987 but more than 44 percent of part-time jobs. Nearly one-half of all sales clerks and workers in service occupations in retail trade were employed part-time, compared with less that 10 percent of those employed in administrative, managerial, and supervisory positions. Of the 6.6 million part-time workers in retail trade in 1987, 71 percent were employed in sales clerk or service worker occupations. In restaurants and hotels, 79 percent of part-time workers are employed in service worker occupations, while in education, nearly half the part-time workers are found in clerical and service worker jobs. Thus, opportunities for part-time workers are restricted to a rather narrow range of jobs, virtually assuring that part-time employment will

Table 3.9 Earnings of Wage and Salary Workers (in dollars),[a] 1987

Industry	Median Hourly Wages Paid by the Hour		Median Weekly Earnings (Usually Full-Time)
	Usually Full-Time	Usually Part-Time	
Extractive	6.67	4.33	309
Information-knowledge manufacturing	8.43	5.01	422
Other industry	8.08	5.27	384
Construction	9.05	5.81	395
Nondurable manufacturing	6.73	4.84	332
Durable manufacturing	8.46	5.27	409
Transportation, public utilities	9.96	6.51	451
Information-knowledge services	7.85	5.06	418
Education	6.91	4.90	416
Professional services	9.20	6.21	471
Communications	11.81	8.02	501
Finance, insurance, real estate	6.54	5.20	365
Business services	6.19	4.89	359
Public administration	9.82	5.10	454
Other services	6.25	4.04	314
Hospitals	8.44	8.77	373
Other health	5.96	5.54	272
Social welfare	5.56	4.22	321
Personal and recreation	5.19	4.16	267
Private household help	3.67	3.49	152
Eating, drinking/hotels	4.24	3.58	212
Vehicle sales	5.64	3.94	318
Retail trade	5.54	4.03	277
Wholesale trade	6.74	5.05	383
Auto services, repair	6.10	4.23	287
Guard/cleaning/repair	5.98	4.03	268
All industries	7.24	4.24	369

[a]Excludes self-employed and self-employed incorporated. First-quarter averages, 1987.

Source: U.S. Department of Commerce, *Current Population Survey* (March 1987).

continue to be unattractive to men who might otherwise prefer a reduction in hours (for example, older workers who desire partial retirement.[7]

Recent concern over the growth of part-time work in the United States is related to the involuntary nature of much of the growth in part-time employment since 1979 and to the low wages and lack of health and pension benefits in many of these jobs. In 1987, approximately 5.5 million people were employed as involuntary part-timers, people who want full-time employment, but who are unable to obtain and who must work part time instead. About 42 percent of part-time workers have no health insurance coverage and 70 percent have no retirement benefits.[8] Average hourly wages of part-time workers in 1987 were only $4.24 compared with $7.24 for full-time workers paid by the hour. The average weekly earnings of all full-time wage and salary workers was $369, or approximately $9.22 an hour (see Table 3.9).

Union and Earnings Characteristics. The extent of unionization in the United States is by now quite low. Only 17 percent of wage and salary workers currently belong to unions (see Table 3.8). The relatively high rate of unionization in the other industry groups, where 27 percent of workers are union members, reflects the traditional strength of American unions in old-line manufacturing industries and in construction and transportation. More surprising, perhaps, is the relative strength of unionization in information and knowledge service industries with communications the most heavily unionized (49 percent union members), followed by education (32 percent) and public administration (30 percent).

Employment growth since 1979, however, has been low in sectors where unions are the strongest. Employment has declined in nondurable goods and durable goods manufacturing since 1979, following a strong recovery in manufacturing productivity. Strong rationalization in communications has meant slow employment growth despite strong growth in output.[9] Demographic shifts and the fiscal priorities of the Reagan Administration contributed to slower employment growth in public sector activities (education and public administration) since 1979. Thus, highly unionized industries in both the other industry sector and the information-knowledge services sector accounted for only 13.8 percent of net new jobs between 1979 and 1987.

The recent decline in union membership results in part, from the inability of unions to organize workers in the relatively newer sectors of the information and knowledge services, where employment is growing the fastest, and from their long-standing failure to organize workers in the other service group. Union membership in information and knowledge manufacturing is only 10.5 percent; in finance, insurance, and real estate, and in business and professional services, it is a mere 3 percent. Unionization in other services averages 8.4 percent, and only in hospitals, where 16 percent of workers belong to unions, does it approach the national average.

With the exception of information and knowledge manufacturing and professional services, where workers paid hourly have above average earnings, hourly waged workers earn much less in industries where unionization is relatively weak than in those in which it is relatively strong. When weekly earnings of all workers (salaried and hourly workers) are considered, a similar result emerges. While weekly earnings are above average in all of the more heavily unionized industries, they are below average in nonunionized industries with the exception, again, of information and knowledge manufacturing and professional services (see Tables 3.7 and 3.8).

Employment of Women and Blacks. Labor force participation rates of women have increased steadily in the United States since 1973. Between 1973 and 1987, women increased their share of total employment from 38.5 percent to 45.0 percent (see Tables 3.7 and 3.8). Women's share of employment rose in nearly all industries. But the pattern of female employment by industry is little changed today from two decades ago.

By 1973, women were already 50 percent or more of the work force in education, finance, insurance, and real estate, business services, hospitals, other health services, other social welfare services, personal and recreation services, domestic services, eating and drinking places and hotels, and retail trade. These are the very same industries in which they held more than 50 percent of the jobs in 1987 as well. Women were also well represented in information-knowledge manufacturing, nondurable goods manufacturing, professional services, communications, and public administration by 1973, holding between one-third and one-half of all jobs in these industries. By 1987, women held between two-fifths and one-half of all jobs in these industries but less than 30 percent of jobs in the traditional male strongholds—the extractive industries, construction, durable goods manufacturing, transportation and public utilities, motor vehicle sales, wholesale trade, automotive services, and guard, janitorial, and repair services.

While the overall pattern of women's employment by industry shows little change over a decade and a half despite rising female labor, women have made notable gains in a few industries. Thus, women's share of employment increased from 13 percent of all jobs in 1973 to 21 percent in 1987 in transportation and public utilities; from 33 to 41 percent in public administration; and from 51 to 69 percent in other social welfare services. These services are either publicly regulated, publicly subsidized, or government provided. As such, they may have been more amenable to programs put in place during the 1970s to enforce affirmative action in hiring. In addition, women's employment in finance, insurance, and real estate increased from 51 percent of all jobs in 1973 to 60 percent in 1987, partly as the result of two successful affirmative action suits brought by the Equal Employment Opportunities Commission against the insurance industry, which previously had had a poor record in hiring women in nonclerical positions. Finally, women raised their share of jobs in professional services substantially, from 35 to 45 percent of employment.

Blacks were 10.6 percent of the U.S. labor force in 1987 but, because of their very high unemployment rate (14.7 percent in March 1987), represented only 9.8 percent of the employed work force.[10] This is only marginally higher than the 9.5 percent share of jobs they held in 1973 (see Tables 3.7 and 3.8). In 1973, blacks were underrepresented in industriès engaged in trade (motor vehicle sales, other retail trade, and wholesale trade); they remain so today. They are also substantially underrepresented in professional services, where their share of employment slipped from an already low 3.7 percent of all jobs in 1973 to 3.5 percent in 1987.

However, important improvements in the employment position of blacks can be noted. While their share of jobs in agriculture and domestic service has declined, their share of jobs in several information and knowledge intensive industries has increased. The share of blacks employed in information-knowledge manufacturing increased from 5.9 percent in 1973 to 7.2 percent in 1987; in finance, insurance, and real estate, their share increased from 6.2 to 8.3 percent; and in business services, from 4.6 to 8.7 percent. Blacks are still underrepresented in these industries, but their share of jobs has increased substantially in the last decade and a half. Blacks have also made gains in industries where they were strongly represented by 1973. Their share of employment increased from 11.8 to 14.6 percent in nondurable goods manufacturing; from 12.7 to 13.8 percent in communications; from 11.2 to 13.2 percent in public administration; and from 10.5 to 14.8 percent in tertiary business services (guard and janitorial services) and repair.

Occupational Composition

The occupational composition within a sector depends as much on the organization of work within firms in the sector as on the nature of the sector's output. Thus, important differences in occupational structure emerge when industry and services are classified according to information and knowledge intensity.

Sectoral Differences in Occupational Composition

Table 3.10 compares occupational distributions among our major industry groups in 1987. Changes in occupational definitions after 1984 make it difficult to compare 1987 with earlier years.

Table 3.10 shows a very high proportion of employees in executive, administrative, or in management-related positions in 1987 in both I-K manufacturing and I-K services: 16.2 percent in such occupations in the I-K manufacturing sector; 17.4 percent, in the I-K services sector. The corresponding proportions for other industry and other services are 10.9 percent and 8.8 percent, respectively. Supervisors, however, make up 9.4 percent of the labor force in other services—triple the proportion in I-K services and double the proportion in I-K manufacturing.

I-K manufacturing industries make the most intensive use of professional employees with specialties in engineering, mathematics, computer

Table 3.10 Occupational Distribution of Employment by Industry, 1987

			Industry			
	All	Extractive	Information-Knowledge Manufacturing	Other Industry	Information-Knowledge Services	Other Services
Total employment (in thousands)	109,854	3,964	3,561	29,071	30,395	42,862
Occupation (in percent)						
Executive/administrator	9.8	35.3	13.1	8.9	10.4	7.3
Management-related	3.2	1.4	3.1	2.0	7.0	1.5
Supervisor	6.5	4.0	4.5	6.4	3.2	9.4
Professional[a]	3.0	2.4	7.6	4.1	4.5	0.7
Other professional	10.3	1.3	7.7	0.9	20.7	10.4
Health technician	1.0	0.5	0.1	0.1	0.3	2.3
Engineer/scientific technician	1.9	1.3	5.4	2.2	3.6	0.4
Sales representative	3.4	0.5	5.4	2.1	5.9	2.5
Sales worker	5.4	0.0	2.0	0.2	0.7	13.0
Secretary/typist	4.6	1.3	3.6	2.6	8.9	3.3
Information clerk/computer operator[b]	5.2	2.1	5.1	3.1	8.5	4.7
Other clerical	6.0	1.2	8.1	4.8	10.5	3.9
Precision services	7.4	0.3	0.0	0.1	4.6	15.8
Service operator	5.4	0.5	1.1	1.8	4.6	9.3
Farm worker/fisherman/ hunter/logger	1.6	35.0	0.1	0.2	0.4	0.5
Mechanic/repairer	3.8	2.7	2.7	5.1	2.2	4.2
Precision production/craft	6.2	4.1	4.5	18.0	1.0	2.3
Operator/fabricator/ laborer	15.2	6.2	25.8	37.5	3.0	8.7
Total	100.0	100.0	100.0	100.0	100.0	100.0

[a]Engineer, mathematician, computer specialist, scientist, social scientist.

[b]Includes other peripheral operators.

Source: U.S. Department of Commerce, Current Population Survey (March 1987).

sciences, natural sciences, or social sciences, while other services makes the least intensive use of these labor skills: 7.6 percent of all employment in I-K manufacturing but only one-tenth that figure (0.7 percent) in other services.

Engineering and science technicians are used more extensively in the information and knowledge sectors than in the other industry or other services sectors. They represent 5.4 percent of the labor force in I-K manufacturing and 3.6 percent in I-K services but only 2.2 percent in other industry and 0.4 percent in other services.

Information clerical workers and computer and peripheral equipment operators are used most extensively in I-K services where they constitute

8.5 percent of the work force. This contrasts with other services, where they represent only 4.7 percent of the work force. A similar difference can be observed between I-K manufacturing and other industry, where the proportions of information clerical and related workers are 5.1 percent and 3.1 percent, respectively.

Service occupations are concentrated in other services where they account for just over 25 percent of the labor force compared with just over 9 percent in the I-K services sector. About 16 percent of the work force in other services is in skilled service occupations ("precision services") and 9 percent in less skilled ("service operators"). Service and sales occupations account for more than 40 percent of employment in other services but less than 16 percent in I-K services.

Production workers are more highly concentrated in other industry than in I-K manufacturing. Mechanics, precision production, operators, laborers, and related occupations account for more than 60 percent of employment in other industry but only 33 percent in I-K manufacturing.

In short, the intensity of use of information and knowledge skills is highest in I-K manufacturing, where 18.1 percent of the work force is employed as professional specialists (engineers, mathematicians, etc.), engineering or science technicians, or information and related clerks. It is nearly as high in I-K services where the proportion of such workers is 16.6 percent of all employees. In contrast, only 9.4 percent of the work force in other industry is employed in such occupations, and only 5.8 percent in other services. If executive and managerial positions are added, the share of all such occupations is 34.3 percent in I-K manufacturing and an almost identical 34.0 percent in I-K services. The corresponding shares for other industry and other services are only 20.3 percent and 14.6 percent, respectively. The contrast between I-K services and other services, in this regard, is most striking.

Educational Attainment, Work Time, and Gender Differences by Occupations Between Information-Knowledge and Other Services

Differences in Educational Attainment and Work Time by Occupations. It is sometimes argued that occupational differences are more relevant than industry differences when discussing skill requirements and work time.

A comparison of educational attainment and work time differences between the two service sectors, by detailed occupational category, points to two observations (Table 3.11). First, within occupations the educational attainment requirements are generally much lower in other services than in information-knowledge services. For example, the largest differentials in educational attainment requirements can be found among executives

Table 3.11 Occupational Characteristics, 1987

Occupation	In Occupation	Percentage With College Degree	Part-Time	1986 Median Earnings[a] (in dollars)
Information and knowledge services				
Executive/administrator	10.4	52.8	7.7	31,298
Management-related	7.0	55.7	6.4	26,102
Supervisor	3.2	23.8	3.4	26,703
Professional[b]	4.5	77.7	5.7	35,249
Other professional	20.7	85.5	16.7	25,830
Health technician	0.3	32.1	16.7	19,198
Engineer/scientific technician	3.6	41.0	14.3	25,950
Sales representative	5.9	43.6	11.7	28,266
Sales worker	0.7	9.9	59.4	14,794
Secretary/typist	8.9	10.7	18.5	15,947
Information clerk/computer operator[c]	8.5	15.5	21.4	15,869
Other clerical	10.5	12.0	22.0	18,088
Precision services	4.6	12.4	18.0	24,176
Service operator	4.6	5.2	40.7	14,451
Farm worker/fisherman/hunter/logger	0.4	7.5	15.7	15,644
Mechanic/repairer	2.2	6.2	2.8	27,475
Precision production/craft	1.0	4.9	10.7	21,666
Operator/fabricator/laborer	3.0	6.7	37.2	17,562
Total	100.0	40.3	16.5	23,033
Other services				
Executive/administrator	7.3	31.1	7.3	24,265
Management-related	1.5	39.4	10.5	22,648
Supervisor	9.4	18.5	7.6	21,726
Professional[b]	0.7	76.5	10.0	33,744
Other professional	10.4	60.6	23.4	23,548
Health technician	2.3	21.9	23.4	17,518
Engineer/scientific technician	0.4	40.5	9.8	25,662
Sales representative	2.5	36.8	8.0	26,505
Sales worker	13.0	9.3	47.4	12,628
Secretary/typist	3.3	9.1	24.1	14,911
Information clerk/computer operator[c]	4.7	9.4	26.4	14,258
Other clerical	3.9	8.9	27.6	15,966
Precision services	15.8	5.5	39.9	10,898
Service operator	9.3	3.6	47.4	11,050
Farm worker/fisherman/hunter/logger	0.5	4.1	28.7	11,095
Mechanic/repairer	4.2	3.4	8.5	19,715
Precision production/craft	2.3	6.4	16.4	23,054
Operator/fabricator/laborer	8.7	3.4	29.8	18,660
Total	100.0	17.1	28.1	17,772

[a]For full-time wage and salary workers.
[b]Engineer, mathematician, computer specialist, scientist, social scientist.
[c]Includes other peripheral operators.

Source: U.S. Department of Commerce, Current Population Survey (March 1987).

and administrators (53 percent with a college degree in information-knowledge services compared with 31 percent in other services), managers (56 percent compared with 40 percent), sales representatives (44 percent compared with 37 percent), information clerical workers (15 percent compared with 9 percent), and precision service occupations (12 percent compared with 5 percent).

Second, other services generally make greater use of part-time workers than I-K services, not only in sales occupations and service operators occupations but also in administrative support occupations, in precision service occupations, and in health professional and technician positions.

Gender Differences by Occupations. Women have found increased employment opportunities since 1973 in both information and knowledge services and other services. They currently make up about 55 percent of employed workers in both service sectors. However, the experience of women in these two sectors differ sharply from that of men, both in terms of occupational composition and, within occupations, in terms of the full-time salaries that they command (Table 3.12).

In both service sectors, women hold between 70 and 99 percent of health technician, sales worker, secretary, information clerical, and other clerical jobs. They also hold 75 percent or more of the precision service positions in other services. They are underrepresented in upper, middle, and lower management ranks and in professional and technical positions, although, overall, they do hold a significant proportion of these jobs.

Women, like men, are generally better paid in information-knowledge services than in other services. However, the pay differentials between men and women within occupational categories is striking. For example, women supervisors earn $5,000 more a year in information-knowledge services than in other services. But this is $11,000 less than male supervisors in information-knowledge services and $5,000 less than male supervisors in other services. Female information clerical workers in information-knowledge services earn $1,500 more a year than their counterparts in other services but $7,500 less than their male counterparts in information-knowledge services and $5,500 less than males in the same occupational category in other services.

Trends in Educational Attainment

Educational Attainment of the Labor Force

Before turning to an analysis of the utilization of college-educated workers by sectors, it is useful to review briefly the rise in educational attainment in the U.S. labor force since 1973. Not only has the size of the U.S. labor force increased, from 87.4 million in 1973 to 118.1 million

Table 3.12 Occupational Characteristics by Gender, 1987

Occupation	Percentage in Occupation		Median Earnings (in dollars)[a]	
	Male	Female	Male	Female
Information and knowledge services				
Executive/administrator	56.1	43.9	37,279	24,860
Management-related	53.9	46.1	31,214	21,293
Supervisor	59.1	40.9	32,194	20,837
Professional[b]	77.4	22.6	37,739	29,175
Other professional	41.1	58.9	30,233	22,874
Health technician	26.9	73.1	18,199	20,061
Engineer/scientific technician	61.2	38.8	28,007	21,974
Sales representative	62.2	37.7	32,514	21,455
Sales worker	26.4	73.6	17,085	13,962
Secretary/typist	*	98.5	*	15,968
Information clerk/computer operator[c]	17.7	82.3	22,641	14,984
Other clerical	30.3	69.7	24,482	15,849
Precision services	64.8	35.2	26,191	12,444
Service operator	58.1	41.9	15,573	12,357
Farm worker/fisherman/hunter/logger	94.0	6.0	14,993	16,573
Mechanic/repairer	92.2	7.8	27,581	26,525
Precision production/craft	96.4	3.9	22,272	11,530
Operator/fabricator/laborer	64.2	35.8	19,202	14,634
Total	45.5	54.5	28,828	18,886
Other services				
Executive/administrator	56.8	43.1	29,427	19,113
Management-related	46.9	53.1	28,398	19,700
Supervisor	66.0	34.0	25,551	15,754
Professional[b]	56.6	42.8	36,974	22,050
Other professional	36.3	63.7	26,316	22,655
Health technician	13.0	87.0	21,196	16,975
Engineer/scientific technician	58.9	41.1	29,699	19,536
Sales representative	81.4	18.5	27,930	19,867
Sales worker	31.1	68.9	18,158	10,050
Secretary/typist	*	98.8	*	14,925
Information clerk/computer operator[c]	9.8	90.2	20,604	13,677
Other clerical	27.0	73.1	19,228	14,915
Precision services	24.4	75.6	13,109	10,363
Service operator	44.4	55.6	12,774	9,534
Farm worker/fisherman/hunter/logger	90.3	10.3	11,026	12,332
Mechanic/repairer	98.6	*	19,697	*
Precision production/craft	75.2	24.8	24,861	12,710
Operator/fabricator/laborer	79.7	20.3	20,019	10,901
Total	44.5	55.5	21,479	14,379

[a]For full-time wage and salary workers.
[b]Engineer, mathematician, computer specialist, scientist, social scientist.
[c]Includes other peripheral operators.
*Occupational share is insignificant. Median earnings not computed because of sample size.

Source: U.S. Department of Commerce, Current Population Survey (March 1987).

Table 3.13 ⁻Percentage Distribution of the Educational Attainment of the U.S. Labor Force, 1973 and 1987

Educational Attainment	Total	Men	Women	White	Black
1973					
High school dropout	32.2	34.2	29.1	30.4	48.9
High school graduate only	39.4	35.8	45.1	40.2	34.0
Some college (1–3 years)	14.2	14.5	13.8	14.6	10.3
College graduate	14.2	15.6	12.0	14.8	6.8
4 years only	8.5	8.8	8.1	8.9	4.4
5+ years	5.6	6.7	3.9	5.9	2.3
Total	100.0	100.0	100.0	100.0	100.0
1987					
High school dropout	17.9	20.0	15.4	17.1	25.5
High school graduate only	40.1	37.5	43.3	40.2	42.6
Some college (1–3 years)	20.1	18.9	21.6	20.1	19.7
College graduate	21.8	23.5	19.7	22.5	12.1
4 years only	12.8	13.3	12.3	13.2	7.9
5+ years	9.0	10.2	7.4	9.3	4.2
Total	100.0	100.0	100.0	100.0	100.0

Source: U.S. Department of Commerce, *Current Population Survey* (March 1973 and March 1987).

in 1987, but workers today are much better educated. The number of college graduates in the labor force more than doubled between 1973 and 1987, increasing from 12.4 million to 25.8 million.[11] College-educated men increased from 8.3 million to 15.3 million; college-educated women, from 4.1 million to 10.4 million. This more than 150 percent increase in the number of college-educated women is the result of both the increase in the number of women graduating from college and the rise in female labor force participation. Among blacks, the rise in college-educated workers between 1973 and 1987, from 591,000 to 1.5 million, is even more dramatic than among women. This is nearly a 160 percent increase in the number of college-educated blacks, and virtually all of it is due to improvements in the number of blacks graduating from college since the proportion of blacks in the labor force has increased only marginally since 1973.[12]

Table 3.13 shows the distribution of the U.S. labor force by educational attainment in 1973 and 1987. The table shows very little change since 1973 in the share of workers with a high school degree only: 39 percent of the labor force in 1973 compared to 40 percent in 1987. However, the table shows a dramatic decline in the proportion of high school dropouts, from nearly one-third to well under one-fifth of the labor force, and a corresponding increase in the proportion of workers educated above high school. The proportion of workers with some college education (one to three years) increased from 14 to 20 percent of the labor force, that of workers with a bachelor's degree (four or more years of college education) rose from 14 to 22 percent, while the proportion of those educated beyond the bachelor's degree (five or more years of college) increased from less than 6 to 9 percent of the labor force.

Women continue to be less likely than men to drop out of high school but also less likely to pursue graduate work beyond the bachelor's degree. About 12 percent of women in 1987, compared with 13 percent of men, have a four-year college degree only. But only 7 percent of women, compared with 10 percent of men, have completed some graduate work. Finally, women are more likely than men to attend a two-year college or to drop out before completing four years of college: 22 percent compared to 19 percent.

The high school drop-out rate for blacks in the labor force has been cut by nearly one-half since 1973. Still, one-quarter of black workers did not graduate from high school in 1987 compared with only 17 percent of white workers. Also, part of the apparent improvement may simply reflect lower labor force participation rates among poorly educated blacks. Nevertheless, blacks have made very real gains in educational attainment over the 1973–1987 period. The proportion of blacks with only a high school degree increased from 34 to 43 percent, and the proportion with some college education nearly doubled, from 10 to almost 20 percent. The proportions of black workers in these two categories are about the same as those for white workers. The proportion of blacks with four or more years of college education also increased substantially over this period, from 7 to 12 percent. However, this is still far below the nearly 23 percent of whites who are college graduates. In addition, only 4 percent of blacks, compared with 9 percent of whites, have gone beyond the bachelor's degree.

Changes in Educational Attainment by Sector

As early as 1973, information and knowledge intensive industries employed large proportions of college graduates. Fifty-six percent of those employed in education were college graduates, and 28 percent had completed five or more years of university education. Forty-seven percent of those in professional services were college graduates and 28 percent had completed five or more years of college. Finally, almost 20 percent of those employed in finance, insurance, and real estate, business services, and public administration were college graduates, as were almost 16 percent of information-knowledge manufacturing workers. Communications was the only information and knowledge intensive industry in which employment of college graduates was below the economy-wide average—7 percent of employees in communications had college degrees compared with nearly 15 percent overall (Table 3.7).

In the other services sector, social welfare services and health services other than hospitals also utilized college graduates extensively by 1973. In the other industry sector, wholesale trade was the only sector in which the utilization of college graduates approached their proportion in the work force in 1973. But college graduates made up 7 percent or less of the work force in all other subsectors of the other service and other industry sectors.

Between 1973 and 1987, the proportion of college graduates among all employed workers increased from 14.6 percent of the work force to 22.9 percent (Tables 3.7 and 3.8). This translates into increased shares of college graduates in every sector but social welfare services, where the proportion was virtually unchanged.

To assess where some of the most important changes occurred, we examined in which sector the 13 million additional college graduates were hired between 1973 and 1987. Table 3.14 shows the increase in employment of college graduates by sector between 1973 and 1987. Over 44 percent of the new college graduates and nearly 55 percent of those with five or more years of university education were hired by the information and knowledge sector compared with 35.3 percent of all new workers hired by the sector during 1973–1987. The large other services sector absorbed 33 percent of the new college graduates and 28 percent of those with five or more years of college compared with 45.7 percent of all new workers hired by the sector between 1973–1987. Other industry absorbed 16 percent of the new college graduates and 12 percent of those with education beyond the bachelor's degree, despite near zero growth in the sector between 1973–1987. In fact, despite a net employment decline in durable and nondurable goods manufacturing between 1973 and 1987, together these two sectors increased their employment of college graduates by almost 1.3 million, absorbing nearly 10 percent of the new college graduates over the period. Finally, the small information-knowledge manufacturing sector absorbed 5 percent of the new college graduates and 4 percent of the increase in those with five or more years of college, in both cases a share larger than the sector's share of all new hires.

Turning to specific subsectors, it is apparent that much of the absorption of new college graduates has been concentrated in particular industries. For example, despite a marginal increase in the already high proportion of its college-educated work force, education hired the largest number of new college graduates—over 1.3 million or 10.2 percent of the total. Furthermore, education alone absorbed 24 percent of the 1973–1987

Table 3.14   Increase in Employment of College Graduates, 1973–1987

Industry	Increases in College-Educated Workers (in thousands)	Percentage Distribution of Increases in College-Educated Workers
Extractive	247	1.9
Information-knowledge manufacturing	640	4.9
Other industry	2,089	16.1
Construction	323	2.5
Nondurable manufacturing	408	3.1
Durable manufacturing	856	6.6
Transportation, public utilities	501	3.9
Information-knowledge services	5,741	44.2
Education	1,326	10.2
Professional services	918	7.1
Communications	314	2.4
Finance, insurance, real estate	1,304	10.0
Business services	1,017	7.8
Public administration	863	6.6
Other services	4,277	32.9
Hospitals	967	7.4
Other health	693	5.3
Social welfare	521	4.0
Personal and recreation	318	2.4
Private household help	1	0.0
Eating, drinking/hotels	384	3.0
Vehicle sales	89	0.7
Retail trade	716	5.5
Wholesale trade	466	3.6
Auto services, repair	37	0.3
Guard/cleaning/repair	84	0.6
All industries	12,993	100.0

Source: U.S. Department of Commerce, *Current Population Survey* (March 1973 and March 1987).

increase in the number of workers with education beyond the bachelor's degree. Finance, insurance, and real estate absorbed almost as large a share of the new college-educated workers—10 percent or 1.3 million workers. These two sectors plus business services, hospitals, and professional services hired over 40 percent of the new college graduates. Finally, just ten of the 23 industries in Table 3.14 absorbed over 70 percent of the increase in college graduates. The only surprise is that the retail trade industry ranked eighth in terms of increased use of college graduates, and tenth in terms of its use of workers with education beyond the bachelor's degree. But this is due to the large size of this industry, not to any above-average use of college-educated workers.

Table 3.15 ˜Ratio of Industry Share of College Graduates to Industry Share of Total Employment, 1973, 1979, and 1987

Industry	1973	1979	1987
Extractive	0.43	0.54	0.54
Information-knowledge manufacturing	1.06	1.07	1.31
Other industry	0.47	0.52	0.59
Construction	0.36	0.40	0.38
Nondurable manufacturing	0.51	0.55	0.63
Durable manufacturing	0.50	0.54	0.69
Transportation, public utilities	0.49	0.54	0.66
Information-knowledge services	2.29	2.01	1.77
Education	3.82	3.03	2.50
Professional services	3.24	2.86	2.42
Communications	0.46	0.68	0.84
Finance, insurance, real estate	1.30	1.23	1.27
Business services	1.28	1.37	1.55
Public administration	1.34	1.45	1.35
Other services	0.70	0.76	0.75
Hospitals	0.99	1.22	1.43
Other health	1.84	1.63	1.38
Social welfare	2.34	1.98	1.47
Personal and recreation	0.44	0.53	0.62
Private household help	0.12	0.07	0.11
Eating, drinking/hotels	0.19	0.29	0.33
Vehicle sales	0.33	0.40	0.38
Retail trade	0.48	0.53	0.52
Wholesale trade	0.98	0.95	0.92
Auto services, repair	0.14	0.17	0.17
Guard/cleaning/repair	0.34	0.34	0.34
All industries	1.00	1.00	1.00

Source: U.S. Department of Commerce, *Current Population Survey* (March 1973, March 1979, and March 1987).

To compare the utilization of college graduates by sector, we created an index of utilization defined by the share of all college graduates employed by sector divided by the industry's share of total employment (Table 3.15). A score of 1 indicates that the proportion of college graduates which the industry utilizes is the same as its share of total employment; a score greater than 1, that the industry's use of college graduates exceeds its share of total employment; and a score below 1, that the industry utilizes less than its proportionate share of college graduates. For example, a score of 1.31 in 1987 for information-knowledge manufacturing shows that this industry employs much more than its proportionate share of college graduates, while a score of 0.52 for retail trade shows that this industry employs far less than its proportionate share of college-educated workers.

Based on the scores shown in Table 3.15, it is possible to rank the sectors according to the intensity of their use of college graduates. In 1973, ten sectors utilized college graduates in proportion or above their share of total employment: information-knowledge manufacturing, all of the information-knowledge services except communications, hospitals, other health services, social welfare services, and wholesale trade. In 1987, the same ten sectors remained the only ones with average or above-average use of college graduates, although there had been some reordering among them.

Conclusion

It has been suggested by others that despite its obvious success in generating employment growth, the U.S. economy has not escaped the crisis that confronts the industrialized nations of Western Europe.[13] In contrast to Europe, however, where the main dimension of the crisis has been high unemployment, adaptation to change in the United States has taken the form of low-wage employment in low-productivity growth industries for a large and increasing segment of the labor force. The much vaunted flexibility of the U.S. labor market has translated mainly into expanded employment in the other services sector. The availability of a low-wage labor force has slowed the pace of technological change in this sector. Productivity growth in this sector has been slower than in manufacturing and information-knowledge services and has also lagged far behind the rates of productivity growth in similar activities in Europe.[14]

The result, we would argue, has been the revitalization of a dual economic structure in the United States, characterized by an increase in income inequality, a rise in poverty, and slow overall productivity growth—attributes generally associated with underdevelopment and which are ordinarily expected to wither in technologically progressive economies.[15] This economic dualism can be traced to employment growth in the service industries—particularly once the distinction between information-knowledge services and other services has been established. The gendered nature of employment relations in the United States in permitting the extension of this dualistic structure also stands out; for it is largely women who continue to fill many of the lowest paying jobs in other services.

The deindustrialization thesis, which emphasizes the decline in employment in traditional manufacturing and notes the small employment contribution—documented here as well—of the expanding information-knowledge manufacturing sector, loses some of its urgency in light of the employment expansion in information and knowledge service industries. This sector of the economy has generated more than 9 million additional jobs since 1973, and absorbed more than 5.7 million college-educated workers, at earnings that compare favorably with those in other industry. Over the same time period, however, other services have added 11.2 million jobs, 7.7 million of them in sectors in which the median earnings of full-time workers in 1986 were one-third or more below the average for other industry and in which the proportion of part-time jobs ranged from 25 to 40 percent of employment.

The long-term impact of the continuing, simultaneous expansion of a technologically progressive, high-wage information and knowledge service sector and a low-wage other service sector on the U.S. economy remains uncertain. The key role of mass production manufacturing in fueling rapid economic growth in the 25 years following the end of World War II, by providing for the rise in real wages and the spread of mass consumption, is well established. However, the period since 1979 suggests the feasibility of robust employment growth and rapid economic expansion in the presence of rising income inequality. Low wages in the other services keep the costs of these labor-intensive activities from rising too rapidly relative to the cost of the outputs of the technologically progressive sectors. Meanwhile, high wages among a significant proportion of workers in information and knowledge intensive sectors, especially male workers, mean that there will continue to be consumers with sufficient discretionary income to purchase these services. Apart from the question of the social desirability or political viability of such a pattern of economic growth, it remains to be seen, however, whether such a pattern of employment growth can be sustained or whether increases in income inequality will undermine economic growth via the saturation of markets for mass-produced items and the slow diffusion of technologically sophisticated consumer goods and services.

Notes

1. P.S. Albin and E. Appelbaum, "Productivity and Employment Implications of Computer Rationalization," Paper presented at the American Economic Association Meetings, Chicago, December 1987; E. Appelbaum and P.S. Albin, "Structural Change and Employment Dynamics in the US," Working Paper, Temple University, Philadelphia, 1989; and U.S. Congress, Office of Technology Assessment, *International Competition in Services*, OTA-ITE–328 (Washington, DC: GPO, July 1987).

2. For a detailed explanation, see Appelbaum and Albin (n. 1).

3. F. Machlup, *The Production and Distribution of Knowledge in the United States* (Princeton, NJ: Princeton University Press, 1962); and M.U. Porat, "The Information Economy: Definition and Measurement," U.S. Department of Commerce, Office of Telecommunications (Washington, DC: GPO, 1977).

4. U.S. Department of Commerce, Bureau of the Census, *Current Population Survey* (March 1987).

5. L.C. Thurow and B. Waldstein, "Services in the American Economy," Draft report prepared for the Economic Policy Institute, Washington, DC, March 1988; and L.C. Thurow, "The End of the Post-industrial Era," Paper presented at the Economics Association Meetings, New York, December 1988.

6. E. Appelbaum and C.S. Granrose, "Hospital Employment Under Revised Medicare Payment Plan," *Monthly Labor Review* (August 1986).

7. H. Kahne, *Reconceiving Part-Time Work* (Totowa, NJ: Rowman & Allanheld, 1985).

8. M. Pollock and A. Bernstein, "The Disposable Employee Is Becoming a Fact of Corporate Life," *Business Week* (December 15, 1986): 52–53.

9. J.W. Kendrick, *Productivity in Services. National Academy of Engineering Symposium on Technology in Services Industries: The Next Economy* (Washington, DC: January 1988).

10. Bureau of Labor Statistics, unpublished data from the *Current Population Survey*, March 1973, March 1979, and March 1987.

11. Bureau of Labor Statistics (n. 10).

12. Bureau of Labor Statistics (n. 10).

13. B. Harrison and B. Bluestone, *The Great U Turn* (New York, NY: Basic Books, 1988); and P. Petit, *Slow Growth and the Service Economy* (London: Frances Pinter Publishers, 1986).

14. Thurow and Waldstein (n. 5).

15. Petit (n. 13).

APPENDIX

Census Codes of Industries Listed in the Tables

Extractive industries (agriculture, forestry, fisheries, and mining)	A(010)–050
Information and knowledge manufacturing	C(171),172,321,322,341,371–382
Other industry	B(060),100–162,180–222,230–320,331,332,340,342–370,390–392
Construction	B(060)
Nondurable goods manufacturing	100–162,180–222
Durable goods manufacturing	230–320,331,332,340,342–370,390–392
Transportation, public utilities	400–411,420–432,460,472
Information and knowledge services	412,440–442,G(700)–712,721,730–740,742,841,L(842),M(850)–861,882–892,900–932
Education	L(842),M(850)–861,891
Professional services	730,841,882,890,892
Communications	440–442,412
Finance, insurance, real estate	G(700)–712
Business services	721,731,732,740,742
Public administration	900–932
Other services	400–411,420–432,460–472,500–571,580–691,722,741,750–760,J(761)–802,812–840,862–881
Hospitals	K(831)
Other health services	812–830,832,840
Other social welfare services	862–881
Personal and recreation	770–791
Private household	J(761)
Eating and drinking places, hotels	F(641),762
Motor vehicle sales, service, supply	612–622
All other retail trade	580–611,630–640,642–691
Wholesale trade	500–571
Automotive services, auto repair	750,751
Janitorial, protective, repair	722,741,752,760

Source: U.S. Department of Commerce, Bureau of the Census.

4

A Special Focus on
Employment Growth in
Business Services and Retail Trade

Robert Bednarzik

As noted by Eileen Appelbaum and Peter Albin in the previous chapter, the strength of the U.S. job market during the 1980s has drawn worldwide attention. Unemployment has declined drastically, to the point where many economists think that we are now near full employment. A major part of the story is the unabated rise in the number of jobs in the service sectors.

This chapter examines employment growth in the U.S. service sectors over the past fifteen years and takes an in-depth look at two service-producing industries: business services and retail trade. Both have experienced rapid job growth. In addition, the business services industry is characterized by a mix of high-wage and low-wage employment, and retail services, predominantly by low-wage jobs.[1]

It is often assumed that high industry earnings reflect the high-skill level of an industry's work force. Average hourly earnings in the business services sector in 1987 were $8.73, ranging from $12.20 in the computer and data processing services industry to $6.68 per hour in the services to buildings industry. In retail trade, average hourly earnings in 1987 were $6.11, ranging rather narrowly from $7.80 in auto dealers and service stations to $4.42 in eating and drinking places. This latter figure does not include tips. Estimates of tipped occupations in the hotel and motel industry in 20 large cities in 1983, derived from the Bureau of Labor Statistics *Industry Wage Survey*, showed that 43.4 percent of total average hourly earnings was received in tips among the approximately 30 percent of the workers who hold tipped occupations.[2] Using these numbers to estimate wages, including tips, in eating and drinking places raises the per hour wage in this industry to $5.44. Average hourly

Table 4.1 -Number and Percentage Distribution of Jobs by Major Industry, 1987, and Net Changes, 1986–1987

Industry	Total Jobs, 1987		Net Job Change, 1986–1987		
	Number of Jobs (000)	Percentage Distribution	Number of Jobs (000)	Percentage Change	Percentage Distribution
Goods-producing	24,784	24	226	0.9	8
Mining	721	1	−56	−7.2	−2
Construction	4,998	5	182	3.8	7
Manufacturing	19,065	19	100	0.5	4
Service-producing	77,525	76	2,558	3.4	92
Transportation & public utilities	5,385	5	130	2.5	5
Wholesale trade	5,872	6	119	2.1	4
Retail trade	18,509	18	579	3.2	21
Finance, insurance and real estate	6,549	6	266	4.2	10
Services	24,196	24	1,143	5.0	41
Government	17,015	17	322	1.9	12
Total	102,310	100	2,785	2.8	100

Source: U.S. Department of Labor, Bureau of Labor Statistics, *Employment and Earnings* (March 1987 and March 1988).

earnings for production or nonsupervisory jobs in private sector, non-agricultural establishments were $8.98 in 1987.

Overall Job Growth

Recent Growth

Employment growth accelerated in 1987, the fifth straight year of economic expansion. The number of nonagricultural payroll jobs increased 2.8 million in 1987, following a 2 million increase in 1986. From 1982, when the recovery began, to 1987, employment grew an average of 2.7 percent per year.

Although the number of jobs in manufacturing increased in 1987, following two years of decline, the vast majority of the job growth has been among service-producing industries. Of the 102.3 million jobs in 1987, three-fourths were in service-producing industries. In every state in the United States, there are more jobs in this sector than in manufacturing, agriculture, construction, and mining combined. The distribution of jobs by major industry in 1987 and changes in 1986–1987 are shown in Table 4.1.

The goods-producing sector showed renewed strength in 1987, gaining a quarter of a million jobs over the year. After experiencing substantial job losses in 1985 and 1986, manufacturing added 100,000 jobs in 1987. Job gains in the construction industry were the most robust.

The service-producing sector continued to expand at a rapid pace, adding 2.6 million jobs in 1987. Since 1982, the beginning of the economic recovery, this sector has added nearly 12 million new jobs, accounting for nine out of ten new jobs. This represents a 3.4 percent average annual rate of growth. In 1987, as was the case throughout most of the decade, the largest and most significant increases were in the service, retail trade, and finance, insurance, and real estate divisions.

The service division, which includes personal, business, social, automobile and other repair, health, legal, educational and entertainment services as well as hotels, accounted for over 40 percent of all non-agricultural jobs added in 1987. The service division is now the largest major industry division in the United States, accounting for 24 percent of all jobs, surpassing the 19 percent share of manufacturing and the 18 percent share of retail trade.

Long-Run Changes

The purpose of this chapter is to examine secular, not cyclical, changes. In Table 4.2, observations are made at the same points in the business cycle as those selected by Appelbaum and Albin: 1973, 1979, and 1987. Nineteen-seventy-three and 1979 are business cycle peaks as designated by the National Bureau of Economic Research. Although 1987 is not an officially designated peak period, it is the most recent year for which complete data are available and is also a year characterized by a strong labor market.

While manufacturing recovered strongly between 1975 and 1979 from the severe job losses of the 1973–1975 recession, reaching an all time high of 21 million in 1979, the sector never completely recouped from the back-to-back economic downturns of the early 1980s. Factory employment fell to 18.4 million in 1983. By 1988, the number of jobs in manufacturing had inched back up to 19.5 million, but this was still 1.5 million short of the 1979 peak level.

In sharp contrast, the service-producing sector added over 25 million jobs between 1973 and 1987. This growth was led by the service division, where the number of jobs almost doubled between 1973 and 1987, from 12.9 to 24.2 million. Retail trade and finance, insurance, and real estate industries also posted strong job growth over the period. The weakest job growth was in the transportation and public utility industry, due in part to the breakup of the telephone monopoly. Following the 1982

Table 4.2 Number of U.S. Jobs by Detailed Industry, 1973, 1979, and 1987

Industry	Total Employment (in thousands)			Percent Women			Average Hourly Earnings in 1987[a] (in dollars)
	1973	1979	1987	1973	1979	1987	
Goods-producing	24,893	26,461	24,784	24.7	26.1	27.8	10.58
Mining	642	958	721	6.7	9.5	13.3	12.52
Construction	4,097	4,463	4,998	5.9	8.0	10.6	12.69
Manufacturing	20,154	21,040	19,065	29.1	30.7	32.9	9.91
Service-producing	51,897	63,363	77,525	44.0	47.6	52.2	8.32
Transportation and public utilities	4,656	5,136	5,385	21.2	24.1	28.6	12.03
Transportation	2,747	3,021	3,166	12.2	15.9	23.8	11.36
Communication	1,180	1,309	1,293	46.1	47.0	45.6	12.44
Public utilities	729	806	925	15.0	17.5	21.5	13.79
Wholesale and retail trade	16,607	20,192	24,381	40.2	43.1	47.4	7.06
Wholesale trade	4,277	5,204	5,872	23.1	25.3	29.6	9.59
Retail trade	12,329	14,989	18,509	46.2	49.2	53.0	6.11
Finance, insurance, and real estate	4,046	4,975	6,549	52.8	57.9	62.4	8.73
Finance	1,865	2,368	3,275	59.9	65.3	67.9	8.56[c]
Insurance	1,383	1,630	2,022	53.9	60.0	64.3	9.59[c]
Real estate	798	977	1,252	34.5	36.5	44.7	7.84[c]

Services[b]	12,857	17,112	24,196	54.6	58.0	60.4	8.48
Hotels and other lodging places	854	1,060	1,481	51.6	53.8	55.1	6.16
Personal services	906	904	1,147	64.0	67.5	71.4	6.37c
Business services	1,935	2,906	5,172	38.7	43.0	46.2	8.73
Auto repair services and garages	422	575	796	14.0	16.7	19.5	7.80
Misc. repair services	205	282	320	15.6	20.2	22.2	9.16
Motion pictures	207	228	234	37.2	37.3	44.0	11.92
Amusement and recreation services	535	712	894	34.0	38.6	41.5	6.95
Health	3,641	4,993	6,828	80.2	81.3	82.3	8.70
Legal	295	460	797	72.2	70.9	72.0	11.99
Educational	975	1,090	1,436	45.1	50.7	55.7	8.52c
Social	552	1,081	1,493	67.4	73.7	76.4	6.12c
Membership organizations	1,410	1,516	1,580	—	—	—	—
Misc. services	684	941	1,321	26.0	30.5	38.8	12.07
Government	13,732	15,947	17,015	43.8	46.7	51.0	—
Total	76,790	89,823	102,310	37.7	41.3	46.3	8.98

aPrivate-sector, production or nonsupervisory workers only.

bIncludes a number of jobs in museums, botanical, and zoological gardens and in private households that are not shown separately.

cUnpublished BLS data.

Source: U.S. Department of Labor, Bureau of Labor Statistics, Employment Earnings (March 1974, March 1980, and March 1988).

consent decree, American Telephone and Telegraph (AT&T) was divided into one long distance and 12 regional companies. Some of the divisions of the new companies, like sales and service divisions, became separate companies and were reclassified from the communication industry to the most appropriate Standard Industry Classification (SIC), resulting in a shuffling, rather than a loss, of jobs.

Although job growth was visible among all the major service-producing industries throughout the 1973–1987 period, it accelerated in the latter part of that period, especially in the service and the finance, insurance, and real estate divisions (see Table 4.2). Led by business services, which accounted for 18 percent of all new jobs between 1979 and 1987, nearly all industries in the service division recorded disproportionately high growth. That is, their share of net new jobs was disproportionately much larger than their share of total employment in the industry. Similarly, disproportionate job growth occurred in the finance, insurance, and real estate industry and was led by growth in banking and other financial institutions.

Women

Seven of every ten jobs added between 1973 and 1987 have been filled by women. Since the early 1970s, the rate at which women have entered the work force is very impressive. Between 1973 and 1987, the labor force participation rate for women aged 20–64 years increased from 51.7 percent to 67.3 percent. The rate for men in the same age group declined from 90.6 percent to 87.7 percent.

In 1987, women held 46 percent of all jobs, up from 38 percent in 1973. At this rate, women and men will soon share equally the number of jobs in the United States. As shown in Table 4.2, women have increased their share of jobs across nearly all industries with only two exceptions: communications and legal services.

Of course, substantial differences remain. In 1987, women held only 10.6 percent of the jobs in construction but 82.3 percent in health. In 1987, women held more jobs than men in the following major industries: retail trade, services, government, and finance, insurance, and real estate. As noted earlier, in the rapidly growing health services industry, over 80 percent of all jobs were held by women in 1987. Women hold over 70 percent of the jobs in personal services, legal services, and social services.

Business Services[3]

The business services industry has drawn much attention in the last few years. Some of this is due to its tremendous job growth. More

Table 4.3 Number and Percentage Distribution of Jobs in Business Services, 1987, and Net Changes, 1973–1987

	Total Jobs, 1987		Net Job Change 1973–1987	
Industry	Number of Jobs (000)	Percentage Distribution	Number of Jobs (000)	Percentage Distribution
Advertising	212	4.1	89	2.7
Credit reporting, collecting	99	1.9	18	0.6
Mailing, reproduction, stenographic	212	4.1	126	3.9
Services to buildings	710	13.7	346	10.7
Personnel supply services	1,196	23.1	940	29.0
Computer and data processing services	647	12.5	527	16.3
Misc. business services	2,087	40.4	1,182	36.5
Total	5,172	100.0	3,237	100.0

Source: U.S. Department of Labor, Bureau of Labor Statistics, *Employment and Earnings* (March 1988 and March 1974).

importantly, however, business services probably best typifies the changing relationship between manufacturing and service industries. To cut costs, improve flexibility, and implement new technologies, manufacturing firms are increasingly relying on business service firms to provide needed functions, talent, and know-how. The industry is on the frontier of change.

The business services industry in 1987 provided 5,172,000 jobs (5 percent of the total), making it a larger employer than construction and almost as large as transportation and public utility, and wholesale trade. The number of jobs in business services has increased unabated ever since data were reported for the industry beginning in 1958. Job growth since 1958 has averaged 7.4 percent per year, although the industry's growth slows significantly during recessionary periods. The objective here is to examine the makeup of the industry and changes in the 1973–1987 period.

The distribution of jobs in the business services industry in 1987 and changes between 1973 and 1987 are illustrated in Table 4.3. Although job growth occurred in all 3-digit SIC business service industries between 1973 and 1987, the share of job increases in personnel supply services (SIC 736) and in computer and data processing services (SIC 737) exceeded their share of all jobs in the industry. Together, these two industries accounted for nearly half of the 1973–1987 increase in the number of jobs in business services.

Job counts at the 4-digit SIC level were first available in many service-producing industries in 1982. Table 4.4 exhibits the number of jobs in business services by detailed industry. In personnel supply services, the temporary help supply services industry has been the main engine of job growth in the time period for which detailed data are available, 1982–1987. The industry more than doubled the number of jobs over that period. Although data processing services reported more jobs than computer programming and other software services in 1987, computer services added more jobs between 1982 and 1987. Job growth in miscellaneous business services (SIC 739) has been led by job increases in management, consulting, and public relations services and in equipment rental and leasing services. Part of the 1982–1987 increases in rental and leasing employment is due to growth in video tape rental stores. The 1987 changes in the SIC will move video rental stores from the equipment, rental, and leasing industry to the motion picture industry, and make them a separate 3-digit industry.

Women held 46 percent of business service jobs in 1987. Interestingly, women were underrepresented in both the industry characterized as high wage/high skill (computer and data processing) and the industry characterized as low wage/low skill (services to buildings) (see Table 4.4). In contrast, over half of the jobs in credit reporting and collecting, personnel supply services, and advertising were held by women in 1987. However, between 1982 and 1987, the proportion of jobs held by women in personnel supply services, including the temporary help industry, declined. The proportion of women in computer and data processing services declined as well. In miscellaneous business services, women workers were most likely found in management, consulting, and public relation services and photofinishing labs and least likely found in detective and protective services.

Retail Trade

Retail trade, which added over 6 million jobs from 1973 to 1987, is now nearly as large as manufacturing in the United States. It totalled 18.5 million jobs, 18 percent of all nonagricultural payroll employment in 1987. Jobs in the manufacturing industry accounted for 19 percent of the total. Average hourly earnings for production or nonsupervisory jobs in 1987 were $6.11 in retail trade, compared to $9.91 in manufacturing. All of the major retail trade industries participated in the 1973–1987 job increase.

The distribution of jobs in retail trade in 1987 and changes between 1973 and 1987 are shown in Table 4.5. Eating and drinking establishments constituted the largest subsector in 1987, with over 6 million jobs or one-third of all retail trade jobs. Food stores (mainly grocery stores), general merchandise stores (mainly department stores), auto dealers and

Table 4.4 Number of Jobs in U.S. Business Services Industry, 1973, 1979, 1982, and 1987

SIC	Industry	Total Employment				Percent Women				Average Hourly Earnings in 1987[a] (in dollars)
		1973	1979	1982	1987	1973	1979	1982	1987	
73	Business services	1,935	2,906	3,286	5,172	38.7	43.0	44.5	46.2	8.73
731	Advertising	123	146	161	211	39.8	45.9	49.7	55.2	11.88
732	Credit reporting, collecting	81	78	75	99	75.3	74.4	70.7	72.7	—
733	Mailing, reproduction, stenographic	86	113	135	212	44.2	48.7	49.6	50.5	—
734	Services to buildings	364	487	524	710	33.2	36.6	38.4	38.6	6.68
736	Personnel supply services	256	527	555	1,196	52.0	58.6	63.8	59.7	—
7361	Employment agencies	—	—	124	181	—	—	74.2	66.9	—
7362	Temporary help supply services	—	—	401	939	—	—	63.8	61.1	—
737	Computer and data processing services	120	271	365	647	47.5	47.2	46.6	44.0	12.20
7372	Computer programming, software	—	—	112	243	—	—	40.2	39.1	—
7374	Data processing services	—	—	199	296	—	—	53.8	50.3	—
739	Misc. business services	905	1,284	1,465	2,087	32.0	35.4	36.5	39.0	—
7391	R&D laboratories	—	—	170	194	—	—	28.2	30.9	—
7392	Management and public relations	—	—	366	585	—	—	52.7	53.8	—
7393	Detective and protective services	—	—	349	455	—	—	12.9	15.4	—
7394	Equipment rental and leasing	—	—	131	242	—	—	25.2	25.2	—
7395	Photofinishing laboratories	—	—	74	81	—	—	62.2	58.0	—

[a]Nonsupervisory workers only.

Source: U.S. Department of Labor, Bureau of Labor Statistics, unpublished data.

Table 4.5 Number and Percentage Distribution of Jobs in Retail Trade, 1987, and Net Changes, 1973–1987

Industry	Total Jobs, 1987		Net Job Change 1973-1987	
	Number of Jobs (000)	Percentage Distribution	Number of Jobs (000)	Percentage Distribution
Building materials and garden supplies	741	4.0	207	3.3
General merchandise	2,432	13.1	203	3.3
Food stores	2,957	16.0	1,102	17.8
Auto dealers and service stations	2,004	10.8	226	3.7
Apparel and accessory	1,108	6.0	314	5.1
Furniture, home furnishings and equipment	800	4.3	267	4.3
Eating and drinking places	6,127	33.1	3,074	49.7
Misc. retail	2,338	12.6	787	12.7
Total	18,509	100.0	6,180	100.0

Source: U.S. Department of Labor, Bureau of Labor Statistics, *Employment and Earnings* (March 1988 and March 1974).

service stations, and miscellaneous retail each accounted for another 2 to 3 million jobs. Apparel and accessory stores employed slightly over one million workers; furniture, home furnishings, and equipment stores, slightly under one million workers.

Over the 1973 to 1987 period, the two largest subsectors, eating and drinking places and food stores, also recorded disproportionately high job growth. Together, they accounted for slightly over two-thirds of the 1973–1987 increase. Average hourly earnings for nonsupervisory workers in the eating and drinking places industry were $4.42 (excluding tips) in 1987. Average hourly earnings in food stores were $6.95 in 1987. Surprisingly, this is a decline from $7.64 in 1984, primarily as a result of a decline in average hourly earnings in the grocery store industry.

Table 4.6 shows the employment levels for all of the 3-digit SIC industries in retail trade for the years under study. The retail industries in which the share of the job increase over the 1973–1987 period exceeded their share of jobs in 1973 (not shown in Table 4.6) were: radio, television, and music stores (SIC 573); family clothing stores (SIC 565); miscellaneous shopping goods stores (SIC 594); bakeries (SIC 546); grocery stores (SIC 541); and retail stores, not elsewhere classified (SIC 599). Job growth in the radio, television, and music store industry occurred primarily in radio and television stores, which added nearly 100,000 jobs between 1982 and 1987. This industry includes stores that sell computers and

Table 4.6 Number of Jobs in U.S. Retail Industry, 1973, 1979, and 1987

SIC	Industry	Total Employment (in thousands)			Percent Women			Average Hourly Earnings in 1987[a] (in dollars)
		1973	1979	1987	1973	1979	1987	
52–59	Retail trade	12,329	14,989	18,509	46.2	49.2	53.0	6.11
52	Building materials and garden supplies	535	629	741	19.4	24.8	27.7	7.03
521	Lumber and other building materials	286	338	409	13.6	18.6	21.5	7.36
525	Hardware stores	122	148	157	30.3	35.8	38.9	5.95
53	General merchandise stores	2,229	2,287	2,432	69.4	67.4	69.0	6.48
531	Department stores	1,768	1,878	2,033	68.9	66.1	68.4	6.79
533	Variety stores	311	276	240	75.2	77.5	77.5	4.84
539	General stores	150	133	160	64.0	65.5	64.4	5.01
54	Food stores	1,856	2,297	2,957	36.8	41.7	49.5	6.95
541	Grocery stores	1,624	2,002	2,604	34.6	39.8	47.9	7.10
542	Meat and fish markets	44	54	57	25.0	33.3	37.9	—
546	Retail bakeries	106	128	172	54.7	59.4	65.1	5.64
55	Auto dealers and service stations	1,778	1,812	2,004	13.5	17.2	22.6	7.80
551,2	New and used car dealers	846	881	980	12.1	14.1	16.8	9.49
553	Auto and home supply stores	205	268	319	14.1	18.3	19.1	6.68
554	Gasoline service stations	651	577	610	14.7	21.1	33.6	5.53

(continues)

Table 4.6 (Continued)

SIC	Industry	Total Employment (in thousands)			Percent Women			Average Hourly Earnings in 1987[a] (in dollars)
		1973	1979	1987	1973	1979	1987	
56	Apparel and accessory stores	795	949	1,108	66.0	69.2	74.6	5.56
561	Men's and boys' clothing stores	135	140	107	40.0	43.6	46.7	6.57
562	Women's ready-to-wear stores	294	353	388	87.4	88.7	92.0	5.21
565	Family clothing stores	130	174	257	71.5	75.3	76.7	5.50
566	Shoe stores	157	185	221	38.9	42.2	51.6	5.62
57	Furniture, home furnishings, and equipment	533	615	800	29.8	32.5	38.5	7.49
571	Furniture/furnishings, except appliances	339	377	446	32.2	35.3	41.9	7.62
572	Household appliance stores	90	86	88	24.4	26.7	34.1	7.41
573	Radio, television, and music stores	104	153	266	26.9	28.8	34.2	7.31
58	Eating and drinking places	3,054	4,513	6,127	54.8	56.6	57.3	4.42
59	Miscellaneous retail	1,551	1,886	2,338	48.9	53.1	58.2	6.32
591	Drug and proprietary stores	461	489	580	59.2	61.6	65.5	5.88
592	Liquor stores	98	128	124	19.4	25.0	36.3	—
594	Misc. shopping goods stores	399	569	783	55.6	60.1	63.6	5.88
596	Nonstore retailers	256	285	277	53.5	56.5	58.8	7.19
598	Fuel and ice dealers	105	106	108	19.0	21.7	25.9	9.05
599	Retail stores not elsewhere classified	195	253	382	39.5	47.4	56.3	6.49

[a]Nonsupervisory workers only.

Source: U.S. Department of Labor, Bureau of Labor Statistics, unpublished data.

software. The 1987 changes in the SIC will make it possible to disaggregate this industry.

There were a few retail sector industries where the number of jobs declined between 1973 and 1987. They were, in order of the absolute magnitude of their decline, variety stores (SIC 533); men's and boy's clothing and accessories (SIC 561); gasoline and service stations (SIC 554); and household appliances (SIC 572) (see Table 4.6).

Women now hold 53 percent of retail trade jobs, up from 49 percent in 1979 and 46 percent in 1973. However, there is a real mix across industries. There are eight 2-digit and 24 3-digit retail industries. In about half of them, women held the majority of the jobs. The highest proportion was in women's ready-to-wear stores (SIC 562) where women held 92 percent of the jobs in 1987, and the lowest proportion was in new and used car dealers (SIC 551,2) where women held only 17 percent of the jobs. Average hourly earnings in the new and used car dealer industry were $9.49 in 1987, the highest industry in the retail sector. In contrast, the women's ready-to-wear industry, at $5.21 in 1987, was among the lowest. Generally, retail trade industries with a large proportion of jobs held by women had lower average hourly earnings in 1987 than industries with a large proportion of jobs held by men (see Table 4.3).

Nearly all of the retail industries listed in Table 4.3 posted a larger percentage increase in the number of jobs held by women than those held by men over the 1973–1987 period. The one exception was in department stores (SIC 531), which showed a slight decline in the percentage of jobs held by women.

Notes

1. Unless otherwise indicated, the data discussed in this chapter are unpublished data from the Bureau of Labor Statistics.

2. U.S. Department of Labor Statistics, *Industry Wage Survey*, 1983.

3. The term "business services" is often used by economists to refer to sectors included in Standard Industrial Codes SIC 73 (Business Services), SIC 81 (Legal Services), SIC 87 (Engineering, Architectural, Accounting and Auditing Services), and SIC 89 (Miscellaneous Services). The discussion in this chapter focuses on SIC 73 only.

5

The Changing Face
of Retailing

Thomas M. Stanback, Jr.

Retailing is of major importance in the U.S labor market. Not only is it one of the largest employment sectors (accounting for 17 percent of all nonagricultural jobs in 1987, up from 15 percent in 1950), it is the largest employer of youth (47 percent of 16- to 19-year-old workers in 1987) and a major employer of women (19 percent in 1987).[1]

The decades since World War II have brought dramatic changes in the retailing sector. Competition has changed; new types of retailers have appeared, along with new product lines and new arrangements for merchandising, buying, warehousing, and distribution; and firms have altered their utilization of labor.

This chapter deals with the period since the late 1970s and treats a broad segment of retailing, including department stores (both traditional and discount), apparel specialty stores, supermarkets, drug stores, convenience stores, and certain new forms of discount outlets. Information is drawn from trade literature, government publications, interviews with investment analysts specializing in various segments of the industry, and interviews with human resources training executives and store managers.

New Modes of Retailing

General Merchandise

Department Stores and Discount Department Store Chains. Prior to the 1960s, traditional department stores and department store chains dominated the general merchandise segment of U.S. retailing. The large independent department store, a long-established, highly popular downtown institution, thrived in the early days of burgeoning suburbanization by establishing outlying branches, as did the few existing chains, Sears, Roebuck, J.C. Penney, and Montgomery Ward, which grew rapidly on a nationwide scale by building look-alike branches.

From their early days at the beginning of the 1960s, the discount department store chains took off. By 1966, they had surpassed traditional department stores in total sales.[2] With low overhead store locations, highly centralized operations, and mass buying they were able to effect substantial economies, offer low prices, and increase their appeal to the cost-conscious customer.

Discount department store chains are of two types, national and regional. The largest national, K mart, enjoyed spectacular growth during the 1970s. More recently, however, the rates of expansion of the national chains have moderated, and the industry is increasingly dominated by a handful of regional chains. Among the regionals, Wal-Mart is by far the most successful and has become the fastest growing large retail organization in the United States today. Wal-Mart stands second only to K mart among the discounters and is rapidly closing the gap (Table 5.1)

In spite of continued growth, the discount department chain segment of retailing has not increased significantly its market share (about 22 percent of total sales of general merchandise, furniture, and appliance stores) since the beginning of the 1970s.[3] The reason lies in the failure or slow growth of a number of discounters due to unwise investments in high-cost real estate, unimaginative merchandising, and inefficient operating procedures: one-half of the 20 leading discounters in the industry in 1975 were no longer in existence in 1987.

Regarding the success of the leading regionals, one retail investment analyst observes:

The nation's three largest discounters—K mart, Wal-Mart, and Target— are still growing as they enter their second quarter century, growth records of rare duration in the retailing business. Most other discounters, however, are struggling, and in our view many of these chains have significant operational and competitive problems. . . . We believe that many discounters have, over the years, simply confused being *low-cost distributors* with *being cheap*, a situation that we believe is now "coming home" to haunt a number of discounters.

The aggressive introduction of technology (scanning, electronic data interchange with vendors, satellite networks) by the leading chains and the development of new competing formats . . . are upping the competitive ante in the business.[4]

Table 5.1   Sales and Annual Sales Growth of Selected Publicly Held Retailers, 1987 and 1978-1987

Retailer	Sales, 1987 (in millions)	Annual Growth Rate of Sales, 1978-1987	Type of Retailing
Department store			
J.C. Penney	15,332.0	3.9	Department store chain
Sears, Roebuck	48,440.0	11.7	Department store chain
Federated[a]	11,300.0	8.5	Holding company
May[b]	10,800.0	17.3	Holding company
Nordstrom, Inc.	1,920.2	23.0	Department store chain
Discount department store			
Ames	2,112.0	29.0	Discount department store chain
K Mart Corp.	25,626.0	9.1	Discount department store chain
Rose's Stores	1,337.1	11.5	Discount department store chain
Wal-Mart Stores	15,959.0	37.0	Discount department store chain
Zayre	6,186.5	18.0	Discount department store chain
Apparel specialty stores			
Charming Shops	639.0	25.0	Women's specialty store chain
Deb Shops	199.0	26.5[c]	Women's specialty store chain
The Gap, Inc.	1,062.0	16.9	Women's specialty store chain
Limited, Inc.	3,528.0	40.0[d]	Women's specialty store chain
Other specialty stores			
Burlington Coat	481.0	37.5[e]	Off-price apparel chain
Child World	749.0	22.7[e]	Toy supermarket chain
Circuit City	1,350.0	31.9	Video, audio, appliances chain
Claire's Stores, Inc.	105.4	21.4	Costume jewelry (enclosed malls) chain
General Nutrition	350.9	8.8	Health foods chain
Gordon Jewelry	388.1	3.6	Jewelry chain
Heilig Meyers	302.6	17.6	Home furnishings chain
House of Fabrics	322.5	8.9	Fabrics chain
Kay Jewelers	367.9	6.5	Jewelry chain
Lionel Corp.	343.6	7.0	Toy, leisure products chain
Pep Boys	553.8	15.2	Discount auto supply chain
Pier 1 Imports	327.2	10.8	Imports, decor, home furnishings chain
R.B. Industries	103.6	4.1	Furniture showrooms
Royal International Optical	95.0	22.6[d]	Optical stores
Standard Brands Paint Co.	305.5	7.1	Paint, do-it-yourself chain
Sym's	256.8	18.1	Off-price apparel chain
Toys "R" Us	3,136.6	27.7	Toy supermarket chain
Supermarket			
Albertson's Inc.	5,869.4	11.2	Food supermarket chain
Brono's Inc.	1,143.2	15.6	Food supermarket chain
Delchamps	784.9	5.1	Food supermarket chain
Food Lion	2,953.8	29.0	Food supermarket chain
Giant Food	2,721.2	10.8	Food supermarket chain
Great A&P	9,531.8	2.8	Food supermarket chain
Hannaford Bros.	1,033.4	11.8	Food supermarket chain

Table 5.1 (Continued)

Retailer	Sales, 1987 (in millions)	Annual Growth Rate of Sales, 1978–1987	Type of Retailing
Kroger Co.	17,659.0	9.5	Food supermarket chain
Lucky Stores	6,924.0	4.5	Food supermarket chain
Marsh Co.	848.1	8.9	Food supermarket chain
Drug Store			
Genovese Drug	315.0	15.6	Drug store chain
Long's Drug	1,772.5	11.5	Drug store chain
Rite Aid Corp.	2,486.3	16.2	Drug store chain
Walgreen	4,281.6	15.2	Drug store chain
Convenience Store			
Circle K Corp.	2,619.8	22.0	Convenience store chain
National Convenience	828.0	13.1	Convenience store chain

[a]Abraham & Strauss is a subsidiary.

[b]Lord & Taylor is a subsidiary.

[c]1981–1987.

[d]1979–1987.

[e]1980–1987.

Source: Sales from Value Line Investment Survey (New York: Value Line, Inc., 1988–1989). Value Line lists over 1,600 companies whose stocks are publicly held. Stocks were selected to provide a representative list of public companies in the retail sectors analyzed.

As competition from discounters increased during the 1960s, independent department stores reacted in two ways. The first was to join national holding companies (e.g., Federated Allied Stores Corporation, May Department Stores Co., and Dayton-Hudson Corporation), in order to achieve greater economies of scale through centralized purchasing arrangements and opportunities to benefit through cooperative advertising programs with manufacturers.[5] A second strategy was to move out of certain lines of goods in which they were no longer able to compete and to give greater emphasis to apparel and furnishings, thereby trading up to take advantage of increasing affluence.[6]

The traditional department store chains were also affected by the increasing competition and forced to find new strategies. At Sears, the largest of the big three, management was finally forced (in 1989) to convert to a discount chain mode, slashing prices and sharply altering store layouts and merchandising. At J.C. Penney the adjustment came earlier (late 1970s) as the firm shifted its emphasis to soft goods (where margins are more generous) and targeted the broad middle-priced segment of the market.

The Apparel Specialty Chain. For a while, many department stores enjoyed considerable success though their strategy of giving greater emphasis to apparel and upgrading their lines, but this was not meant to last. By the late 1970s, they were experiencing sharp competition from apparel specialty chains.

Independent apparel specialty stores are one of the oldest forms of retailing, but they lack buying power and, frequently, skillful merchandising. Apparel specialty chains, however, have brought a formidable new concept to the marketplace. Through proliferation of numerous, nearly identical outlets, they are able to buy on favorable terms and assemble talented merchandising staffs. Their outlets are large enough (frequently over 16,000 square feet[7]) to offer a wider selection than the competing single department of the department store. Customers find sought-after items with greater ease and frequently enjoy superior service since sales people, specialized in a single line of goods, have greater product knowledge.

Since the late 1970s, leading apparel specialty stores, such as Limited, Inc., The Gap, Inc., Esprit, and others, have grown rapidly (Table 5.1), largely at the expense of conventional department stores.

Other Specialty Chains. Along with the rise of apparel specialty chains, other specialty chains have entered areas which were traditionally controlled by the department stores: toys (e.g., Toys "R" Us), electronic, audio appliances, and related items (e.g., Circuit City), auto supplies (e.g., Pep Boys), home maintenance and repair (e.g., Home Depot), and optical services (e.g., Royal International). A number of these chains have grown extremely rapidly (Table 5.1).

These chains incorporate strategies similar to those of apparel specialty stores: nearly identical stores and centralized buying and advertising. Also similar is the merchandising strategy of offering a much wider range of goods within their product line than is possible for either the discount department store chain or the traditional department store. Typically, margins are razor-thin and prices well below those of discount department stores and department stores. Since success depends on a substantial sales volume in each store, they tend to be located in larger urban and suburban markets. In these markets, discount department stores cannot compete head-on, and, accordingly, operate most successfully in less populated suburban markets, and in nonmetropolitan areas.

Food Retailing

Supermarket Chains.[8] The supermarket concept—low prices, self-service, and cash and carry policies—was introduced during the early

1930s and quickly gained popularity. During the decades of the 1950s and 1960s, supermarkets burgeoned along with suburbanization and increased automobile ownership. Management adopted a policy of operating look-alike stores with more or less similar merchandising. Beginning with the 1970s, however, various store formats were developed. Management experimented with larger stores, exerted increasing leverage over suppliers, and affected substantial economies through more effective warehousing and distribution. In recent years, service and specialty departments have increasingly been added (e.g., delicatessen departments, florists, pharmacies), and, through greater emphasis on higher value added products, operating margins have increased sharply, from below 3 percent in the late 1970s to well above 4 percent in 1987.[9]

In the prewar years, it was generally thought that national grocery chains would dominate the industry through superior buying power, but such has not proven to be the case. No truly national chain exists today. A&P, once the largest and most successful national chain, collapsed during the 1970s and was forced to retrench drastically, to reemerge, once again successful, but as a regional operation.

Along with the rise of the regional grocery chains, the development that has affected the supermarket industry most significantly is market segmentation. Increasingly, the industry is splitting into major groups of firms: those emphasizing low prices and those emphasizing quality foods and service, partly at the expense of price. The first segment is giving rise to new types of retailers employing new strategies to decrease costs and attract customers—hypermarkets and warehouse clubs. The second has moved into upscale supermarkets and broader product lines (e.g., Food Emporium, a subsidiary of A&P, in the New York area, Giant Food in the Washington D.C. area, and Ralph's Grocery in the Los Angeles area).

Hypermarkets.[10] These huge stores (typically over 200,000 square feet) originated in Europe and as yet have not appeared in great numbers in the United States. The basic strategy of the hypermarkets is to offer one-stop shopping for both food and general merchandising. Pricing is aggressive and well below that of the average supermarket (gross margins are typically 13–15 percent compared to 20 to 25 percent for supermarkets and 25–30 percent for discount department stores). Operating costs are minimized through utilization of warehouse-like structures, efficient restocking procedures, shelf pricing (i.e., using computerized point-of-sale terminals), and centralized checkouts. Economies of operation depend on locating within heavily populated areas drawing customers from distances as great as 50 miles. Hypermarkets are operated by two French firms, Euromarche and Carrefour, and by Wal-Mart. K mart and several other U.S. firms are also in the process of opening such stores.

Warehouse Clubs.[11] Warehouse clubs represent a quite different mode in that they sell to both wholesale and retail customers who are members and pay an annual membership fee. Many of these stores sell both food and general merchandise while others specialize in a single broad category (e.g., office supplies and home improvement).

Successful operation depends on mass buying and very heavy sales volume to make possible the lowest prices offered by any type of retail outlet. With annual sales of $60 million and over, a warehouse club is highly profitable; at lower volume levels, it is not. At present $10 billion of the industry's $14 billion sales are accounted for by three companies: Price's Club, Sam's (Wal-Mart), and Costco. The average population per warehouse in those cities which currently have club stores is approximately 500,000.

Drug Chains. Drug chains predate World War II, but it was only in the 1960s that the self-service drug chain began to thrive. Since then, this format has evolved into one in which the store combines essentially two businesses, the pharmacy with its associated proprietary products and the convenience section, with cosmetics, toiletries, tobacco products, and so on. In recent years, drug chains have sought to exploit a strong health care image, using computer technology, particularly in the pharmacy department, to increase efficiency.

Convenience Store Chains.[12] The extremely rapid growth of convenience stores throughout the 1950s, 1960s, and 1970s was fostered by the rapid growth of the suburbs and the increasing use of the automobile. Growth since the late 1970s has continued apace with the total number of stores rising from about 37,000 in 1978 to close to 65,000 in 1986. The two largest chains, The Southland Company (parent of 7-Eleven) and The Circle K Corporation, operate 8,200 and 3,500 stores, respectively; and all of the top twenty operate 480 or more.

The single most important product featured by these small stores (1,000 to 3,200 square feet) is gasoline, and leading petroleum products firms have entered the field aggressively in recent years (six gas distributors operate chains that are large enough to be numbered among the top 20). In addition to gasoline, convenience stores carry a broad line of quick purchase and impulse items, e.g., tobacco, beer, soft drinks, fast foods, dairy products, snack foods, and confectionery goods. In recent years, many firms have introduced delis, broadened fast-food lines, and added services such as video rentals.

Key Factors in Recent Change

Three factors have played major roles in the transformation of retailing since the beginning of the 1980s: changing patterns of consumption and new forms of competition, computer technology, and the changing nature of scale economies.

Changing Patterns of Consumption and New Forms of Competition

The postwar years have brought dramatic changes in consumer demand. Following World War II, there was a general rise in per capita income and purchasing power, opening up new opportunities for vendors to introduce new products. In the broad U.S. market, it was now possible to target individual segments, designing products and services to cater to the tastes of specific groups, segmented by income, age, sex, lifestyle, ethnic identification, special leisure habits, and so on.

At the same time, there were major demographic shifts and changes in employment, changes that gave rise to new patterns of consumer demand. The baby boom of the late 1940s and 1950s altered the age composition of the population and as the years passed gave rise to shifts in market emphasis, culminating in the 1980s with a much larger adult population and a new emphasis on consumption.

Along with the above shifts have come two other major changes: the increase in the employment of women and the rising importance of white-collar work. More women in the work force has brought an increase in two-income families, more disposable income for these families, and major shifts in consumption, including an increased demand for work and leisure apparel, "take-home" meals and quickly prepared foods, and furnishings and equipment for the home. Moreover, with both men and women finding work increasingly in the office rather than in the factory, there has been a new emphasis on clothing generally.

Thus, we see that the retail market has been characterized by increasing disposable incomes, increasing segmentation among consumer groups, and a new and broader range of consumer needs. In response, firms have aggressively sought new ways of establishing a competitive advantage. This continuous search for a niche has taken a variety of forms: increasing price competition through discount strategies, changing merchandising emphasis, introducing new store formats, and extending the scope of merchandise lines.

Computer Technology

Successful retail firms of significant size rely heavily on modern computer systems which support functions at headquarters, distribution centers, and individual stores. Integrated through telecommunications, they make possible increased efficiency and substantial cost savings.

Distribution and sales can be synchronized to permit automatic replenishment, resulting in major savings in inventories (store stockroom inventory levels may be sharply reduced or virtually eliminated). Vendors may even be integrated into the system for "quick response," receiving sales and inventory information and taking on the responsibility of shipping goods as needed.

Recently the cost of scanning has fallen sharply and larger retailing firms are adopting the technology at an accelerating pace. Scanning makes possible pricing and repricing without marking goods, resulting in substantial cost savings. The technology also permits the store to feed competitor's prices into the computer for automatic repricing when company policy calls for matching all competition. At the same time, checkout is facilitated, providing improved customer service.

With such modern systems, managerial responsibility and organization are changed. Store managers are largely relieved of the responsibility of making purchasing decisions and maintaining stock records. Such responsibility shifts to management at higher levels where it is carried out with greater ease and effectiveness by utilizing computerized procedures. Store managers have more time for overseeing operations and supervising and training, while middle and higher level managers assume greater responsibility for planning and for carrying out such functions as advertising, merchandising, purchasing, store location and design, and the oversight of company-wide training and recruitment programs.

The Changing Nature of Scale Economies

In previous years, economies of scale in retailing were seen as largely related to the ability of very large firms, particularly nationwide retailers, to extract more favorable purchase terms from vendors than were available to their smaller competitors. The fear of such unfair competition in the 1930s gave rise to the Robinson Patman Act which required that price reductions be justified by cost savings and that prices be made available on an even-handed basis.

Today, in spite of this legislation, larger buyers still purchase on favorable terms. Vendors frequently offer special deals, and advertising allowances are offered on lots of such size that only very large buyers can take advantage of them. Moreover, in recent years the rapid increase of stock-keeping units (SKUs) offered by vendors has outrun the space available in retail stores, resulting in a shift of bargaining power to the retailer, principally to the large buyer.

In this new environment, regional chains are frequently large enough to extract the most favorable terms available. Accordingly, firms operating nationwide have no special advantage. Wal-Mart, a very large regional discount department store chain, and Food Lion, one of many regional supermarket chains, are regarded as two of the most successful buyers in U.S. retailing. Even Rose's, a medium-size regional discount department store chain, reported that its purchasing department was able to buy on highly favorable terms.

This does not mean that all chain retailers command sufficient purchasing power on their own to make deals at lowest possible prices for all items they sell. Three of the firms interviewed, Abraham & Strauss, Lord & Taylor, and High's, find it advantageous to purchase through their holding companies. Nevertheless, it does seem clear that a large number of retail chains have not been significantly disadvantaged by an inability to purchase on favorable terms.

In any event, purchasing power is today but one source of economies of scale. The ability to take advantage of sophisticated computer systems is still another and the list extends even further. Large chain retailers by operating a number of identical or similar outlets can standardize operations and dedicate considerable human and financial resources to merchandising, advertising, pricing, and training programs, giving them significant advantages over smaller firms.

An additional observation is that regional chains appear to be better positioned than national chains to cater to the special tastes of their regions and to establish themselves as employers who understand the ways and needs of their workers.

Skills and Skill Formation:
Highlights from the Interviews

This section presents key findings from interviews and store visits at six regional retail organizations: a department store chain (Abraham & Strauss); an apparel specialty department store chain (Lord & Taylor); a discount department store chain (Rose's Stores, Inc.); five supermarket chains (Publix Super Markets, Food Lion, Inc., Ralph's Grocery Company, Schnuck's Markets, Marsh Supermarkets, Inc.); a drug store chain (Jack Eckerd's Drug Stores); and a convenience store chain (High's).

The interviewed firms vary widely in terms of store size, merchandising objectives, and number of employees. At one extreme lies Abraham & Strauss with its large stores, each with numerous departments and a staff of sales people and managers numbering into many hundreds; at the other, High's, with its tiny outlets, each offering a limited range of goods and operated by a handful of people.

Yet to a remarkable degree, these firms have adopted similar strategies and face a common set of problems. Each operates a number of branches and pursues a strategy of gaining acceptance in the marketplace by projecting a single image throughout all stores in terms of price policy, range and presentation of merchandise, and quality of service. Each has sought to bring about scale economies and increase merchandising effectiveness through concentrating and centralizing purchasing, distributing out of a limited number of centers, and utilizing computer systems to link all parts of the organization. Each has in recent years sought to bring about changes in organization and in the responsibilities of management. And each has sought to increase the effectiveness of its store personnel.

The principal findings from the company profiles may be presented under four general heads: the new emphasis on customer service and human resources; strategies for building more effective work force; a new emphasis on training; and the changing role of middle management.

The New Emphasis on Customer Service and Human Resources

Without exception, the executives interviewed stressed the importance to their companies of improving customer service. With a larger number of stores fighting for the customer's dollar, efforts to improve merchandising and pricing strategies do not suffice: Customers will go elsewhere if the shopping experience is not efficient and pleasant. Moreover, in a multibranch operation the reputation of all stores tends to be sullied by the poor performance of any one store.

The widespread concern about service goes hand-in-hand with a new emphasis on building a more effective staff of store personnel. Accordingly, the task of improving customer service may be approached in several ways: by more careful selection of employees with an eye to employing only those who appear to have the necessary aptitude for dealing with customers, by reducing the turnover of part-time personnel through a policy of hiring fewer individuals who appear likely to work for a limited period of time, by training all store personnel and increasing supervision, by trying to build company loyalty and commitment to long-term employment with the company. No one of these approaches excludes the other, and each firm interviewed was committed to several of these approaches, if not all of them.

Strategies for Building a More Effective Work Force

Recruitment of Store Personnel. Most, if not all, of the companies studied are currently giving increased attention to recruitment of store personnel. More and more, assistance is being provided by the personnel and human resources departments and greater care is given to the selection of job candidates.

All companies admitted that labor shortages existed in some of their labor markets, although only four (Lord & Taylor, Publix, Schnuck's, and Eckerd's) explicitly recognized the emerging problem of a generally declining labor supply in the 1990s. These companies were planning to recruit more heavily among the retired population and were facing the attendant problems of utilizing these workers.

Selection of Management Trainees. Policies differed among companies regarding method of recruiting new managers. Some recruited managers from college campuses; some did not. There does appear to have been a new interest, however, in recruiting from the ranks of store personnel. Such a trend is consistent with the strong interest of all firms interviewed in building company loyalty and emphasizing the advantages of seeking a career within the firm.

Yet there is evidence that firms in their search for managerial talent are likely to give preference to those with college training. The ranks of young part-time workers regularly include college students and college-bound youngsters, and it is from these upwardly mobile workers that firms are likely to find many of their best prospects for management training programs. Publix, Eckerd's, and Lord & Taylor managers readily conceded that if they were to be faced with a choice between a college and noncollege candidate for promotion from within they would choose the college graduate; and Schnuck's encourages its management-bound employees to attend college, offering tuition assistance. Given the administrative demands on store managers and the new recognition of the need for continuous training of management at all levels, it seems clear that the progressive, growth-minded firms interviewed seek to enlist managerial candidates who have demonstrated an aptitude for learning.

This does not mean that those with only a high school diploma are never chosen for management training programs. Indeed, it is quite clear that in many organizations, particularly the supermarket chains which customarily draw their management trainees from the floor, a substantial number of high school graduates will be included although promotion to top managerial ranks is likely to be reserved for college graduates. In the large multidepartmental stores where organizational structure is taller, opportunities for the noncollege employee appear to be sharply restricted (see Abraham & Strauss and Lord & Taylor profiles).

The implication for those with less than a high school degree is clear. Dropouts will find little opportunity for advancement in any of the retail organizations surveyed.

Benefit Programs. An emphasis on company *esprit de corps* was apparent not only in the training programs but in benefit programs. All companies provided a well-rounded package of benefits several of which include quite attractive retirement benefits as an inducement to remain in the organization as a career employee.

A New Emphasis on Training

Perhaps the most solid finding is that there has been a new emphasis on training in recent years. Each of the firms interviewed has revised sharply its training program. There is greater use of video presentations, an increase in formal classroom training, and a change in focus.

In training store personnel, several important changes are apparent. The first is the insistence that everybody be trained; no distinction is made between part-time and full-time employees, nor between very low-wage occupations, such as baggers in supermarkets, and those with higher responsibilities. The second is that training programs are more formalized and make greater use of video and manuals. A third is that substantial attention is given to customer service, company policy (dress code, regulations, etc.), and product knowledge as well as to specific skill attainment (such as mastery of the electronic cash register). Customer service training includes not only "friendliness" programs but confrontational, role-playing training in which the new employee is required to demonstrate how to handle difficult customer-related problems.

Product training varies according to the task performed. For a supermarket cashier it may involve simply a comprehensive knowledge of what the store carries and where it is located; for the meat attendant, some knowledge of how to prepare a given cut of meat or seafood; for the cosmetician, rather detailed knowledge of individual products, and how they are suited to the customer's needs. In the latter case, company training may be supplemented by training by the vendor.

In training new managers, more attention is being given to "people" skills (how to supervise, train, handle difficult situations) in addition to familiarizing trainees with all aspects of the company's operations. Furthermore, most firms are requiring that managers periodically improve their skills through additional training.

The Changing Role of Middle Management

In a branch store operation, the store manager plays a key role. Store managers are responsible for carrying out the merchandising objectives of the firm, for maintaining employee relations, and for overseeing the day-to-day efficient and profitable operation of the store.

Paradoxically, in recent years a number of the burdens of the store manager's tasks have been lightened, yet more is expected. The buying functions have been shifted to the centralized buying organization and the day-to-day ordering and record-keeping functions substantially lightened by computer systems. New emphasis has been given to providing assistance to the store manager by higher level management. In some instances, though not in all, the human resources department assists in hiring. District managers or some upper-level management representatives visit the store frequently to both monitor operations and provide assistance. Company specialists provide expert advice in merchandising. Human resources training personnel design training programs, prepare training manuals and videos, and frequently conduct, or assist in conducting, in-store training.

Yet at the same time the store manager has assumed heavier responsibilities. Given the firm's greater emphasis on customer service, the broader range of merchandise, more frequent introduction of new products, and the longer hours of operation of a store, store managers must pay closer attention operations, assuring the proper display and attractiveness of the floor and, above all, training and supervising personnel. Store managers must keep abreast of changes in competitors' prices and merchandise as well as the changing tastes of clientele, continuously feeding back pertinent information to top management through district managers.

Above the store level, middle managers are assuming responsibility previously handled at least in part at the store level. As computer systems provide more information, buying and merchandise planning become more demanding and the role of managers becomes more critical. Human resources staffs increase the scope of their duties. District managers and regional merchandise specialists play more important roles in monitoring store operations and providing assistance.

Profiles of Six Firms

This section presents profiles of six of the firms interviewed as evidence of how retailers are responding to the challenge of competition, with special attention to organization, recruitment, and training of personnel.

Abraham & Strauss

Abraham & Strauss (A&S) is a chain of 14 full-service department stores catering to the moderate and upper moderate income trade. Stores are located in the boroughs of Brooklyn (flagship store) and Queens, in Westchester County and Long Island, New York, and in New Jersey. Total employment is 12,000. Stores are supplied from two distribution centers. Virtually all departments are operated by A&S with franchise arrangements only in a few stores in books, optical, and bridal departments.

A&S is a member of the Federated Department Stores holding corporation which controls seven major chains (Jordan Marsh, A&S, Bloomingdale's, Stern's, Richie's, Burdines, and Lazarus). Federated, itself, became a part of the Campeau organization (which also controls Allied Stores Corporation) in the spring of 1988. Sharp retrenchment at A&S followed the takeover, resulting in the reduction of employment by 1,000, mostly in purchasing, checking rooms, loss prevention, and back-office clerical personnel.

A&S now maintains a buying staff of 95 buyers and 45 clerical assistants (prior to the takeover there were 125 buyers and 125 to 130 clerical assistants). About 95 percent of buying is done centrally for all stores. Although some merchandise is bought to meet the special merchandising needs of certain stores, all stores for the most part carry the same merchandise and the chain engages in common promotional advertising for all.

A primary objective of the merger of the Federated and Allied stores within the Campeau organization was to bring about greater scale economies through increased centralization, especially through combining the buying power of the various chains that had previously functioned largely autonomously. Under the new arrangement, A&S buyers decide what merchandise is needed, and Federated combines the orders of the several divisions for special "deals." Federated continuously attempts to arrange very large purchase contracts with vendors contingent upon their acceptance by division (e.g., A&S) buyers and then tries to get the division buyers to "come aboard." Such buying occurs across a wide range of goods (e.g., furniture, electronics, women's ready-to-wear). Increasingly, A&S is taking advantage of such buying.

In addition to its role in buying, Federated allocates capital and gives final approval to sales projections and expense budgets. It exercises no direct control over day-to-day operations, however.

Federated is playing a key role in introducing a new computer system throughout all its stores. This system, SABRE—to be fully operative in 1991—will automate and link a variety of functions including personnel, buying, inventory, sales, and warehousing. Until now, the A&S operations have made only partial use of computer systems. In buying, for example, orders are still handwritten.

Competition. Management reactions to questions relating to competition were of two sorts. It recognized that local electronics specialty chains like Crazy Eddie and The Wiz were selling merchandise at prices below those which they could offer, but stated that there was a residual demand from customers who preferred to buy where they could depend on the store backing its product and accepting returns when goods were faulty. They saw the discount chains as treating customers badly and resorting to such practices as not stocking goods in sufficient quantities to meet demand when special prices were advertised.

Regarding specialty apparel stores, management observed that The Gap was doing a superior job. It was noted that with its narrowly specialized line and only 1,500 square feet in comparison to a department store's 300,000, The Gap is able to maintain a highly attractive store, offer appealing merchandise, and, typically, good service. A&S has endeavored to compete by offering new color lines and style trends.

Among other department stores, A&S sees Macy's as it's chief competition and meets all prices advertised by Macy's. It plans to open within a year a large store (the old Gimbel's store) across the street from Macy's flagship store in Manhattan.

Management observed that there was a new emphasis on service within the trade. The success of Nordstrom, with its superior customer service, has been widely recognized and discussed. A&S's principal effort to improve customer service has been to move to a commission basis for remunerating *all* of its sales personnel. It sees this change as a means of raising salary levels and thereby attracting a better performing staff, but recognizes that the new salary policy will have to be accompanied by better training. The new effort has been under way since late 1988.

Along with the shift to a commission basis, management would like to shift away from its heavy reliance upon part-time sales personnel (currently 60 percent part-time, 40 percent full-time) to a predominantly (60 percent) full-time selling staff. In addition, it is acting to increase sharply the amount of time department heads spend on the floor selling and actively supervising.

Management Staffing. The A&S organization is sufficiently "tall" to allow good opportunities for career advancement for management trainees. At the store level, the manager is assisted by two (three in the case of the flagship store) divisional group managers. Reporting to each divisional group manager are one or two group managers. Department managers report to group managers or, in the case of larger departments, directly to a divisional group manager. Each department manager is typically assisted by two sales managers (assistant department managers) and supervises in all some 15 to 20 people. During evening hours, the entire store is run by six to eight department managers, with each department manager working one night each week.

Given this organizational structure, successful trainees have an opportunity for advancement along a fairly extended career ladder. After 13 weeks, trainees become sales managers. After an average period of nine months, they advance to department manager positions. Department manager positions last an average of 18 months and are followed by a move to associate buyer, group manager, or into advertising, personnel, or some other specialization.

A&S recruits about 300 persons for its management training program annually. Traditionally, trainees have been recruited on major college campuses in the Northeast, but recently there has been a significant increase in the number recruited from among the ranks of sales associates. Five years ago, the number of sales associates accepted for management training was from 10 to 15. This past year it has been around 100. A&S is now emphasizing career opportunities in recruiting sales associates. Previously, this was not the case.

Sales Employee Staffing. Part-time sales associates (60 percent of the sales force) fall into two categories: the permanent part-time employees working during regular store hours and the "T's." T's are employed to work principally at seasonal peaks and to staff the store during evening hours (Thursday's at the Brooklyn store) and on Saturdays and Sundays. Turnover is relatively low among permanent part-time associates. Among temporaries, turnover rates and absenteeism are extremely high.

The company's major staffing problem is during evening hours and on weekends. Full-time and permanent part-time employees work mostly during weekdays, leaving stores staffed largely with inexperienced "T's" during evenings and weekends. The problem is particularly serious for Sunday operations when sales volume is heavy.

Under the new policy of increasing the number of full-time sales associates, new full-time hires will be expected to work two nights a week and to take turns on Sundays.

Recruitment of sales personnel is seen by management as a major problem. We were told that every year it becomes more difficult to find good people. This was blamed partly on the educational system, but management also conceded that beginning pay for inexperienced persons was low, below wages currently offered by McDonald's. Recently, a more careful policy of recruitment has been instituted, with department heads as well as a human resources department staff member interviewing applicants.

Management Training. The 13-week initial program for management trainees emphasizes the skills required to manage within the store: how to supervise, how to motivate, how to set a floor, how to take markdowns, how to execute required paperwork, how to schedule personnel, how to interview, etc. Seminars of 2½ hours are held weekly, and there are two advanced courses. The balance of the training is on the job. There are no video presentations.

Department managers are given some advanced training, but no systematic program was mentioned by interviewees. A&S does not provide tuition assistance for college courses and only rarely sends managerial personnel to attend outside courses.

Sales Personnel Training. The A&S training program was strengthened about two years ago. Each store now has a trainer and assistant trainer and classes are given every week for new sales people. Each new sales associate receives about 27 hours of formal training (other than on the job). A nine-hour module is devoted to selling, utilizing classroom video and instruction. This instruction includes situational training in which the associate is given a manual to read and then called upon to demonstrate how to respond to specific customer-related situations. In addition, five to six hours are given over to company policy, security provisions, company benefits, etc., and 12 hours are devoted to training on point-of-sales (POS) terminals. The latter training focuses principally upon the technical aspects of making sales, handling returns, and the like.

The principal difference between the new and old training program is the current policy that employees at all levels receive training and the emphasis given to selling and customer service. Previously, training was not given to all sales people, was of shorter duration, and less well-organized.

Following the initial sales associate training, there are short presentations amounting to perhaps one-half hour weekly in which the department head gathers together staff for 10 to 15 minutes to relate what is new in merchandise, in policy changes, and so on. Other than some special instruction for the selling of electronics, shoes and furs, and dresses (fundamentals of color and texture, types of dresses, complementary colors), there is little product training.

Lord & Taylor

Lord & Taylor, one of the oldest and best-known department specialty store chains in the United States, appeals principally to upper-middle income and upper-income women. Its merchandise line includes not only a wide variety of women's apparel but also apparel for children and men, cosmetics, home furnishings, and jewelry.

Today, Lord & Taylor employs 12,000 persons (about 10,000 of whom are store personnel) and operates 53 stores and five distribution centers. It projects a near-doubling of sales over the coming half decade.

Since October 1986, Lord & Taylor has been owned by May Department Stores Company, which took over from the former parent company, Associated Dry Goods. May leadership has brought no reduction in staff but stronger support and stronger leadership than was obtained under the more laissez faire approach of Associated Dry Goods. Evidence of change is seen in a more focussed merchandising policy (a strengthening of basic lines and elimination of certain peripheral lines), installation of more comprehensive and effective computer systems (POS terminals were installed in early 1988), a strong new emphasis on customer service, and a significantly strengthened training program.

Merchandising Policy. Management has seen rapid changes in demand and competition in recent years. A major factor has been the increased employment of women and the need of career women for work, social, and leisure clothes. Lord & Taylor's response has been to emphasize being the first with new and attractive merchandise and to move goods quickly. This policy of quick turnover of fairly highly styled merchandise is facilitated by the capability of moving goods from one store to another. When an item is selling poorly in one branch, it may be shipped to another where demand is stronger.

Recent years have brought new challenges in merchandising. Whereas some years ago leading women's apparel manufacturers had featured four (seasonal) lines each year, they now offer six. In addition, there has been an increase in the breadth of product lines (i.e., the number of stock-keeping units) across a broad spectrum.

Nevertheless, Lord & Taylor's management has been able to reduce stock-turn through aggressive merchandising and innovations in distribution and stock control. A major effort has been made since 1987 to focus merchandise lines more carefully, providing, "more meaningful stock levels where it counts" and eliminating peripheral lines.

Two examples illustrate this policy. The first relates to home furnishings. Under current policy, a very complete line of bedding, towels, and table top items (crystal, vases, and so on) is offered, but kitchen utensils and equipment are not included; and, recently, lamps have been removed in order to feature in the furnishings line only those items that the company can offer in a comprehensive fashion with careful attention to customer needs.

The second illustration is men's wear in several of the company's smaller stores. Unable to offer a comprehensive line in these stores, management opted to eliminate the department altogether, making it possible to offer a fuller assortment in other departments.

Evidence of management's efforts to improve its response to merchandising needs is seen in the company's modernized delivery arrangements. In contrast to methods of some years ago when large deliveries were made on a weekly basis to be uncrated and stored in each retail outlet, deliveries are now made on a daily basis. Merchandise arrives "floor ready" (ticketed, on hangers, and with sensormatic devices attached) and is moved directly into selling departments. Whereas older stores might have been built with a total of 120,000 to 150,000 square feet or more with over 30,000 square feet of storage, new stores range from 90,000 to 120,000 square feet yet operate with roughly the same selling space.

Competition. In discussing clientele, management pointed out that its market is women 25 to 45 years of age, many of whom are career women. Not only do these customers have little time to shop, they also have little store loyalty and are increasingly knowledgeable as to shopping alternatives. In such a market, specialty stores, such as The Gap, the Limited, and Anne Taylor, often have an advantage in that they can offer a particular kind of merchandise in a store in which customers can find quickly what they want.

The proliferation of specialty stores was viewed as the greatest challenge facing Lord & Taylor in today's marketplace.[13] The company's response has been to make the shopping experience in its stores less confusing, with more focussed merchandising, better product knowledge by sales personnel, friendlier service, and faster execution of transactions.

Organizational Structure and Function. In its relationship to Lord & Taylor, the May Company sets overall budgets, provides general policy leadership and staff expertise, and acts as a central purchasing organization. The May buying staff purchases large volume, more staple merchandise, especially from overseas, but Lord & Taylor retains the right to buy independently merchandise it requires to protect its special market niche.

In the area of training, the May organization has played a substantial role, supplying materials and direction based on its considerable experience.

Notwithstanding the change in top-level control, Lord & Taylor has retained autonomy in the management of all matters relating to merchandising—the shaping of its image through selection, promotion, and presentation. It also controls recruitment, training, and housekeeping activities.

In practice, merchandising strategy is formulated at Lord & Taylor headquarters and conveyed to the store level through store managers (managing directors) who then meet and work with the various branch store division managers and department managers who work under them. Stores are visited frequently (weekly at the Stamford store), not only by the regional vice president (the immediate superior of the store manager) but by his senior, the director of stores (who reports directly to the chief executive officer).

Lord & Taylor stores are relatively large, multidepartmental outlets. The organizational structure comprises a store manager (managing director), operations manager (responsible for human resources, receiving, housekeeping, and cashier departments), and, reporting to the store manager, one or two branch store divisional managers and a number of department managers.[14] The position of branch store divisional manager is new (created within the last year or two). It is planned to increase the number of these managers in the years just ahead.

It was pointed out that a decade ago, store management was deeply involved in keeping stock record books and communicating with buyers or even vendors regarding purchases. This is no longer necessary because of computerization.[15] As computerization has freed department heads of earlier chores, they now spend more time on the floor to improve supervision and enhance training.

Store Hours. Store hours have been increased over the years in response to changes in shopping habits and the actions of competitors. This has been especially true over the last two years as the company has become increasingly aware of the special needs of its large clientele of working women. Currently, the company is moving toward a policy of operating its branch stores five nights a week. In the Stamford store, the Christmas season shopping hours (10 A.M. to 9 P.M., Monday through Saturday) plus Sunday, 12 A.M. to 6 P.M., are now a permanent arrangement. According to the store manager, the results have been "very gratifying."

Reduction of Part-Time Personnel. Lord & Taylor has responded to changing market conditions and increasing competition not only through its merchandising, store operations, and organizational arrangements but through changed policy toward employment of full-time sales personnel and through increased emphasis on training.

High turnover (currently, 35 to 40 percent for all sales associates) is primarily the result of the employment of a large number of part-time workers (about 70 percent of sales associates) and has posed a major obstacle to the company in building a well-trained sales staff.

To remedy this situation, Lord & Taylor is now moving toward increasing the use of full-time personnel from present levels of about 30 percent to a target of about 60 percent. The company recognizes that pay levels will rise with this change, but improvement in competitiveness along with reduction in recruitment and training costs through lower turnover are expected to result in higher efficiency and better profits.

There is evidence that the new policy is producing results. The manager of the Stamford store stated that his current ratio of full-time sales associates was 50 percent and that reduction in part-time employment had lowered turnover rates dramatically.

Management Training and Recruitment. Until roughly 1987, training for managerial and buyer positions took place at New York headquarters with trainees recruited largely from college campuses. Emphasis was given largely to the training of buyers, although some of those completing the program filled department manager vacancies in branch stores. More frequently, managers were hired locally or to a limited extent promoted out of the ranks.

Under the new arrangement there are two training programs: a central store program solely for buyers and a branch store program for both store executives and sales associates. Both programs make substantial use of May materials and procedures.

For both the central office and store management training programs, recruitment is carried out on college campuses. The two programs recruit separately and, frequently, on different campuses (the store program recruiting tends to be restricted to campuses in the general market area). Central office program recruiting is done by the human resources staff; store office program recruiting, by the store manager. In describing recruiting procedures, the store manager stressed the importance of also recruiting from among competitors' personnel—visiting stores, observing well-run departments, and later interviewing persons interested in working at Lord & Taylor. Fifteen to 20 percent of trainees in the store program are persons who were recruited from the ranks of sales associates. This is a markedly higher percentage than five years ago. We were told, however, that a college degree was still important. Those without a degree would be at a disadvantage in applying for the program.

The central store program lasts 13 weeks and includes 180 hours of classroom training at headquarters. In addition to lectures by management and staff, manuals and video are utilized. The program features substantial situational (i.e., problem-oriented) training.

The branch store program for management trainees also lasts 13 weeks and is carried out entirely within the store. One day out of every two weeks is spent in class (roughly 40 hours in all) with lectures by the store manager, store operations manager, and store human resources director. In addition, there is one-on-one training by store managers to whom the trainee is assigned. Following the 13-week period, training continues with monthly two-hour seminars. An important feature of this program is that it is accompanied by a career path for trainees in store management. Previously, there had been little opportunity for promotion beyond department manager unless the individual was willing to relocate to New York City. Taking advantage of the newly created position of branch store divisional manager, along with the hierarchy within the store in terms of size and gross sales of departments and responsibility and salaries of their managers, Lord & Taylor now offers trainees an opportunity to advance in rank among sales managers, and then to move upward to branch store divisional manager, operations manager, and store manager.

Recruitment and Training of Sales Personnel. Recruitment of sales associates is based largely on advertising or applications received by the store human resource department. The principal finding relating to recruiting is that in recent years there has been a greater emphasis on hiring only the most promising applicants. This policy is, of course, consistent with company objectives of reducing part-time employment and labor turnover and improving customer service.

Training of sales associates, which takes place at the store level, has been extended by 30 to 40 percent since 1985. A major change has been the increased attention devoted to customer service. Initial training (administered by the store personnel administrator) is carried out at the store in a classroom environment over a three-day period (21 hours) and covers point-of-sale technology, systems procedures, company policy, benefits, and so on, along with the May "friendliness program" (2½ to 3 hours).[16] Video, classroom instruction, and class participation are utilized, including situational training (how to behave in customer-related situations). This structured training is followed by daily on-the-job instruction and supervision. After an initial four to five weeks on the floor, new sales associates return to the classroom to talk about friendliness, sales tips, team effort, and special problems they have encountered.

General Employment Policy. Wage and salary scales were not revealed although the Stamford store manager did state that wages for sales associates ranged from $7 to $12 an hour, quite competitive for the area.

The human resources administrator stated that they were developing a new wage administration policy to enable the company to be more competitive in hiring from a reduced pool of applicants. He predicted that there would be an increased emphasis on compensation during the next four to five years and that training would become more important as a result of the continued introduction of new technology and increased competition.

Role of Vendors and Leasees. A major innovation in the vendor's role in the last year has been the appearance of "rotators" on the store floor. These rotators, representing leading apparel manufacturers, such as Liz Claiborne, Jones of New York, J.H. Collectibles, Leslie Faye, S.K. and Co., Cambridge Dry Goods, Ralph Lauren, train sales managers and sales associates in product knowledge and merchandise presentation. The women's apparel rotators visit weekly, appearing an hour before opening time to work with store personnel and remaining on the floor to discuss the product with customers. The Ralph Lauren (men's apparel) rotator comes somewhat less often (once every two to three weeks) but performs essentially the same role in training store personnel.

In cosmetics, vendor representatives have visited stores for a number of years.[17] Their early appearance illustrates the need for vendor-store cooperation where product knowledge is important and merchandise lines are complex. In cosmetics, the number of stock-keeping units offered by a given manufacturer may run into the hundreds (Estee Lauder's product line was estimated to exceed 600 items), creating a baffling problem in terms of both purchasing and sales presentation. To provide assistance (and to promote the product line), the manufacturer's account coordinator once a month checks inventory and sales in the stock control book and prepares the next month's order with the department head. The account coordinator also introduces new products and explains the features of the various items to the department manager and sales personnel. Based on such product knowledge and clientele familiarity, the manager winnows down the vendor's offerings to provide an appropriate mix for the store. At the same time, sales people gain information and expertise that boost sales volume and create customer confidence and loyalty.

As regards franchising, there were only three leased departments in the Stamford store: fine jewelry, furs, and men's shoes, all merchandising areas regarded as lying outside Lord & Taylor's area of specialization. Sales associates in these departments receive Lord & Taylor training in point-of-sale procedures as well as the friendliness program. Changes in franchise departmental managers must be approved by the store manager.

Rose's Stores, Inc.

Rose's Stores, Inc. operates about 250 mass market discount department stores in 13 southeastern states, predominantly in North Carolina, South Carolina, Virginia, and Georgia. Stores range in size from 54,000 to 70,000 square feet, but most are about 54,000 square feet, with new stores ranging from 54,000 to 60,000 square feet. Stores are located in nonmetropolitan areas and sell predominantly to lower middle income ($15,000 to $20,000) families, frequently with two earners.

Competition. Rose's was slow to react to the increasing competition that began in the mid-1970s, but in the early 1980s, it embarked on a program to upgrade management information systems, renovate stores, broaden product lines, and expand. From 1983 to 1988, employment increased from 10,678 to 17,933 and sales, from $829 million to $1.5 billion. New store growth continues, with 25 branches added in 1988. Rose's chief competitors are K mart and Wal-Mart, with the latter making increased inroads into Rose's traditional market areas.

Buying and Merchandising. Rose's current sales mix is 50 percent hardgoods, 31 percent apparel, 19 percent soft home goods. In recent years, it has broadened its lines substantially, adding or broadening offerings in ready-to-assemble furniture, stationary, automotive supplies, toys, and horticulture products.

Management notes that there has been a marked increase in the number of products and in vendors in the market during the last decade. Its vendors have increased from 10,000 ten years ago to over 18,000 today.

Organization. The Rose's organization is highly centralized in merchandising, buying, and operations. One large computerized warehouse (over 500 employees) in Henderson, N.C. (its headquarters) supplies stores with twice weekly deliveries utilizing company trucks (110–115 drivers). Stores are stocked according to planograms prepared at headquarters.

The company has markedly increased its efforts to buy directly (about 90 percent) from manufacturers for delivery to its warehouse. It has tripled its buying staff over the last five years and increased the number of employees engaged in distribution by 50 percent. When possible, purchase contracts include arrangements for vendors to ticket merchandise prior to shipment. Management noted that forward buying and special deals have made possible substantial economies, well above the additional cost involved in centralizing and enlarging the buying function.

Administration of store operations is headed by a senior vice president with two regional vice presidents and a director of loss prevention under him. Each regional vice president presides over 12 district managers. A district manager is responsible for the operations of about ten stores.

Store employment averages about 60 including a sizable number of managers and specialists in addition to sales associates, stock clerks, and other lower level personnel.

The human resources manager expressed some concern over the fact that store management and personnel were so specialized by function that there were too few people on the floor to provide the level of customer service desired. One plan under consideration to remedy this situation is to reorganize the store under several merchandise department managers and put more people on the floor. It was noted that the computer system with electronic cash registers captures all the information necessary to permit sales incentive arrangements to be introduced on a departmental basis.

Part-Time Employment and Turnover Levels. About 50 percent of nonmanagement store-level employees work part-time. This proportion is regarded as too low and is expected to be raised to the industry level, about 65 percent. In new stores, the percentage is approximately at the industry level.

Turnover rates vary widely among different types of employees. For store managers it is about 15 percent, and among all full-time store personnel the rate was said to be quite low. Among part-time personnel, however, turnover rates were quite high.

Recruitment of Management. Until about 15 years ago, the Rose's organization functioned largely as an internal labor market with management drawn from the ranks of lower level employees. Since that time, prospective managers have been largely recruited from college campuses. The company brings very few individuals up from the store floor, although district managers are instructed to look for promising talent. Recently, the company found it necessary to hire store managers directly from outside. This has been largely due to the fact that they have lost managers to competitors, especially Wal-Mart. It was noted that Rose's managers are well trained and sought after by competitors.

Management Training. The management development training program is carried out in selected stores and usually involves one move to provide the trainee with experience in more than one store. Training is designed to provide hands-on experience in all merchandise and operations areas and is divided into five sections: orientation (2 months), home furnishing (3 months), apparel (4 months), operations (1 month), and hardgoods (2 months). During the entire period the trainee is required to complete assignments, involving operational and merchandise projects. Training is provided through on-the-job training, classroom training by human resources staff, and some specialized training by outside instructors. The promotional ladder for management trainees is: assistant manager, after six months; senior assistant merchandise manager, after completion of the training program (15 months); store manager, usually after three to five years of employment.

In addition to the management development training program, there is a continuous educational program for middle and top management. All managers are expected to complete a masters in retailing certificate (an in-house degree awarded after completing 12 Cornell University correspondence courses). Every manager is appraised at regular intervals and must also appraise himself and set interim goals to improve performance.

Rose's also offers college tuition assistance of up to 90 percent for those receiving a grade of "A."

Training of Sales Personnel. Rose's has a well-developed training program for store personnel which has been markedly changed and improved during the last five years. Store personnel receive about 40 hours of training including on-the-job training, with everyone trained to be a sales person and to use the cash register. Videos are used for customer service, company culture, and technical material pertaining to specific occupations. Training manuals are used for teaching the skills of every position.

Efforts to Improve Customer Service and Productivity. Management maintains that Rose's has a solid reputation for fair and friendly customer service, a reputation which it is acting to maintain. At the same time, it is also attempting to raise productivity.

Efforts to improve customer service involve not only explicit instruction during the training programs but also a strong emphasis on the image of the Rose's organization as a "family" working together to serve the customer. Employee morale and a sense of belonging are given major emphasis. An important part of its drive to improve employee enthusiasm and company spirit is its annual "Recognition Program." In this program, store employees in each store nominate a candidate (management or hourly worker) to compete at the area level for an award for outstanding contribution to the organization during the preceding 12 months. Winners (chosen by judges) then compete at the company-wide level. Some 90 persons are finally chosen for top honors. These employees and their spouses receive a trip to Disneyland, are given a dinner, awarded cash prizes, have their pictures taken with the chief executive officer, and are taken on a cruise to the Bahamas. The company budgets $250,000 annually for its Recognition Program.

A more basic approach to building employee morale is a carefully designed benefits package. Rose's provides employees with a broad array of benefits: group insurance (the employee chooses a package from a variety of plans and the company shares the cost); retirement/profit-sharing plan (the company pays the entire cost with contributions based on annual income and Rose's profits; employees are eligible after one year's service); variable investment plans (employees are eligible, after age 21 or 1,000 hours, to invest, tax-deferred, in Rose's stock or alternative portfolios); paid vacations and holidays; and a Christmas bonus.

Rose's program to enhance productivity extends to all levels of the company's operations. For example, cashiers are monitored for sales, mistakes, hours on the job; stock handlers, for time required to load and unload and the number of products handled; district managers regularly review store productivity with the store manager; and store managers formally appraise the operations of their stores.

Publix Super Markets, Inc.

Publix Super Markets, Inc., with 371 stores and 55,000 employees, is one of the oldest and best-run U.S. supermarket chains, operating entirely in the state of Florida. It has grown rapidly throughout the postwar period, adding new stores and increasing sales as the economy of Florida has flourished. Growth has accelerated in the past 3½ years.

Publix was founded in 1930 by George W. Jenkins, who is presently chief executive officer and whose concepts of innovative quality merchandising and superior customer service still dominate company philosophy. Several family members play important roles in top management and on the board of directors. The company's stock is owned entirely by company employees, including family members of the management team.

Publix enjoys a national reputation as a top-of-the-line supermarket chain with clean, well-kept outlets and superior service. Although it does not feature a policy of everyday lowest prices, management asserts that its price policy is very competitive. Low-cost operations and efficient provisioning are made possible through three large distribution centers and two dry stores distribution facilities (over 5 million square feet in all) and Florida's largest truck fleet (almost 400 tractors and more than 700 trailers). In addition, it maintains production facilities for baking, deli, milk products, fruit drinks, and bagged ice, and operates its own printing plant.

The large majority of Publix stores range from 35,000 to 40,000 square feet. Twenty-five are somewhat larger (five are 48,000 and 20 are 56,000 square feet) and offer a broader variety of merchandise and services (e.g., pharmacy, floral and cosmetic departments). All stores are open seven days a week, typically from 7 A.M. to 9 P.M.

Merchandise Policy and Competition. Publix has been extremely aggressive in its merchandising policy. It has featured bakery products through in-store bakeries in many of its stores since 1956, store delicatessen departments for over a decade, and salad bars for five years. For more than three years it has operated pharmacy departments in a number of its larger stores. Today 26 of its stores make available to customers electronic fund transfer facilities (for credit cards) and a much larger number offer automatic teller machines.

Although competition has been intense, Publix has been successful in maintaining its market share. Kroger, the largest U.S. supermarket chain, deserted the Florida market some years ago to be replaced by expanding Cash 'n Carry stores. Other chains have come and gone. Today Winn Dixie is the leading competitor, but Cash 'n Carry, Albertson, and a highly aggressive newcomer, Food Lion, are important contenders for market share.

Use of Technology. In striving to continue sales and profit growth, Publix relies heavily on electronic technology. All stores are equipped with point-of-sale scanning which is linked to purchasing and distribution to assure appropriate, timely buying, prompt deliveries, and effective inventory control. In one store, the company is currently experimenting with fully automated self-service scanning that eliminates checkout by the cashier.

Organizational Structure. Although distribution, purchasing, and control are key factors in maintaining profitable operation, Publix management places its greatest emphasis on providing the highest possible level of service through efficient store operation and the maintenance of a friendly and well-trained staff of managers and store personnel. To this end, it has in recent years revised its organizational structure and training program.

Roughly three years ago store organization was revamped to place the store manager squarely in charge of all operations with an assistant manager/managers and departmental managers (meat, baking, produce, deli) under him. Such a plan had as its purpose the strengthening of lines of authority and the creation of a single profit center (the store) which along with a storewide bonus plan encourages employees to improve their performance. Under the older arrangement, store managers were in charge of operations related to dry stores and produce, but other operations were under meat, bakery, and produce managers who were answerable to higher level executives.

Under the reorganization, the upper level managerial structure was revamped to bring it in line with the new store organization and to provide greater assistance to store managers and their personnel. Under the new scheme, the district manager became the principal link between top management and the retail outlet. With seven to eight stores, district managers are able to visit frequently (twice a week), be familiar with personnel, and offer counsel in a variety of matters, with particular emphasis on handling personnel problems and maintaining customer service. In addition, produce merchandise supervisors (with surveillance over 45–50 stores), meat supervisors (18–20 stores), and bakery supervisors (18–20 stores) monitor stores less frequently, working through the district manager to address particular problems and provide specialized advice.

Use of Part-Time Workers and Employee Turnover. Publix makes substantial use of part-time personnel—about 60 percent. Part-time employees are found principally among "front-end" workers (cashiers and baggers), deli, and bakery personnel.

Turnover rates vary sharply between full-time and part-time sales associates (i.e., nonmanagerial store personnel), 11 percent for the former group, 103 percent for the latter.

There was no evidence that management was making efforts to shift toward greater use of full-time personnel, although it is clear that in its recruitment, training, and benefits policies Publix strives to build a work force of loyal employees who carry out tasks according to a well-defined standard and who make a long-term commitment to the company.

Recruitment and Training of Management. Publix has a sizable management staff, 5,500 to 5,800 (including store managers and assistant store managers) out of a total work force of 55,000, and, accordingly, must continuously enlist new managerial talent. Yet it does not recruit on any college campus and only about 5 percent of its current managerial force has a college degree. In its managerial recruitment, it "goes outside" to fill specialized staff positions but draws entirely from its store personnel in recruiting management trainees.

Management training is of two sorts. The first is the basic leadership program, a three-day program for new managers and assistant managers, presented 12 times a year at the training center (50 to 60 persons attend each session). The second is the advanced leadership program, a four-day program for both new and old managers, presented at an off-site resort with 30 to 45 persons attending. All Publix managers attend this latter program each year.

In addition to the above training, every manager must take the Cornell University sanitation correspondence course and at least two other courses paid for by the company. Publix also provides tuition assistance for courses completed at the college level ($650 for junior college, $750 for a four-year college).

Recruitment and Training of Store Personnel. Hiring of sales associates is the responsibility of store managers who rely on referrals and, in particular, close contacts with high schools. In addition, the company frequently recruits retirees to fill seasonal requirements for extra workers during the winter peaks that characterize its sales in the coastal areas of Florida.

The Publix training program for store personnel is the most thorough and well-organized that we encountered in our investigation. The present program was instituted about five years ago as a result of a survey which showed that, although there had long been a commitment to training, standards of performance had been slipping under conditions of rapid growth and extension of store hours. While management training was considered satisfactory, training at the store level, delegated to store managers, was uneven. A major objective of the new program was to standardize training and bring about accountability.

In its training of sales associates, Publix emphasizes not only job competence (e.g., cashier training, product knowledge) but also company values (integrity, friendliness, customer service), store cleanliness (all personnel are expected to help), and a strict dress code (all personnel must be dressed neatly, with clean uniforms or aprons and shirts, pants and shoes as prescribed, no jeans for men or women, no long hair for men, white shirts except for pastel shirts in the south Florida area).

Bagging people are given nine hours of formal training; cashiers and sales persons, 20 to 24 hours. Product knowledge training is simple for front-end personnel (i.e., knowledge of location of items) but more intensive in other departments such as meat and deli.

The program is unique in its attention to detail and in the thoroughness with which accountability is enforced. New employees are given assistance in completing the paperwork requisite to joining the organization and are carefully oriented (including location of the bathroom). Associates must sign an acknowledgment that they have received a copy of all rules, regulations, and the associate's handbook, and understand their contents. In addition, the employee's trainer must sign a form indicating that the training program has been completed. A quarterly report is submitted throughout the duration of employment indicating training completed and evaluating performance.

The Publix training organization consists of seven persons at headquarters who prepare training materials and operate the large, modern training center. Extensive use is made of video tapes and training manuals as well as on-the-job training. At the store level, there is a trainer for sales associates (this trainer works also as a cashier or section person).

New Store Program. Special programs are provided for both sales associates and managers in preparation for the opening of a new store. Prospective sales associates meet at the store from 4 to 7 P.M. ten days to two weeks before the opening for orientation and instruction by one or two trainers. Store management personnel attend a one-day team building workshop. This session focuses on situation training (handling problems and crisis situations) and is followed up after opening day by visits from the district manager.

Jack Eckerd's Drug Stores

Jack Eckerd's Drug Stores is a chain of 1,600 stores operating in the South, Southwest, and East. Founded in 1952, the company was a pioneer in the self-service store format but nevertheless has established a reputation for convenience and good customer service. Eckerd's grew rapidly until it went private through an leverage buyout in 1986. Since that time, it has largely redirected investment to remodeling, updating, and upgrading its older stores, eliminating some inefficient stores and adding others in desirable locations. Employment in 1988 was 36,344.

Eckerd's sales strategy is to combine a "back-end" full-service, pharmacy operation with a "front-end" assortment of cosmetics, toiletries, and convenience items. The company does well in cities as well as in suburbs and nonmetropolitan areas, frequently operating at a high traffic corner location close to or near a major supermarket. Eckerd's chief competitor is Walgreen, a national drug chain. In recent years, it has experienced increasing front-end competition from the discount department store chains, especially Wal-Mart.

Stores vary in size but are typically about 10,000 square feet with standardized layout stocked according to planograms prepared at headquarters. Stores are supplied twice weekly from six major distribution centers with purchasing carried out almost entirely by headquarters buyers. Pricing decisions are made centrally with zone-by-zone adjustments. Stores operate seven days a week, typically from 9 A.M. to 9 P.M. or 9 A.M. to 7 P.M. In a number of large metropolitan areas, stores operate on a 24-hour basis, but this practice peaked a few years ago and there is no trend toward increasing its use.

Merchandising. Merchandising strategy is focused on providing convenience of shopping for customers oriented to its full-service pharmacy and extensive line of proprietary drug items. For some years, the company has emphasized its photofinishing service, a product line that attracts customers and at the same time provides a generous gross margin. Recently, it has experimented with adding fast-turnover food items (e.g., cookies) and soft drinks.

Currently, a major emphasis is on maintaining a high level of customer service throughout the store. In discussing this policy, management cited the success of Nordstrom stores with its emphasis on customer service.

Although the company has increasingly made use of computer systems, it has not been a leader in this area. Currently, no use is made of scanning, and application of point-of-sale electronics is limited to cash registers in a number of key stores. In several of its smaller markets, Eckerd's is testing a new system (RAY) which integrates stores with the buying operation and with major vendors. The system promises to improve buying by providing information on sale and stock of individual items thereby alerting management to new trends and providing faster shipment and better inventory control. Management sees the principal advantage of scanning as an opportunity to improve customer service by reducing waiting time at the cash register.

All pharmacies are equipped with computer systems that not only provide a file of prescriptions but provide on-line communication with third-party payers (e.g., health maintenance organizations, Medicare) to verify customer eligibility.

Organization. Eckerd's stores operate with a lean staff. All personnel, including the manager, are involved in unpacking and stocking merchandise and in keeping the store clean and neat.

Store organization varies with size. In a small store there may be as few employees as a pharmacist manager, a front-end clerk, a cashier, and a drug clerk. In a large store, however, there could be one or two assistant managers, an additional front-end clerk, two pharmacists, a drug technician, a drug clerk, one or two cosmeticians, depending on store hours. It was noted that there is a trade-off between numbers of employees in the store and pilferage: reducing staff increases losses from theft.

Each of the eight regions of the company is headed by a regional vice president, to whom one or two operating managers, a pharmacist service manager, a merchandise manager, controller, human resources manager, and loss prevention manager report. A real estate manager typically supervises property acquisition and disposal in two regions.

The key link between stores and upper level management is the district manager who is responsible for 12 to 20 stores. District managers visit stores frequently and are responsible for seeing that stores run smoothly in every aspect of the operation: personnel, merchandising, customer service, store appearance. There has recently been a change in policy regarding the district manager's role. Whereas previously they often functioned as an inspector looking for omissions and mistakes, under the new policy district managers act as counselor to the store manager, a source of advice and assistance. Merchandise managers, pharmacist service managers, human resources managers, and loss prevention managers visit stores less frequently and provide assistance of a more technical nature. Human resources managers play an important role in training and actively assist in recruitment in some instances.

Staffing. Store personnel were said to fall into three categories: full-time, part-time, and on-call. Full- and part-time personnel work on a regular schedule; on-call personnel are available to fill in when personnel are absent or when sales volume is heavy. Full-time personnel include managers, pharmacists, cosmeticians, drug technicians, and may include other workers. From 55 to 60 percent of store personnel work full-time. Part-time people are used largely as front-end workers. On-call arrangements are especially important for pharmacist positions since a registered pharmacist must be on duty at all times and since the sales volume in the pharmacy department varies widely both during the week and seasonally. Cosmeticians also often work on an on-call basis.

Recruitment of Pharmacists and Management. Recruitment of registered pharmacists is a constant problem since these well trained (five years of college), well-paid professionals are in short supply. The company recruits through advertising and visiting college campuses. It makes considerable use of retired pharmacists especially on an on-call basis and especially in Florida. The company has made a major effort through the human resources department to locate and enlist pharmacists who have moved to Florida by offering two- to three-day training sessions to help them pass their state qualifying board examinations.

The company typically does not visit college campuses to recruit other than pharmacists and specialists such as accountants and computer systems people. New store managers may be applicants with managerial experience elsewhere, often with competitors. Trainees may be drawn from the Eckerd hourly ranks. Roughly 25 percent of those who become store managers are in the latter category. Recently, the human resources department has been working with the University of Florida School of Retailing to enlist qualified students as summer interns who may subsequently become trainees.

Recruitment of Store Personnel. Hourly workers are recruited for the most part by store managers; in metropolitan areas, by human resources staff. Pharmacists, working with human resources, recruit drug clerks and drug technicians. Opportunities are provided for hourly employees to move upward within the store. Cashiers may receive training to become cosmeticians, drug clerks, or drug technicians.

Training. The Eckerd training program for management and store personnel has been significantly broadened and stiffened under the new director of human resources, who was brought in several years ago.

Management trainees are trained through the use of manuals, making use of a self-instructional technique by which they are assigned problems to work through. In addition, they receive on-the-job training. Store managers are responsible for the training of assistant managers and are required to "sign off" on training completed.

All new store personnel are given four to six hours of "survival training" at a regional classroom. Such training includes orientation (hours, dress code, company policy) and customer relations. A special feature is the use of board games by which the new employee is introduced to various types of transactions and carried through the various types of merchandise in the store. Following this initial session, there is more specialized instruction. All personnel are trained in use of the cash register through video and on-the-job training. Cosmeticians are given special product training some of which is provided by vendors.

Training, particularly product training, is updated through video tapes prepared by the headquarters human resources staff. These video tapes are regarded by management not simply as a training device but as a total communications tool and are used to provide information on a variety of topics, including new products and how to sell them, instructions relating to seasonal merchandising efforts, managerial techniques, and technical matters of concern to pharmacists. Video equipment and tapes are made available at all times in the store "break" room.

In assessing the importance of training, the human resources administrator stressed the need to emphasize customer service but also noted the increasing importance of training store managers to manage. An important new problem he noted was how to train store managers to work with older retired persons, many of whom held responsible positions in their earlier years. With smaller labor force cohorts of younger workers these individuals must be looked to as an important source of labor in the years ahead.

Turnover. Turnover rates vary widely among the several types of personnel. Part-time, front-end personnel have the highest turnover—roughly 130 percent. Rates for drug clerks run at 30 to 40 percent; pharmacists, 10 to 15 percent. Turnover of management above the store level is less than 25 percent.

High's

High's is a convenience chain of 255 stores operating in the District of Columbia, southern Maryland, and part of Virginia, West Virginia, and Pennsylvania. Founded by a dairy cooperative in the late 1940s to provide an outlet for its output, High's until recently operated ice cream and milk processing plants. Over the years, the company established a niche in its market area by offering hand-dipped ice cream and other dairy products along with more typical convenience store products. High's was acquired in 1987 by the Southland Company, the nation's largest convenience store chain (and owner of the 7-Eleven chain) following which the High's manufacturing facilities were divested (although rights to purchase their output were retained) and a number of unprofitable stores were sold or closed. High's outlets are, for the most part, look-alike in design with merchandise arranged according to planograms prepared at headquarters.

Store Operation and Competition. High's stores are located mostly in suburbs and small towns. About 30 operate 24 hours a day, but because of security problems this practice has not increased in recent years. In the majority of existing outlets, store location does not permit the sale of gasoline, but present policy is for all new outlets to sell gas.

High's regards the gasoline service station with convenience store facilities as its chief competitor, but also sees small supermarkets and fast-food outlets as competitors.

Merchandising. Management sees its market changing as a result of suburbanization, increased use of automobiles, and increased employment of women. Each of these changes has acted to increase the popularity of the convenience store with its easy access and extended operating hours. In particular, the increased employment of women has brought a new emphasis on fast-food purchases, as less cooking is being done in the home.

High's has moved aggressively to increase the sale of fast foods that are appropriate for its relatively small outlets (typically, about 2,400 square feet). In addition to hand-dipped ice cream, all stores feature hot dogs, donuts, hot coffee, and ready-made sandwiches, with pizza offered in most outlets. About 20 stores are equipped with deli departments and the company has recently begun to experiment with selling fried chicken. High's outlets also sell lottery tickets and money orders, and recently, video rentals, automatic teller machines, and dry cleaning pickup service have been added to some outlets.

Distribution and Use of Computer Systems. Stores are supplied principally from one of Southland's three very large distribution centers, with deliveries made on a weekly basis. Bread, beer, potato chips, soda, deli products, and donuts are supplied by local vendors with deliveries made two or three times weekly.

All stores are linked directly to High's headquarters and to the Southland distribution system. Store orders are keyed into a Telzon hand computer which transmits orders to High's and Southland via telephone dial-in. Electronic cash registers record sales information which passes to High's marketing department where it is analyzed in order to allocate store space to various product lines.

Organization. High's operates as one of Southland's 36 divisions. Its chief executive, the division manager, is in charge of an operations manager, marketing manager, real estate and development manager, human resources manager, and controller, each with its own staff. Under the operations manager, there are five area managers and under each, five store supervisors, an audit supervisor, and an area trainer. The store supervisor is responsible for overseeing ten stores, visiting frequently and working with the store manager. The audit supervisor is responsible principally for taking a physical inventory of each store monthly. The area trainer is responsible for orientation and operational training at the store level.

High's headquarters has retained operational autonomy but may turn to Southland specialists for assistance (e.g., merchandising). High's has incorporated the Southland employee benefits system and is in the process of adopting its training system.

Stores employ from five to eight persons and organization is simple, with a store manager typically directing the efforts of a full-time assistant store manager, full-time first clerk, and full- and part-time clerks. In addition, where a deli is in operation, there will be a deli manager and assistant. All employees unpack and stock merchandise and man cash registers.

Store managers are responsible for store operations, hiring and firing, on-the-job training, ordering, and attaining profit goals. In practice, they must monitor stocks continuously and be aware of sales of all types of merchandise.

Recruitment. Human resources executives recruit management trainees on college campuses and hire after administering a test to determine the likelihood of a candidate's success. Trainees receive up to six months of training, including on-the-job training, sometimes less. They start at the bottom of the store organization and perform at all levels before being promoted to store manager.

All hourly personnel are hired by the store manager. Under new Southland procedures, applicants are given a standardized test the answers to which are keyed into the computer and the results provide an estimate of the applicant's expected performance, likelihood of staying on the job, integrity, customer relations, and general aptitude. Results of the test are used by the store manager for guidance in conducting the interview.

People coming in at the hourly level were said to be receiving inadequate training in reading, writing, and communication in school. Although no more than a high school education is required, it is important that all employees have mastered the "three r's."

Training. Formal training of management trainees is manual-based. Each trainee is given a series of problem assignments and must work out the answers from manuals and by working with store managers. High's executives noted that at the store manager level, there are increasing demands for familiarity with government regulations (e.g., alcoholic beverage control, equal employment opportunity guidelines), and greater emphasis on profit and loss control, and increasing emphasis on customer relations.

Hourly personnel are given eight hours of classroom training. Video training includes customer service, rules for selling alcoholic beverages, and shortage control. Other training modes cover company policy, customer complaints, cash register operation, use of price book, and stocking procedures. Following this, are eight hours of on-the-job training.

In the small convenience store, with its relatively limited range of fast-turnover merchandise, demands upon personnel for product information are not great. Yet High's management feels its employees should be able to answer customer questions, and, accordingly, store personnel are required, at a minimum, to have a basic knowledge of High's dairy products (percentage butter fat, nature of yogurt, etc.).

The company is shifting to the Southland training program within the near future. Under this program, new associates will receive three days of classroom training with much greater use of video and more extensive role playing. Classroom training will be followed by two days of on-the-job training. Thirty days after this training, area managers will return for a two-hour session in which new employees have an opportunity to ask questions and evaluate their training.

Under the Southland program, a number of special courses are given for management at various levels.

Fringe Benefits. Since the company's acquisition, the Southland program has been instituted. The principal advantage of the Southland

Table 5.2 Percentage of Employment Held by Women and Minorities, Three Retailers

Retailer	All Occupations	Officers/ Managers	Sales Workers	Trainees
A&S (1986)				
Females	75.5	63.0	84.6	76.2
Minorities	33.0	11.2	28.8	12.9
Rose's (1988)				
Females	67.5	12.8	79.9	14.1
Minorities	17.7	7.7	19.5	11.0
High's (1989)				
Females	67.2	60.3	70.3	NA
Minorities	25.8	23.9	27.0	NA
Rose's (1978)				
Females	77.9	15.6	84.0	11.4
Minorities	15.1	7.3	17.0	13.4
High's (1979)				
Females	59.4	44.5	62.8	NA
Minorities	20.1	22.4	20.1	NA

Source: Company EEO-1 data.

program is that it offers more generous profit-sharing and retirement plans. Under the latter, Southland contributes (after a minimum period of service) an increasing amount to match the employee's contribution, ranging from 40 cents on the dollar (for new employees) to four times that amount (after a number of years of service). Funds are invested in a company-managed high yield portfolio. In addition to other benefits, all employees, except store managers, receive a bonus based on Southland sales volume. Store manager bonuses are paid on the basis of individual store profit performance.

Women and Minorities: Some Limited Evidence

From employment data provided by three of the above firms, we can make several observations regarding the employment experience of women and minorities.

The first is that women find jobs rather readily in retailing: in the three firms providing information from their equal employment opportunity reports (EEO–1) women accounted for more than two-thirds of all employment and from 70 to 85 percent of all sales worker jobs in recent years (Table 5.2).

A second observation is that the extent to which women gain admission to the ranks of management varies widely. In A&S and High's, women's share of employment in officer and manager occupations was more than 60 percent; in Rose's, under 13 percent.

The relatively high percentage of women in managerial positions at A&S is not unexpected since department stores cater principally to women and there is a heavy merchandising emphasis on women's apparel, cosmetics, and accessories. Moreover, there are a large number of departments in a typical department store of which many are small, with limited responsibility for department managers and relatively low levels of compensation (this is by no means true for all, however).

The explanation of the high percentage of women in managerial positions at High's (60 percent) lies largely in the nature of convenience stores. Outlets are small and the range of merchandise relatively limited; there are few workers to be supervised. Accordingly, salaries of store managers are low: the average store manager earns about $22,000, with top salaries at around $35,000 to $40,000. As one of High's executive stated, "Actually, we don't find much competition from men for the job." It is interesting that at the next level, area supervisor, only two out of 25 are women; and among the five area managers, all are men.

In contrast, at Rose's stores store manager responsibilities are much greater and compensation much higher—a manager would receive in salary and commissions two or three times the compensation of his counterpart in a convenience store.

It is somewhat difficult to assess the minority experience since information is lacking on the size of the minority population. Once again Rose's record is poorest. Given the fact that this firm operates in a southern area, its equal employment opportunity record raises questions as to the extent to which the firm has made a concerted effort to increase employment of minorities. Management stated, however, that it had experienced difficulty in getting promising black college graduates to come into their training program, since these young people typically preferred to seek careers outside of retailing and were much sought after, especially by banks.

At first glance, the data for High's indicate a more successful experience in hiring minorities. Yet a closer look indicates that blacks are not employed in large numbers: only 36 percent of all minority workers are black and the remainder is largely Hispanic (not shown in Table 5.2).

For the two firms that provided data for two points in time (Rose's and High's), there is evidence of progress in total employment of minorities but little indication that these workers have experienced greater success in gaining access to the managerial ranks.

Publix did not provide EEO-1 data, but we did learn something about their experience in promoting minorities and women. The Publix record in bringing minorities into management is hardly impressive. According to management, the company "had a good number of blacks in the management track" eight to ten years ago, but today has only one black store manager. We were told that its record was somewhat better in production and in its bakery departments. In southeast Florida, there were reported to be eight Asian department managers.

Similarly, Publix has not made major strides in promoting women into the managerial ranks. There are no women in executive positions above the store level and only 15 in store manager positions. Within the stores, women account for 15 assistant store managers, 30 second assistants, three produce managers, and 30 bakery managers.

Taken as a whole this limited evidence tends to support the conclusion that although women readily find employment in retailing, for the most part they do not do well in competing with men for the most responsible and well-paying positions. As for blacks, the evidence indicates that they have fared relatively poorly in finding employment at any level in two of these firms, although the third, A&S, does employ a relatively large number. As regards the success of minorities in finding a place in the ranks of management, the record varies among firms. It is clear, however, that for the two firms furnishing data for an earlier year, very little progress was made over a ten-year period.

Conclusion

There is a widely held view that retailing is largely an unprogressive, unproductive sector of the U.S. economy. Yet the ten firms interviewed, representing major segments of the industry, provide a quite different picture. Although all are, admittedly, among the more progressive firms in the industry, analysis of their operations indicates that competition is moving the industry to a new set of merchandising practices, organizational structures and employment recruitment, and promotional and training practices that are significantly altering its characteristics.

An important conclusion to be drawn from the interviews would seem to be that the new economies of scale offer strong competitive advantages to the well-run regional chain. These organizations compete readily with national firms and appear to be competitively superior to most smaller companies. This does not mean that some small retailers with innovative management cannot find special niches in the market where quality of service, knowledge of product, and attractiveness of merchandise provide a strong appeal to the consumer. But it seems highly likely that strong regionals will not only continue to thrive but will gain a larger share of the market in the years ahead.

If this is, indeed, the case, there are, quite possibly, unfortunate implications for some groups in the labor force. These aggressive, well-run companies are clearly trying to upgrade the quality of their work force through a process of careful selection and training of new workers.

Given their objectives, they may be expected to be less willing than formerly to hire those who are poorly educated and lack in the social skills necessary to provide the targeted improvements in customer service. This augers ill for the minority job-seeker as he or she seeks to find employment.

If indeed these new policies act against the disadvantaged worker, we will see a reversal of an older tradition in which it was the largest and strongest firms with their sheltered internal labor markets that offered the most promising opportunities for work and advancement to the least privileged in our society. Much can be said for the recent developments in retailing as regards improved efficiency and better service to the consumer, but it is by no means clear that they open up new work opportunities for those most in need of them.

Notes

1. U.S. Department of Labor, *Employment and Earnings* (January 1988): 190–193. The percentage for youth employment is for wholesale and retail combined. Wholesale employment is about one-third of retail, but the sector employs relatively few youth.

2. B. Bluestone, P. Hanna, S. Kuhn, and L. Moore, *The Retail Revolution* (Boston, MA: Auburn House, 1981), p. 19.

3. Goldman Sachs, unpublished notes for retailing seminar, 1989.

4. Goldman Sachs (n. 3).

5. Bluestone, et al. (n. 2), p. 25.

6. Bluestone, et al. (n. 2), p. 33.

7. "Research Study: Proof of Rising Store Costs," *Chain Store Executive* (July 1986): 25.

8. This section draws heavily on D.J. Levin, "The Supermarket Industry," Salomon Brothers, Inc., February 1988; and Goldman-Sachs (n. 3).

9. Goldman Sachs (n. 3).

10. This section draws upon material presented in A.M. Hayutin and J.D. Seibald, "The Hypermarket Experiment in America," Salomon Brothers, Inc., 28 July 1988.

11. Material presented in this section is drawn from Goldman Sachs (n. 3).

12. This section is based largely on D.J. Levin, "The Circle K Corporation—A Bumpy Road to Growth," Salomon Brothers Inc., 5 October 1987.

13. Lord & Taylor, as a chain of large department specialty stores, has felt the competition of specialty stores less keenly than the traditional department stores.

14. Not all department managers report to the store manager directly; about half report to the branch store divisional manager.

15. Lord & Taylor has been slow to adopt point-of-sale (POS) computerization although it has utilized computer systems to facilitate the buying operation and

other functions for a number of years. POS computerized registers on line to headquarters were installed as recently as early 1988 in some branches.

16. *All* persons in the Lord & Taylor organization are required to enroll in the May friendliness program.

17. There were six major vendors represented in the Stamford store.

6

Business Services: Accounting, Management Consulting, and Computer Software

Thierry Noyelle

For over four decades now, employment and output in business services have expanded at rates markedly higher than the rest of the economy, with growth accelerating even faster during the 1970s and 1980s. The reasons for this development are many and complex. It is in large part the outcome of a fundamental postwar transformation in the economy's mode of production and is associated with what is sometimes called the rise of the post-industrial or service economy. This transformation is not discussed in this chapter but is addressed in Chapters 3 and 8.[1]

The scope of this chapter is both less ambitious and more focused. It is an effort to assess the kinds of labor markets that have developed in sectors that were once relatively marginal to the economy but are now quite large, the changes such labor markets have undergone as a result of rapid growth, changing competition and new technology, and the skill needs and skill formation problems that these sectors have encountered as they have matured.

To narrow the discussion, this chapter focuses on three business service sectors: accounting and audit, management consulting, and computer software. These three sectors have a large share of their employment in the professional and managerial occupations, typically two-thirds of their labor force. In addition, they are sectors whose labor force is overwhelmingly a college-educated one. Yet, as this chapter indicates, they must confront the same technological and competitive changes that are being met by so many other sectors in the economy, often with remarkably similar implications for skills and skill formation.

In the next section, I review the growth of the three sectors within the context of the overall growth of business services. Thereafter, I highlight broad similarities and differences in the labor market and skill transformations that have been experienced by the three sectors. I also indicate how the sectors have altered their skill formation system to respond to change.

This overall assessment of change in the three sectors is based on interviews conducted with executives and managers in more than 20 firms over an 18-month period. I also draw from information available in the specialized business press and from survey work conducted during 1988 in relationship with another research project.[2]

To further illustrate the nature of change in the three sectors, I then turn to a detailed presentation of recent transformations in five firms: two accounting firms (Coopers & Lybrand and Arthur Andersen & Co.); one management consulting firm (Harbridge House); and two computer software firms (Information Builders and Decision Systems).

In the final section, I return to a discussion of aggregate findings and focus on their long-range implications for firms. In particular, I argue that, despite U.S. firms' remarkable success both here and abroad in the three business services studied in this chapter, both here and abroad, their continuing success cannot be taken for granted. Competition is likely to intensify, especially in foreign markets, and U.S. firms will have to face new challenges. In turn, these new challenges are likely to pose new human resources problems. Specifically, U.S. business service firms will need to strengthen their firm-specific service technologies, and, in turn, they will need to learn how to better transfer these technologies, and the accompanying sets of skills, to their foreign operations.

Business services are sectors that have rarely come under the scrutiny of either labor market economists or education analysts. Perhaps, the predominance of technical, professional, and managerial personnel as well as the very large numbers of college-educated individuals in those sectors have led to the perception that these sectors are either immune from changes or too different from other sectors for their study to be useful. Nothing could be further from the truth, however. As I indicate in the next section, strong competitive and technological forces are making for an environment subject to rapid change. In addition, to the extent that there is continuing transformation and upskilling across sectors of the U.S. economy, issues associated with managing relatively high-skill human resources are becoming important in other sectors as well, and the study of business services can be useful in that respect. Let us not forget that upward of 30 percent of the U.S. labor force is employed in managerial, professional, and technical occupations.

Table 6.1 Employment Growth in Business and Related Services, 1970–1986

	Employment (000)			Growth (%)	
	1970	1980	1986	1970–1980	1980–1986
Total private sector	57,265	74,835	83,380	30.7	11.4
Business services	1,632	2,996	4,613	83.6	54.0
Advertising	115	140	168	21.7	20.0
Computer software, data processing	na[a]	303	553	na	82.5
Management consulting and public relations	288	324	562	12.5	73.5
Temporary employment agencies	na	569	971	na	70.7
Services to buildings	288	497	636	72.6	30.0
Legal services	237	503	746	112.2	48.3
Miscellaneous services	590	925	1,410	56.8	52.4
Engineering, architectural	261	523	706	100.4	35.0
Accounting	200	302	432	51.0	43.1
Total business and related services	2,459	4,424	6,769	79.9	53.0

[a]na = not available.

Source: U.S. Department of Commerce, Bureau of the Census, *County Business Patterns, U.S. Summary,* several years.

The Growth of the Accounting, Management Consulting, and Computer Software Industries

How rapid has growth in business services been and how large has the sector become? Tables 6.1 and 6.2 provide some answers.

The U.S. Standard Industrial Code (SIC) classifies business and related services under three main sectors: business services, legal services, and

Table 6.2 Annual Receipts of Business and Related Services, 1980–1986 ($ billions—current $)

	1980	1983	1986	1983–1986 (% rate of change)
Business services	na[a]	128.8	198.7	54.3
Advertising	na	12.0	17.3	44.2
Computer software, data processing	na	24.7	36.0	45.8
Management consulting and public relations	na	24.8	36.8	48.4
Personnel supply	na	10.6	18.0	69.8
Services to buildings	na	10.0	13.8	38.0
Legal services	25.7	39.7	57.1	43.8
Miscellaneous services	na	na	na	
Engineering, architectural	na	36.3	45.4	25.1
Accounting	na	17.1	24.0	40.4

[a]na = not available.

Source: U.S. Department of Commerce, Bureau of the Census, *Current Business Reports,* Series BS, Service Annual Survey, several years.

miscellaneous services. Table 6.1 shows employment changes from 1970 to 1986 and suggests growth rates in these services at least twice as large as those of total private sector employment during the last two decades or so. The results speak for themselves: By 1986, business and related services accounted for 8.1 percent of total private sector employment, compared to 4.2 percent in 1970. Table 6.2 emphasizes the very rapid growth of business service output during the long phase of economic expansion of the 1980s.

The quality of government's reporting on services, and particularly on business services, however, is notoriously poor. The reasons are many but include the fact that coverage of business services remained nearly nonexistent until the early 1980s. One likely implication is that official statistics vastly underestimate the employment and output size of some of these sectors.

To stay with limitations in employment measurements, consider the following: Based on reasonable extrapolations of the occupational employment data of the 1980 *Census of Population*, data processing and computer software activity probably employed between 2.5 and 3 million individuals in 1986, a far cry from the half million individuals employed by independent data processing and software firms as reported in Table 6.1.[3] To be sure, these larger numbers include all persons employed in data processing and software occupations, be they employed by computer users, by manufacturer of computing equipment, by service sectors others than the data processing and computer software sector, or by that very sector itself. However, there are strong suspicions that the official estimates of employment and output in the independent data processing and software industry, as shown in Tables 6.1 and 6.2, are far too small. Indeed, the industry's own professional associations estimate the sector output at nearly twice the size of that reported by the government and shown in Table 6.2.

Table 6.1 also suggests that while overall business and related service sector growth has been rapid, growth has not been evenly distributed. Employment growth in advertising, for example, has been much slower than growth in other sectors during both the 1970s and 1980s. Two explanations are possible, and, for that matter, not necessarily exclusive of each other. Since slow employment growth was accompanied by seemingly rapid output growth, at least during that 1980s (see Table 6.2), this discrepancy may simply reflect productivity gains in the sector. But slow employment growth may also reflect structural problems within a sector, perhaps a reflection of a sector's own maturing.

Signs of rapid growth followed by market saturation and restructuring can be found in the three sectors detailed in this report. For example, the modern accounting and audit industry is an old industry founded initially in England but institutionalized in this country at the turn of the century with the introduction of required statutory audits for publicly owned companies. The industry has undergone several transformations over the years, most recently during the 1980s.

Beginning in the 1980s, traditional accounting and audit services came under growing pressure as markets matured, as the diffusion of computerized technology helped transform the audit product, and as client demands for management information and financial systems services shifted. Hence, the demand for tax services increased rapidly due, in part, to the complexity of tax planning in a global marketplace and due, also, to major changes in U.S. federal income tax law initiated under the Reagan Administration. Paralleling this development, there was a surge in the demand for management consulting services as well as an inordinate growth in the demand for services to assist firms in the introduction of computerized technology. Tax planning, management consulting, and information technology services are areas in which many accounting firms have expanded during the 1980s in the search for new markets, helped by the special knowledge of basic financial and management information systems that the accountant is uniquely positioned to acquire during the audit process.

Growing competition in the audit market can be explained in a number of ways, including the fact that the torrid pace of mergers and acquisitions during the 1980s and the privatization of many firms previously publicly held resulted in the elimination of some very large, and traditionally, very lucrative, accounts.[4] Growing competition helped put downward pressure on audit fees, which in turn pressured firms to find new sources of revenue. Furthermore, the diffusion of minicomputers, and, to an even greater extent, microcomputers, accelerated the computerization of the audit process. Those firms that were the quickest at computerizing their operations used their initial technological advantage to attract new business by lowering fees. As fees dropped, several of the large accounting firms began using audits as a "price leader," with the intention of making up revenues by cross-selling tax planning, management consulting, and information technology services for which margins are much higher.

Paralleling these changes within accounting, management consulting also underwent some major changes.

Modern management consulting's roots also date back to the turn of the century, specifically to the time and motion studies and related engineering analyses carried out by efficiency experts to assist businesses in their search for greater productivity. The most recent period of transformation dates back to the late 1970s and is most relevant from the point of view of this chapter.

Growth in management consulting services slowed down considerably in the 1970s (Table 6.1). As it turned out, those years marked the end of an era in which the main thrust of management consulting services was oriented toward business-problem *diagnosis*, but in which the consultant remained removed from the risks associated with implementation. Strategic planning consulting, as practiced by Bain or the Boston Consulting Group, two of the most famous and most successful consultancies of that era, epitomized the management consulting of the 1970s. Yet it did not take long for clients to understand that they, themselves, could hire young MBAs to crank out numbers and map out strategies.[5]

In the 1980s, a different focus emerged, one that put major responsibilities in the hands of consultants in not only *developing diagnoses* of problems but more importantly in *implementing solutions* for clients. Consultancies that could assist firms with compensation and pension plans or develop training solutions and information systems have emerged as some of the most successful in the 1980s.

The origins of electronic data processing and computer software date back to the first computers developed by the military at the end of World War II. As a profit-making industry, the sector owes its development to the introduction of IBM's first mainframe commercial computers in the late 1950s.

Today, the industry is organized around several main markets: data processing, customized software, packaged software, systems integration, and so-called "consulting." These segments are not static but rather rapidly changing. Data processing is an industry that came of age at a time when only mainframe computing was available, typically at high cost and necessitating expert personnel to carry out the processing. So-called service bureaus, which bloomed during the early period of computing, sold processing time and processing applications to corporate customers on the bureaus' mainframes. To a large extent, the customized software industry is an industry that also came of age around the heyday of the mainframe, although demand for its product remains large.

The advent of the minicomputer in the mid- and late 1970s, followed shortly thereafter by the microcomputer, is at the origins of the packaged software industry and the slow demise of the data processing industry, at least as a dominant industry. The sharp drop in the price of hardware associated with the minicomputer revolution meant that computing could now be reinternalized by users, while the rapid multiplication in computer users put growing pressure on software producers to develop packaged rather than customized solutions to business applications.

Meanwhile, the growing availability and variety of both hardware and software have given birth to a whole industry of systems integrators

Table 6.3   Worldwide and U.S. Revenues of Accounting, Management Consulting, and Software, 1983–1987 ($ billions)

	1987 Worldwide	1987 U.S.	1983 U.S.
Accounting/auditing	50–60	26.5	17.0
Management consulting	80–90	45.0	28.0
Software/data processing	100–120	60.0	35.0

Source: Author's estimates based on Table 6.2 and U.S. Department of Commerce, International Trade Administration, *U.S. Industrial Outlook, 1988* and *1989* (Washington, D.C.: Government Printing Office, 1988, 1989).

who assist customers and develop particular "turnkey" applications using hardware and software available on the market.

Finally, in and around the periphery of the data processing and computer software industry, has emerged a "consulting" software industry whose primary role is to provide systems analysis and programming staff for software projects being develop by others.

A few additional observations will emphasize the extent of the commingling that has taken place among the sectors that are discussed in this chapter. Accountancies have moved into tax planning (a field of activity which they often share with law firms), into areas of management consulting such as compensation work, executive search, and many other areas which they share with management consultants, as well as in information technology services, typically primarily in areas of systems integration. Some consultancies have evolved to become producers of packaged software, others to specialize in systems integration or in large-scale customized software. And some producers of packaged software, through their products, have de facto cut into markets once controlled by accountants (e.g., small business accounting or tax preparation software) or by consultants (e.g., actuarial software for compensation work). All of this has made for intense competition across many of these fields. It has also pushed many firms into new skill areas.

Before turning to this very issue, a last observation is in order regarding the firm size and competitive structure of the three sectors under scrutiny. Table 6.3 presents revised indicators of the worldwide and U.S. revenue of the three sectors in 1983–1987. Tables 6.4 through 6.7 present lists of the top firms in the three sectors with output measures comparable to those of Table 6.3. In the case of the data processing and computer software industry, the list is actually divided into two lists: a list of the top 15 software firms (mostly firms specializing in packaged and/or customized software) (Table 6.6) and a list of the top 15 computer service firms (mostly firms specializing in data processing and systems integration) (Table 6.7). Note the presence of Arthur Andersen on three of the four

Table 6.4 Eight Largest Accounting Firms Worldwide, 1988

Firm	Country	Worldwide Revenues ($ millions)	U.S. Revenues ($ millions)	Worldwide Employees	Fee Split Audit/Tax/Other
1. KPMG	U.S.	3,900	1,640	62,500	65/20/15/0
2. Arthur Andersen	U.S.	2,820	1,700	45,900	40/20/40/0
3. Coopers & Lybrand	U.S.	2,500	na	45,000	na[a]
4. Price Waterhouse	U.S.	2,218	960	38,500	55/22/18/5
5. Ernst & Whinney	U.S.	2,191	1,174	35,600	58/20/22/0
6. Arthur Young	U.S.	2,053	843	33,000	59/21/20/0
7. Deloitte Haskins & Sells	U.S.	1,921	820	31,000	61/20/14/5
8. Touche Ross	U.S.	1,840	800	33,000	56/17/18/9
		19,443	9,400 (est.)[b]	325,000	

[a]na = not available.
[b]est. = estimate.

Source: International Accounting Bulletin, December 1988.

lists (accounting, management consulting, and computer service), owing to the firm's increasingly varied specializations.

These tables suggest rather different industry structures. In accounting, large firms are dominant both domestically and worldwide. In 1988, the eight largest firms, the so called "Big 8", controlled approximately one-third of the industry's revenue—domestically and worldwide, followed by a group of ten to 15 middle-sized firms (not shown in Table 6.4) which control an additional 15 percent or so of revenue.[6]

In management consulting, where the emergence of relatively large firms ($150 million or more in annual revenue) is a very recent phenomenon, concentration remains very limited, with the top 20 firms listed in Table 6.5 controlling less than 10 percent of total industry revenue worldwide.

Finally, in data processing and software, concentration is somewhere in between the other two sectors, with the top 30 firms listed in Tables 6.6 and 6.7 controlling together about 15 to 20 percent of worldwide sales.

Two points emerge from an examination of these lists. First, large firms play a dominant role in accounting, but they do not in management consulting nor in data processing and software. This is important to keep in mind as we approach a more detailed study of skills and skill formation in these sectors because large firms are likely to have stronger internal labor markets and more resources for training than smaller ones. Second, these tables suggest a clear domination of U.S. firms in world markets, a point that has important human resource implications and to which I return in the last section of this chapter.

Table 6.5   Twenty Largest Management Consulting Firms, 1987

Firm	Country	Worldwide Revenues[a] ($ millions)	U.S. Revenues[a] ($ millions)	Number of Professionals Worldwide[a,b]
1. Arthur Andersen	U.S.	838	522	9,600
2. Marsh & McLennan	U.S.	530	393	6,400
3. McKinsey	U.S.	510	255	1,600
4. Towers Perrin	U.S.	465	380	3,085
5. Peat Marwick	U.S.	438	253	4,700
6. Booz Allen	U.S.	412	345	2,100
7. Coopers & Lybrand	U.S.	381	199	4,700
8. Ernst & Whinney	U.S.	374	230	3,255
9. Price Waterhouse	U.S.	345	160	4,300
10. Saatchi & Saatchi	U.K.	267	176	1,500
11. Touche Ross	U.S.	248	157	2,100
12. Wyatt	U.S.	237	207	1,600
13. Arthur D. Little	U.S.	218	151	1,500
14. Deloitte Haskins	U.S.	209	91	2,300
15. Arthur Young	U.S.	204	133	2,400
16. Bain	U.S.	200	140	800
17. PA Management Consult.	U.K.	175[c]	na	na
18. Alexander Proudfoot	U.S.	170	60	1,100
19. Hewitt Associates	U.S.	161	152	1,400
20. American Management Systems	U.S.	145	145	1,600
		6,527	4,149	

[a]Management advisory service revenues only.
[b]As defined by company; does not include support staff.
[c]1986 revenues.

Source: "A Survey of Management Consulting," *The Economist*, February 13, 1988; *Consulting News, Directory of the Largest U.S. Management Consulting Firms* (1988).

An Overview of Labor Markets and Skill Needs

The widespread commingling of activities across the three sectors has brought labor market and skill formation systems, once intended to serve rather distinct skill needs, increasingly in contact with each other. In addition, the skill needs of each sector have changed under technological, competitive, and other pressures, adding to a reshaping of the systems in place. This section highlights key changes in labor markets and the demand for skills in the three sectors.

Labor Markets

Traditionally, accounting firms have provided for their skill needs by relying heavily on internal labor markets and firm-based training. This owes to both the importance of large and medium-sized firms in the

Table 6.6 The Top Fifteen Software Companies, 1985, 1986 ($ millions)

	1986	1985	Percentage Change
1. IBM	5,514.0	4,165.0	32.4
2. Unisys Corp.	861.0	na[a]	na
3. Digital Equipment Corp.	560.0	300.0	86.7
4. NEC Corp.	507.1	376.2	34.8
5. Fujitsu Ltd.	389.2	250.6	55.3
6. Siemens AG	387.1	221.1	75.1
7. Hewlett-Packard Co.	375.0	300.0	25.0
8. Hitachi Ltd.	331.0	202.0	63.9
9. Nixdorf Computer AG	299.5	192.0	56.0
10. Lotus Development Corp.	283.0	225.5	25.5
11. Microsoft Corp.	260.2	162.6	60.0
12. Compagnie Gen. d'Elec.	238.1	178.2	33.6
13. Computer Assoc. Int.	226.5	143.7	57.6
14. Olivetti SpA	225.3	116.0	94.2
15. Wang Laboratories Inc.	200.0	157.0	27.4

[a]na = not available.

Source: "The Top 15 in Software," Datamation (July 1987 and July 1986).

Table 6.7 The Top Fifteen Service Companies, 1985, 1986 ($ millions)

	1986	1985	Percentage Change
1. TRW Inc.	1,450.0	1,275.0	13.7
2. ADP Inc.	1,298.1	1,102.1	17.8
3. General Motors Corp.	1,125.9	978.3	15.1
4. Computer Sciences Corp.	977.7	800.7	22.1
5. McDonnell Douglas	803.2	650.0	23.6
6. Control Data Corp.	752.0	1,058.7	−29.0
7. Martin Marietta	659.4	564.4	16.8
8. Nippon Teleg., Telephone	577.6	382.0	51.2
9. General Electric Co.	550.0	950.0	−42.1
10. Arthur Andersen	546.0	414.7	31.7
11. Cap Gemini Sogeti	419.9	245.1	71.3
12. NCR Corp.	350.0	300.0	16.7
13. Boeing Co.	300.0	270.0	11.1
14. IBM	300.0	300.0	nc[a]
15. Nomura Comp. Sys. Co.	263.5	151.7	73.7

[a]nc = no change.

Source: "The Top 15 in Services," Datamation (July 1987 and July 1986).

industry, a phenomenon that goes back several decades, and the industry's British origins.

The original British system placed heavy emphasis on a firm-based vocational systems, in which young high school graduates were hired for several years as "articled clerks" and learned on the job, before they could "sit their licencing exams" and, if successful, be hired as permanent staff. Thereafter, individuals were further trained, both on and off the job, and echelons were staffed through internal mobility.

Over the years, the U.S. system has transformed from the original system in several ways. First, educational entry requirements have risen, shifting part of the initial training burden to schools. Today, entry-level accountants are hired with a three- or four-year college degree in accounting. There is even some discussion within the industry to create a five-year degree. As under the old system, however, most young accountants take their licencing exams to become certified public accountants only after having worked for a few years.

The other change is a recent one. Large accounting firms have lately amended their time-honored tradition of nearly exclusive reliance on internal promotion, by turning to the external labor market to hire experienced accountants. The reasons for the shift are several and are discussed in the detailed case studies presented in the next section of this chapter. In a nutshell, technological change (i.e., computerization of the audit process) has altered the ratio between junior and senior personnel, toward a larger number of senior relative to junior personnel. In addition, the audit field has become more specialized, with a growing need for strong industry specializations among auditors. In general, firms have found that the old internal labor market operated too slowly to produce the skills required within their occupational pyramid. To strengthen their specializations, firms have sought to attract individuals with work experience from the business side.

In contrast to accounting, management consultancies have long relied on an open labor market system, with some—often weak—elements of an internal labor market. To some extent, this varies according to the nature of the expertise of the firm.

If the firm offers a relatively standardized service, then there is greater room for a fuller division of labor between junior and senior personnel and greater opportunities to institute an internal labor market system. This remains the case, for example, among firms that specialize in actuarial and compensation work. As in the case of accounting, technological and market changes have put new pressure in recent years on hiring experienced personnel directly at the top of the occupational hierarchy.

Minimum educational requirements in management consulting tend to be even higher than they are in accounting: typically a masters degree from a professional school, except, of course for support personnel. (Support personnel in the kind of business services firms that are discussed in this chapter, including management consulting, typically accounts for less than one-third of total personnel, however.)

In computer software, the existing labor market system is mostly "open," with some elements of internal labor markets in place, particularly among some of the very large users—telephone utilities, airline companies, banks, and insurance companies to name a few. The latter serve as an important training ground for a large number of inexperienced programmers and systems analysts. Their low retention rate, however, provides a foundation for the open labor market systems that tend to dominate elsewhere in the industry.

There is an historical dimension to this dichotomy. In the era of the mainframe, large users, hardware manufacturers, and service bureaus made up the bulk of the industry, so the internal labor market system tended to dominate. But the rise of an independent software industry in the 1980s to serve users of mini- and micro-computers has contributed to the fragmentation of the industry and the shift to a more open labor market system. In addition, technological and market changes similar to those experienced by accounting and management consulting have been felt by the computer software industry, shifting skill requirements both *upward* and *toward greater industry specializations.*

Educational preparation in computer software is more varied than it is in the other two industries. Today, many programmers and systems analysts have a minimum four-year college education, but there is still a large number of self-taught individuals in the field, with backgrounds ranging from educational dropouts to musicians, lawyers, former business executives to even physicians. How important is each group? No one knows for sure because of the lack of data. However, one thing is sure. Most computer science programs are recent creations—late 1970s and early 1980s—and are far from controlling entry into this important labor market.

In conclusion, perhaps the biggest labor market changes have been in the large accounting firms. Their shift to product areas traditionally characterized by more "open" labor markets, as well as the pressures for change within accounting itself, have combined to force them to open up their internal labor markets, at least to a certain point. This development, along with some of the differences in the skills and values of the different occupations that have been brought together under one roof (for example, management consulting puts much greater emphasis on individual salesmanship than does audit), helps to explain some of the turmoil that has rocked large accountancies in recent years.[7]

Skills

Some of the same pressures that have contributed to a transformation of the labor market system of the three industries studied here also have contributed to the transformation of their skill needs. Indeed, the two are related since labor market systems are structured, in part, as a way to develop and supply the skills that are demanded by employers.

In general, four skill areas are emphasized by firms as requiring special attention: (1) technical skills, (2) customer service skills, (3) industry specializations, and (4) salesmanship.

Technical Skills. The three sectors under review are in the business of offering technically sophisticated services. They depend heavily on college-educated labor to fill their ranks; yet, they must also add to their workers' stock of knowledge through firm-based training. In this respect, there is considerable evidence to the effect that the minimum threshold for technical knowledge has risen both because the underlying technology has become more complex and because services have become more advanced.

To the extent that the required technical knowledge falls within a general skill area, e.g., knowledge of operating systems, programming languages, accounting principles, hardware, etc., the tendency is either to demand that individuals acquire such knowledge prior to entry into the labor market or that it be acquired through course work provided by educational institutions, vendors, and others, with financial support from employers if necessary. Where technical knowledge is oriented toward a firm's own products, e.g., the firm's own audit method, the firm's proprietary software, etc., then training is provided by the firm itself. Over time, part of the transformation in the role business service firms have played in the technical training of their employees lies in the increasing distinction that firms have established between these two bodies of technical knowledge. In turn, this reflects attempts by firms, under increased competition, to distinguish themselves from competitors by shifting from the use of generalized techniques in the solution of business problems to the use of firm-specific "service technologies."

Customer Service Skills. Another way in which rising competition has caused skill changes in firms is by forcing employers to focus on quality. Quality can usually be achieved in two ways: through the standardization of proprietary procedures and the thorough training of employees in the use of such procedures and by emphasizing customer service skills.

In business services, customer service skills include a wide range of competencies that individuals must use in their interaction with clients. They range from skills associated with proposal writing and presentation to those needed for effective report writing, presentations, and other situations of interaction with clients. In general, firms feel that these are skill areas that are vastly underdeveloped by traditional educational institutions and need to be nurtured.

But the process of communication is not value neutral. It can be shaped to reflect the company's culture and uniqueness. In other words, it can be a way for firms to leave a stamp on their service. So firms do have a vested interest in developing communications media that are proprietary, ranging from company logos and graphics to training techniques for written or verbal presentations that are unique to the company.

Not surprisingly, with the advent of new computer/video/visual technologies, some firms are strengthening the technological component of their communications training. Employees are being trained in the use of computer graphic software; video equipment is being used during workshops to assist in the teaching process of verbal presentations and public speaking techniques; and so forth.

Industry Specializations. As in many other sectors of the economy, rising competition in business services is fostering greater customization of output, most often along industry lines. The growing need for individuals that have, at once, a knowledge of the business service that the firm delivers and, more importantly, a knowledge and understanding of the needs of the user of the service is a major factor behind the opening of previously closed internal labor markets. Put another way, most firms find it difficult to develop a strong, in-house understanding of the intricate needs of particular client industries, short of hiring individuals that have spent a number of years in those very industries.

This does not exclude development of some of the necessary industry knowledge via firm-based training. Indeed, there is ample evidence of considerable firm-based training to strengthen and update employee knowledge in such areas. Most often, such efforts are aimed at senior professionals, especially those who manage assignments or generate new ones, and take the form of seminars bringing together specialists from the industry.

Salesmanship. As suggested earlier, growing competition is disrupting relationships that once were remarkably stable. In addition, competition cuts into margins and puts pressure on firms to seek new areas of revenue. The implication for business service firms is a shift from a business environment in which a great deal of business tended to be "repeat business," to one in which one-time assignments are becoming more important. The result is growing uncertainty and a new premium on salesmanship.

While this shift is most obvious in accounting firms, it is in no way unique to them. Furthermore, it is not unique to the three business service sectors but can be found in a variety of other sectors. Advertising, banking, and legal services are among some of the sectors in which traditional client relationships have experienced major turmoil in recent years.

The response by firms is two-fold. On the one hand, firms are helping individuals to develop salesmanship skills, partly by strengthening their communications skills, partly by using mentor relationships between junior and senior professionals. On the other hand, firms are applying considerable efforts at strengthening their "institutional salesmanship skills" as an alternative to "individual salesmanship."

Developing and promoting strong industry specializations is one way to strengthen institutional salesmanship, by creating, in the marketplace, an aura of superior quality and knowledge that makes it difficult for potential clients not to use the firm's services. Techniques accompanying such efforts might involve organizing meetings with major past, current, and potential clients at which experts, including, of course, those from the firm itself, are brought together to present cutting-edge developments in their field.

Cross-selling is another way to promote institutional salesmanship. Under cross-selling, the firm tries to build on its old relationships to sell new services to old clients. In practice, as many firms have found out, this is often easier said than done. For it may necessitate bringing together a team of professionals from different divisions (for example, an auditor, a tax specialist, and a management consultant) that are not used to working together.

Another institutional salesmanship method is the use of the "old boy's network." Accounting and management consulting firms, for example, use to their advantage the high turnover rates among junior personnel by maintaining a strong relationship with those that leave the firm and by using those relationships to source new business later on. Not unlikely, those firms will even assist the placement of the leavers with clients. Likewise, McKinsey is known for its very active alumni network, which periodically engages former employees of the firm in a variety of activities, a practice which is in no way unique to the firm.

Five Case Studies

This section illustrates these findings through five case studies of two accounting firms (Coopers & Lybrand and Arthur Anderson), one management consultancy (Harbridge House), and two software firms (Information Builders and Decision Systems).

Coopers & Lybrand

Markets. As one of the so called "Big 8" accounting firms, the firm, like its competitors in the field during the 1980s, has moved aggressively into tax planning and management advisory services (MAS). As of 1987, 60 percent of the firm's revenue came from audit, 20 percent from tax, and 20 percent from consulting. The firm employed approximately 30,000 people worldwide and 14,000 in the United States—including 1,200 partners, 7,800 professionals, and 5,000 support staff. By 1987, its consulting practice was its fastest growing division, generating approximately $400 to $450 million of annual revenue worldwide and employing approximately 3,700 staff—1,700 in the United States and 2,000 abroad. The size of the practice had roughly doubled since 1984 and the firm expected it to double again by 1990.

Coopers & Lybrand's consulting practice includes two major businesses: a general management consulting practice and an information technology (IT) practice. In 1987, the IT practice accounted for 60 to 65 percent of all MAS revenues and employed approximately 2,200 staff (1,000 in the United States and 1,200 abroad).

In its general consulting practice, the firm is trying to grow both internally and through acquisitions of small independent consulting practices. In its IT practice, growth is mostly internal. The firm's main markets in these two areas are manufacturing, health care, financial services, public utilities, and the federal government (including the Department of Defense). The benefits of working on federal government contracts, which accounted for nearly 20 percent of the firm's consulting revenues in 1987, are several: budgets for government consulting work tend to be more stable than those of commercial customers and consulting assignments tend to be longer—often two to three years. Furthermore, technical projects will often be followed by technical and maintenance contracts that can last for periods of five to seven years. The downside, of course, is that federal contracts do not pay as well as commercial ones.

Employment Distribution. As of late 1987, the firm's audit practice operated approximately 120 offices in the United States and an additional 250 offices overseas. However, the firm's tax and MAS practices remained much more concentrated geographically: in the firm's 35 largest U.S. offices and 60 to 70 largest offices overseas in the case of consulting. In the United States, this means a management consulting presence primarily in the first-tier metropolitan centers. Several reasons explain these differing locational patterns.

Audit requires regular contact with clients, necessitating repeated site visits to the client's site(s) for the duration of the audit relationship—not unlikely a relationship that is maintained over a period of many years, sometimes several decades. The demand for accountants is thus rather predictable, both in terms of the number of accountants needed to serve an account or a set of accounts and in terms of the location of that demand. Firms can thus station most of the staff that works on large audit accounts in locations in the proximity of the client's key sites.

In contrast, the consulting relationship is both much more ad hoc and much more unpredictable. The relationship may last only for the duration of an assignment, typically weeks or months at a time, rarely years. It is true that it can also be much more intensive, requiring that part of the consulting staff be on the client's site for a good portion of the assignment. By the company's own estimates, some consulting assignments may necessitate that 50 percent of the work be done on site, the other 50 percent at the home office. As a result, the firm may need to relocate consultants temporarily to serve an account, at times for up to several months. Yet, to the extent possible, the firm will try to commute people from a central location. It cannot commit itself to opening offices and/or developing staff in locations that may not endure beyond a given assignment. In addition, consulting makes greater use of specialists than does audit, and larger geographical markets are required to support demand for their services. Finally, the geographically centralized structure characteristic of management consultancies is consistent with a heavy reliance on external labor markets to staff the ranks of such organizations with experienced professionals, as will be suggested below. Quite simply, larger places are more likely than smaller ones to yield the number and variety of specialists that management consultancies often seek to recruit.

To a lesser extent, a similar centralized pattern prevails in the firm's tax division because the success of the division is also partly dependent on its ability to assemble a staff of highly specialized professionals whose expertise can be supported only on the basis of relatively large geographical markets.

Occupational Structure and Skill Needs. In 1987, the firm hired nearly 1,600 recent college graduates directly from campuses. Of those graduates, 1,300 were directed into entry-level accounting jobs in the audit division; another 200, in the tax division; and another 60 or 70, in the management consulting division. In addition to entry-level recruits, another 200 experienced recruits were hired in audit, 40 or 50 in tax, and 350 to 400 in consulting.

In the case of management consulting, these figures confirm the firm's overwhelming dependency on the external labor market to staff its ranks.

In the case of accounting, they underscore a change from the past. Whereas ten years ago the firm used the external labor market exclusively for the purpose of hiring entry-level professionals (senior positions were staffed through internal mobility), it now turns to the external labor market to find some of its senior personnel.

When asked to explain this shift, senior management gave three reasons: the need to shift the balance between junior and senior personnel, high turnover among junior staff, and quick-fix response. Under pressure for rapid change, the firm found that the internal labor market system was simply too slow to produce the number of senior personnel at the rates needed. With growing computerization of the number-crunching portion of the audit process and under new pressure from clients to deliver a more customized service, the firm was coming under growing pressure to expand its senior staff. But high turnover rates among entry-level accountants—in the 20 to 25 percent range through most of the 1980s—did not help in that respect. Thus, the shift to the external labor market was partly a quick-fix response.

In terms of skills, senior managers from the audit division emphasized the following growing needs on their side of the business: stronger technical skills, stronger "client-servicing" skills, stronger sales skills, and stronger management skills.

These needs are not very different from those expressed by other firms and have been discussed in the previous section. One simply needs to add that the firm's emphasis on its growing need for management skills reflects in part the fact that current pressures on moving junior personnel faster into senior positions leaves less time to develop these skills through on-the-job training.

The great majority of the firm's entry-level accountants come from accounting programs. There are about 400 schools around the country that deliver four-year college accounting diplomas. About two-thirds of the new hires come from 80 or so such schools. Recruitment is done by the partners, with one partner in charge of recruiting on one or a few colleges regularly every year.

Once hired, entry-level accountants are put through a two-week formal training session. Thereafter, individuals will be sent back periodically for training. During the first year, individuals receive a minimum of 120 hours of formal training; during year two, 100 hours; and during year three, 60 hours. Entry-level training tends to emphasize technical and customer-servicing skills. Sales and management skills tend to be developed later in the career progression.

During the first two years, junior accountants work out of a pool and are assigned to several project managers and partners for a total of approximately seven to eight assignments. Most classroom training is done locally, some centrally. In addition, the firm has a central training development division to develop training materials. The current emphasis is on expanding formal training as a way to help move people up the career ladder faster.

Recruitment of entry-level professionals in the tax division is more eclectic than in the audit division. Individuals are hired from a variety of fields, often at a higher level than entry-level accountants: attorneys, MBAs, graduates of masters in taxation programs. Consistent with the division's emphasis on tax planning, training of new hires tends to stress research.

In theory, at least, the occupational structure on the consulting side parallels that which exists on the accounting side. In practice, however, the flow of individuals onto, out of, and through the firm's occupational ladder remains different because of much heavier hiring of experienced personnel.

At the bottom of the ladder are associate consultants, who can next move up to become consultants and then senior consultants. Beginning with the next echelon, that of consulting manager, individuals are increasingly judged on their capacity to sell billable hours. If successful, managers graduate into senior manager, director, and partner positions. In theory, at least, it takes between 11 and 13 years for an individual to be eligible for a partnership position.

Until the mid-1980s, most hiring was done at the senior consultant and manager level, with the firm seeking to hire experienced professionals—typically individuals with a graduate university degree, a strong specialization, and eight to ten years of professional experience, including preferably some consulting experience. As a result, the firm's MAS practice was very top heavy, employing extremely few people in the associate consultant and consultant ranks. As long as the firm's MAS practice focused principally on areas of general management consulting, this model served it quite well. But as more and more of the firm's practice shifted to information technology services, this structure became somewhat misaligned with respect to both the skill needs of that particular area of work and the prices that were being charged. Billing rates were clearly too high compared to those charged by competitors. In the area of information technology services in which this and other accounting firms have expanded, namely systems integration, junior personnel can usefully be employed to fill some of the positions in systems analysis, systems design, and systems development (programming).

In 1986, the firm initiated an undergraduate recruitment program targeted to colleges with computer science programs to try to fill its need for associate consultants and consultants in its information technology practice. Approximately 40 college graduates were hired in 1986,

65 in 1987, and 100 in 1988 in the firm's U.S. information technology practice. By the firm's own estimate, these covered approximately 25 percent of the firm's U.S. "intake," meaning, of course, that other forms of hiring, mostly at higher levels, continue to make up the majority of its recruiting effort.

The undergraduate recruitment program has allowed the firm to better "fill-in" lower tier positions and also to bring in employees that are less experienced, yet much more "malleable."[8] After two years, the firm seemed satisfied with its program, with only a 5 percent annual turnover rate among these new groups. This was to be contrasted to a much higher 30 percent annual turnover rate among more senior consultants.

In terms of consulting needs, senior management stressed four broad areas of skills: technical skills, customer-servicing skills, salesmanship, and intra-corporate communications.

Technical skills are those skills that experienced professionals are supposed to bring to the job, and that younger ones have partly acquired in school and will further develop on the job and through company training. In this respect, the undergraduate recruitment program is tied to a six-week, in-house, full-time training program, carried out in Princeton, New Jersey, during which new recruits strengthen their programming and systems analysis skills.

Salesmanship is the skill that is so crucial to the viability of consulting but also seemingly so difficult to develop. One avowed reason for the high turnover among some of the senior personnel recruited by the firm's MAS division is that many end up not being able to sell their work as effectively as necessary to support their own time and that of their junior professional or support staff. But like other large business service firms, the firm is careful not to rely exclusively on individual salesmanship and tries to develop new clientele by means of various forms of "institutional" sales effort, similar to those described earlier in this report: cross-selling, repeat business, and the "old boy's" network. As part of these efforts, the firm is careful in treating as well as possible those that leave the firm, in particular by outplacing many of them with clients. The firm also convenes high-level annual seminars that bring together experts from academia and industry as well as a few senior members of the firm to present cutting-edge knowledge and solutions in particular domains (e.g., telecommunications, health care management, etc.) to a group of well-chosen past, present, or potential clients.

Another skill area emphasized by senior management in the consulting division is the need to strengthen ties among employees and help them put forth a strong company image when dealing with the outside. As one senior executive of the firm put it: "In professional services, the inventory goes home every night. Unless a firm is able to promote a

strong common culture, sense of mission, and set of loyalties, its capacity
to develop and grow remains weak." The consulting division's relatively
greater emphasis on the need to develop the firm's corporate culture is
consistent with the practice's younger age and its heavy reliance on
experienced professionals who join the firm with a much more disparate
set of experiences.

Arthur Andersen & Co.

Background. The firm's origins date back to 1913 when Arthur Andersen
and Clarence Delany bought the Audit Company of Illinois from the
estate of C.W. Knisely, its previous owner and manager. Clarence Delany
resigned from the partnership in 1918, and the name of the firm changed
to Arthur Andersen & Co. subsequent to his leaving. Based in Chicago,
the firm's domestic expansion began in 1920, with the opening of its
New York office.

Arthur Andersen's foreign expansion began in the 1930s, when it
arranged for several foreign auditors to serve some of its clients in
foreign markets. Over the years, however, Arthur Andersen & Co. grew
increasingly dissatisfied with these arrangements, because of difficulties
in controlling quality of service.

In the mid-1950s, the firm shifted from a strategy based on corre-
spondent relationships to one based exclusively on the development of
its own local practices. The company pursued this strategy exclusively
until 1985, when Sycip, Gorres, Velayo & Co. (SGV), a Philippine-based
partnership with offices in eight Asian and one Middle-Eastern countries
merged with Arthur Andersen. These developments are important because
they point to the firm's very strong culture of internal growth and
internal labor markets during most of the postwar period. And yet, as
in other large accountancies, this culture of self-sufficiency is one which
in several ways has come under question since the mid-1980s.

Markets. The firm offers services in the areas of accounting and audit,
tax services, and management information consulting (principally computer systems integration). As indicated earlier, the firm was highly
successful in the development of an information technology consulting
practice during the 1980s.

Arthur Andersen & Co.'s 1988 worldwide revenues were approximately
$2.2 billion. Its $1.1 billion audit revenues made it the fifth largest audit
firm worldwide (the second largest behind KPMG in the United States).
In tax services ($560 million in revenue in 1988), the firm ranked as
the second largest both worldwide and in the United States, in both
cases behind KPMG. Finally, with over $1 billion in management
consulting revenue, Arthur Andersen ranked as the world's largest

management consulting firm and one of the largest computer service firms.

In 1988, Arthur Andersen & Co. employed nearly 46,000 staff worldwide, a 15 percent increase over 1987 (40,000 staff) but, more importantly perhaps, a near doubling of its worldwide staff since 1983 (24,300)! As of 1988, the staff was distributed almost evenly between the firm's U.S. and foreign practices, with the latter growing at faster rates than the former. To sustain such a rapid rate of growth, the firm, throughout the 1980s, has had to recruit very large numbers of new staff and put in place a formidable training infrastructure.

Skill Needs and Hiring Practices. The firm's skill needs and hiring practices during the late 1980s have been heavily influenced by three sets of factors: its very rapid rate of expansion, high turnover rates, and a growing need for specialists. The first two factors have a direct influence on the sheer number of people that the firm has had to recruit each year.

In 1988, the firm recruited approximately 5,000 new staff to accommodate its expansion. (There was an additional, sizable increment in new staff as a result of the merger with SGV.) This number was in part inflated by high turnover, which the firm estimates at approximately 25 percent or higher among new recruits during the first two years. Over the long run, fewer than one out of ten new hires will stay with the firm until reaching partnership (typically, a process which takes between ten to 13 years to complete). Note that these rates are very much the norm in the industry.

The third factor had an impact on the firm's tradition of exclusive reliance on internal labor markets. As of late 1987, in its U.S. practice the firm already employed over 600 direct-hire specialists which had been recruited directly from the experienced labor market, typically as managers (the rank next below partner). Three years earlier there were none. These new specialists had been recruited to serve either in the firm's tax practice or in its management information consulting practice. As for the remaining years of the decade, one personnel executive projected continued hiring of roughly 500 new specialists annually.

In the tax practice, direct hires were typically individuals with MBAs or law degrees, a specialization in a particular field of taxation, and not unlikely a network of existing or potential clients. In at least one case, the firm had hired someone directly into a partnership position.

In management information consulting, direct hires were people with specializations in systems analysis or systems engineering, increasingly people with a computer science or engineering background, and less likely people with a business school background as was the case when the firm first turned to the external labor market.

The basic reason for the firm's shift to the external labor market was fundamentally the same as for Coopers & Lybrand. In fields in which high-level expertise is paramount and in which external labor markets play a much greater role, the firm had no choice but to turn to these markets if it were to develop the necessary staff at a rate rapid enough to keep up with the explosion of demand for its services.

The firm's massive hiring of new personnel, be it entry-level or experienced personnel, means extensive needs for training. In 1986, the firm's estimated training cost was $135 million, compared to annual revenue of $1.9 billion; in 1987, $195 million, compared to annual revenue of $2.3 billion.[9] For both years, training costs accounted for roughly 8.5 percent of the firm's annual revenue—a truly staggering number. In fairness to the firm, Arthur Andersen & Co. most likely has the most extensive training effort in place in the entire industry. With an estimated 6.8 million training hours per year in 1987, the firm's training effort translates to over 170 hours, or over three-and-a half weeks of training per year, per individual! In effect, the distribution of the training is heavily skewed toward younger employees.

Training is delivered at two levels. Training that is directed to country-specific, technical knowledge tends to be done at the field office level (e.g., local tax laws, local accounting regulations). Training that is methods-oriented or that focuses on behaviors tends to be done centrally.

For nearly 20 years, the bulk of the firm's worldwide, centralized training needs has been carried out at the St. Charles Center for Professional Education, a former four-year college campus located northwest of Chicago, which the firm purchased in 1970. In recent years, however, the firm has begun to decentralize some of its centralized education programs to Segovia, Spain and Mexico City. The extent of decentralization remains limited, however, because the process of bringing everyone together in a single training facility is considered part of the process that contributes to creating a unique firm culture. On average during the first three years, new recruits in the audit division spend a minimum of two weeks per year at St. Charles; three weeks in the case of new hires in the management information consulting practice. The St. Charles facilities are large enough to accommodate 4,000 students at anyone time (both teaching and sleeping arrangements).

The firm also uses training facilities in Geneva, where its world headquarters are located, for advanced training of partners.

As a rule, the firm has very few full-time teachers. Most of the teaching is done by managers and partners. One of the main responsibilities of full-time teachers is to work with partners in a research and development capacity, that is, in developing or improving firm-specific methods and the training that goes with it.

Most of the teaching carried out at St. Charles focuses on the firm's proprietary methods (audit methods, systems analysis methods) and on "behavior." In the area of behavior, the firm has put in place multi-year training sequences for what it calls "management development skills." In the consulting practice, for example, during the first year training period at St. Charles, students receive an eight-hour course on interviewing techniques, to assist them in the development of their systems development skills (i.e., interviewing clients to determine the nature of their systems needs). During year two, students enroll in a "support development" program, during which they are taught how to supervise teams of programmers.[10] During year three, the training sequence emphasizes the development of "interpersonal styles," communication with clients, sales skills, and so on. During year four, training for "management development skills" focuses on "leadership and motivation." Over the following years, students receive additional training in "proposing for new business" and "professional sales techniques." Throughout this entire sequence, a great deal of emphasis is placed on the development of such skills as public speaking, writing, negotiation techniques, counselling, small group facilitating, and so on.

In the area of methods, the nature of the firm's "product" changed substantially over the 1980s owing in part to the introduction of the microcomputer. Prior to 1982, the firm did not teach a single audit course using microcomputers, although mini- and mainframe computers were being used. Today audit is done almost exclusively with the assistance of portable microcomputers, Lotus 1–2–3 (earlier, Visicalc), and proprietary software to extract data from the client's computers and put them in a PC-usable form.

Putting the firm's human resources and training policy into focus, one senior executive summarized it in the form of seven objectives:

1. Hire smart and motivated people.
2. Train people not only for "technical skills" but also for "behavioral" skills. Consistent behavior is fundamental in establishing the firm's image in the marketplace.
3. Train people to work as part of a team, not as individuals.
4. Train people in developing the person below them; train individuals in how to best leverage their time by delegating work and responsibilities to others.
5. Sell aggressively.
6. Train individuals in gauging what they promise and fulfilling their promises.
7. Reward people for their accomplishments.

One might view many of these goals as old truths. Yet, what is striking is how few service firms have a process in place to develop such objectives.

Harbridge House

Historical Background and Markets. Founded in 1950 by three members of Harvard Business School's faculty, the firm employs approximately 150 people with estimated revenue between $15 and $20 million. These numbers put it in the top 50 management consulting firms in the United States, well among middle-sized consultancies but somewhat away from the group of very large billion dollar firms that emerged during the 1980s. The firm remained private until 1974, when it was sold to Allstate Insurance, a subsidiary of retail giant, Sears, Roebuck. Following a Sears reorganization in 1984, Harbridge House became a subsidiary of the ill-fated and now-defunct Sears World Trade Corporation. In 1987, key personnel bought the firm back from Sears and set it as a private partnership. The firm is now owned by the 33 senior staff (five officers and 28 principals).

The firm is organized in 11 business units, each headed by its own manager. All units have a functional orientation, except for one with a geographic orientation. The firm specializes in a broad range of expertise typical of general management consulting services as well as in management/executive training and education services. Indeed, one area of expertise for which the firm is best known is its diagnoses of needs for improving corporate organizational effectiveness and the tailored responses that it proposes and delivers in the form of customized training programs to help managers and executives implement needed changes. Its highly prized training expertise is one of the major ways in which the firm has built its business over the years. One measure of its success is that nearly 75 percent of its business is repeat business.[11]

Employment Distribution. The firm's principal locations are Boston (head office) and Chicago. In addition, the firm maintains branch offices in New York, Stamford, Connecticut, Arlington, Virginia, and London. It operates two small satellite offices in Port Smith, New Hampshire and Cincinnati, Ohio.

The firm employs approximately 120 professionals and 30 support staff. In addition, its has linkages to a group of about 90 outside professionals (including a large number from Ivy League universities) to whom it subcontracts, on a regular basis, approximately 25 percent of the firm's business.

The firm has shrunk since the mid–1980s. In 1984, the firm employed upward of 200 professionals. It is then that the firm decided to shut down its military consulting division. The firm had a long-standing relationship with the Navy as a sole source contractor. But when the Navy was forced to shift most of its business to competitive bidding, Harbridge House decided to leave the business. Since then, the firm has continued to do a small amount of work for other parts of the federal government if only because it may relate to some of the work it does for the private sector. The problem with government work lies in rates that firms can charge: at most $500/$600 a day compared to upward of $1,000 for private sector clients.

The loss of nearly 70 professionals in the firm's military business between 1984 and 1987 was accompanied by continued hiring in some of the other divisions, however. The firm hired 16 new people in 1987 and 20 in 1988.

Occupational Structure. Among its professional staff, the firm has five basic occupational levels: consultants, associates, senior associates, principals, and officers. Consultants are mostly paid out of overhead. Associates are paid through billable hours, on their own projects or on projects managed by others. In other words, associates are expected to start selling and managing their own projects. Senior associates must sell their entire work time plus additional billable time to cover some junior personnel time. The difference between senior associates and principals is mostly based on seniority and volume of business. (Principals in 1987 were expected to bill approximately 60 to 65 percent of their time or an annual equivalent of $300,000 and $400,000.) For someone who enters the firm as a consultant, it will take a three-year minimum to become an associate, two more years to become a senior associate, and a minimum five additional years to become a principal. In practice, however, the firm hires at various levels depending on need. In 1987, for example, of the 16 new hires, two were entry-level MBAs hired as consultants, four were hired as associates, three as senior associates, and two as executive consultants. The remaining three new hires were support staff. Executive consultants are people with qualifications similar to principals but whom, as a rule, the firm would not elect as principals until it had a chance to assess them more fully. In practice, executive consultants are compensated at levels similar to those for principals. (The 1987 pay of a principal was $70,000 base pay plus bonus.)

Except for support staff, almost all new hires have the minimum of a graduate university diploma. Among the 16 individuals hired in 1987, the list included six MBAs, two PhDs, one JD, one JD/MBA, two graduate school level transportation specialists, and three undergraduates (support staff).

The small support staff includes a few secretaries and clerks, accounting office personnel, and a few specialists associated with consulting production (editor, graphic artist, etc.). The introduction of PCs has allowed the firm to reduce the number of secretaries and clerical staff as well as the number of research assistants it employs below the consultant level. As of 1987, there were only four research assistants left.

Almost 40 percent of the firm's employees are women. Four of the 11 division managers are women. At one extreme, one division employs no women; another employs nearly 70 percent women.

Skills. The firm identifies six areas of skills that are critical to the makeup of a strong professional: conceptual skills, capacity to see the big picture, analytical tools linked to one's field of expertise, verbal skills, writing skills, teaching skills, and sales skills.

The need for teaching skills is, of course, in no small part related to the firm's strengths in executive/management training.

While the firm assists employees in developing some skills, it also tends to look for individuals who are already well skilled by the time they join the firm. This requirement might seem a bit unrealistic if the firm hired primarily entry-level professionals. However, the firm is now hiring mostly at senior levels from among experienced professionals. Typically, these are individuals with five to ten years of experience, preferably from industry.

This is a relatively recent development, driven, it would seem, by several factors. First, unless clients are buying relatively standardized services, they increasingly want to see "gray hair." The era of the Bain or Boston Consulting Group sending out armies of young MBAs to prepare corporate strategic plans appears to be largely over. Second, for a time in the mid-and late 1980s, MBAs priced themselves out of the market as Wall Street firms recruited thousands of them at greatly inflated salaries. (Prior to Wall Street's onslaught, management consulting as an industry was the largest hirer of MBAs.) The resulting shortage of MBAs occurred at a time when there was growing pressure on consultancies to maximize the number of "revenue producers" and minimize the number of support staff. The result was indeed considerable trimming at the bottom of the firm's hierarchy.

In the area of sales skill, so crucial in the consulting business, the firm has a mentor system to help younger consultants and associates develop sales skills. But like other firms, it also seeks to institutionalize certain relationships in order to reduce the inherent risks associated with individual salesmanship. This is why, ever since its early days, the firm has emphasized developing long-standing relationships leading to repeat business from a number of clients, largely through its training expertise.

Information Builders

Historical Background and Firm's Markets. Information Builders was founded in 1975, which in any other industry, would make it a relatively young firm. By the standards of the software industry, however, the company is a relatively mature one.

With approximately $125 million in sales in 1988, the firm is already one of the largest producers of packaged software in the United States and worldwide. The firm offers two basic software products: FOCUS, a database software, and LEVEL 5, an expert or knowledge-based information system. Until recently, these products have been directed primarily to the mainframe and minicomputer market. Information Builders' main competitors are firms such as Cullinet and Relational Technology, Inc. with products covering similar domains.

In comparison with a database software, such as FOCUS, an expert system, such as LEVEL 5, is able to keep track of decision rules and procedures and apply them to a new set of data. In database software, decision rules are provided externally.

FOCUS and LEVEL 5 are based on fourth-generation programming languages (4GL). Compared to older programming languages—third-generation languages such as Fortran, Cobol, Pascal, and others—these newer languages, like their equivalents for microcomputers such Lotus or dBase, are quite easy to use, even by the nonspecialist. In 4GL, programming sequences, which in third-generation languages had to be programmed as often as they were needed, are built into the software package and can be recalled automatically by the user when needed. The user needs only to specify the parameters specific to their particular use. The result is much greater ease of use and enormous productivity gains for the final user.

The firm's products are now available for use on a variety of operating systems available on mainframes (IBM), minicomputers (DEC-VAX machines, WANG, Hewlett Packard), and even microcomputers (DOS, OS/ 2, MacIntosh for LEVEL 5). The shifts to mini- and microcomputer systems—beginning respectively in the late 1970s and the late 1980s— have in both cases resulted in important shifts in the firm's sales strategy.

The firm's original commercial success hinged on a few factors. First, the firm was one of the pioneers in the development of 4GL software for mainframe computers and when FOCUS was introduced it was clearly a technically superior product. Second, the firm's initial product, FOCUS, was heavily targeted to the service bureaus.

At a time when computing power remained more expensive and less widespread than it is today, service bureaus served many corporate clients by processing large-scale data applications (payroll, accounts payable, account receivable, personnel, etc.) on their behalf or by selling them processing time on a time-sharing basis on large mainframe computers. But, with the rapid advent of minicomputers beginning in the mid–1970s, service bureaus began losing business as customers bought computers and brought back in-house, work that they had previously contracted out. As the shift was occurring, leading eventually to the demise of many small data processing houses, a number of service bureaus began assisting former customers in setting up their in-house systems, partly as a way to recoup lost revenue, often recommending the use of the very same software that they had used on their own mainframes. According to one of the firm's executives, FOCUS was a major beneficiary of this process of "technology transfer" and the firm was quick in adapting its original mainframe product to work on the new series of mid-range machines introduced by IBM in 1978 which were being bought by many of the new converts. Eventually, this shift provided a powerful impetus for the development of a strong in-house sales force, as the firm's clientele base quickly grew from a few hundred data processing houses to thousands of corporate users.

The most recent shift, to microcomputer-based products, is also taking the firm into new sales territories since it must now learn how to sell its product to distributors, who then turn to third-party vendors—mainly computer chain stores. As happened with the shift to minicomputer users, this is also forcing the firm to reassess the kind of sales effort it needs.

Employment. As of early 1989, Information Builders employed approximately 1,250 people, including 850 in the United States and the rest abroad. The firm's principal location in the United States is New York where it maintains its executive office, a large computer center for software development, a warehouse, and a full-scale regional office. The company maintains another 14 full-scale regional offices around the country (including in Minneapolis, Dallas, Boston, Washington, D.C., Silicon Valley, Seattle, Chicago, and Los Angeles) as well as several smaller scale offices. In addition, the company has recently opened a new software development center in Florida. Full-scale offices typically employ between 30 and 50 people, covering sales, customer education, technical assistance, and consulting. Smaller offices typically employ mostly consultants (see below).

Outside the United States, the company maintains two offices in Canada, and one each in England, France, Holland, and Japan. In addition, the company is opening a development center in Paris. Today between 30 and 40 percent of the firm's sales come from abroad, with France, Germany, England, and Sweden among its strongest foreign markets (the firm has supplier agreements with Honeywell-Bull, Siemens, Olivetti, and Phillips).

Occupational Distribution and Skill Needs. The company employs approximately 200 people in software development, ranging from junior programmers to project managers; 700 people in sales and training (mostly sales); 300 people in technical support; and 150 consultants. In addition, the executive offices employ nearly 100 people, ranging from clerical staff to senior managers.

Discussion with the firm's executives would suggest that, to a large extent, each group of employees behaves largely as autonomous labor markets, with little mobility across groups.

Employees in the software development group are typically four-year college educated individuals with a background in computer sciences. New recruits are hired with either some or no work experience. One pattern in the industry, however, is for large users such as banks, insurance companies, airlines, and others to serve as a training ground for large armies of inexperienced programmers, who, after a few years, will try to land a job with more prestigious companies such as this firm.

As regards this functional area, the firm expressed three sources of discontent: first, difficulty in finding good programming managers, people who are both knowledgeable technically and able to lead team work; second, difficulty in finding programmers specialized in networks and telecommunications, an increasingly hot area for software applications; and third, the fact that whenever the market become tighter, Wall Street will pay any price to recruit programmers and get a project done. Complained one executive: "For an investment bank on Wall Street, the costs of programmers compared to the returns they can derive from a data processing project are often so low as to be irrelevant."

The software development group also employs a small number of computer operators to staff the computer center. Typically, these come from some of the local community or four-year colleges with specialization in systems operations or are hired away from competitors.

The sales and education group employs a small group of trainers who assist clients in the use of Information Builders' products when first installed and a relatively large group of salespeople. Salespeople are almost all college educated and almost all experienced (30 years old or older). In finding salespeople, the firm looks primarily for people with strong sales skills—aggressiveness, intuitiveness, and agility—in short, people with a capacity to move quickly when they sense a potential deal. Sales staff productivity can be measured directly through their actual sales and is rewarded accordingly through commissions. The company complains that sales personnel are hard to find in New York: the supply is short; the demand, heavy; the turnover, high. Recruitment of sales personnel is based on hiring away from competitors. Some people from the technical areas of the firm try to shift to sales, partly because the money is better, but they usually do not have the skills to handle the job.

In technical support, the firm employs mostly four-year college educated people with a technical background. A good part of the technical support involves the staffing of hotlines set-up to assist customers in solving problems beyond the early stages of training and software installation. Personnel must be trained extensively, from the ground-up, in the many possible uses, intricacies, and complexities of the company's products. They also must be able to communicate with customers from a variety of business environments.

Finally, consultants include systems analysts that assist customers in developing applications of the firm's products specific to their needs. They come with a four-year college education at the minimum, and not unlikely a degree from a masters program with a specialization in management information systems. The firm employs a mix of experienced and junior consultants.

Training. Each group has its own training structure. Because the sales group is by far the largest group of employees, this is the group on which much of the firm's effort at improving productivity focuses. For example, with the shift to PC-based products, the firm is learning that it has to be more sophisticated in creating demand from customers, since it no longer sells directly to final users. The firm is becoming more sophisticated in using advertising and in creating a marketing image.

Training of technical support personnel is perhaps the most intensive, product-oriented training provided by the firm. Everyone must be fluent in the use of the company's products, since support staff must ultimately be able to assist any customer in problem-solving. In addition, because of the nature of its contact with users, this group plays a major role in maintaining customer loyalty and projecting the firm's image of expertise and quality.

In the programming group, training is also primarily product oriented, although it tends to focus on training programmers in the use of new hardware or in improving their use of programming languages. Vendors serve an important training function with this group.

Special Characteristics of the Firm's Labor Force. The firm's average annual turnover is approximately 20 percent in the United States, somewhat lower elsewhere. This compares to turnover rates of between 30 and 40 percent for data processing personnel of large users such as banks or insurance companies.

The firm employs very few part-time employees, a few percentage points at most. The firm discourages homework, except among sales people. Sales staff can operate on their own as long as they have a car and a phone and come regularly to the office to meet with sales managers.

Among other groups of workers, the firm finds homework dysfunctional in that it makes it difficult to maintain communication among employees. In the software development area, people tend to be organized in project development teams that are disbanded and reshaped as old projects conclude and new ones begin. In the consulting area, consultants tend to spend most of their time working on customer premises.

The firm employs very few "independent consultants," partly because their wages tend to be inflated and because they are more difficult to manage which has implications for quality control. In addition, recent changes in tax laws have made it more difficult for people to declare themselves as independent consultants if they work for one client exclusively.

It is true, however, that the status of the firm gives it an edge in seeking labor, which smaller firms often do not have. One executive interviewed admitted that "body-shopping" and "independent consulting" are widespread in programming in some parts of the industry, especially in the PC software area.[12]

Approximately 30 percent of the firm's employees are women. The highest ratio of women is in the executive office (with a large number of female clerical personnel), followed by programmers (35 percent), and technical support staff and consultants (30 percent each). The lowest ratios are in sales, with approximately 10 percent. Minority workers account for approximately 10 percent of employment, including a large number of Asians.

Decisions Systems

Historical Background and Main Markets. Decisions Systems is a publicly owned company and its stock is traded on the over-the-counter market. The company differs from the previous one in at least two major respects. First, it is a much smaller firm, employing in 1988 approximately 70 people in the United States. Second, the firm primarily provides customized software and consulting services to clients developing their own software projects. The firm has little experience in the difficult packaged software market, although, at the time the firm was interviewed, it had developed its first product for that market.

The firm dates back to 1960 when a group of four individuals working for ITT in the New York area started their own business. Not surprisingly, their first project was a contract from their former employer.

The firm's principal markets are military and aerospace contractors and commercial clients: roughly 55 and 45 percent of sales, respectively. U.S. sales in 1987 were approximately $5 million. In the military/ aerospace market, the firm has a long roster of clients including Fortune

500 companies located in the greater New York area: Grumman, RCA, ITT, Singer, and others. In this market, most of the firm's work is carried out on mainframe computers and/or involves the programming of dedicated electronic gear. In the commercial market, the firm has two major groups of clients: financial firms (Equitable Life, Metropolitan Life, Manufacturers Hanover, Bankers Trust, and Citibank) and government agencies (the New York Metropolitan Transit Agency, the Long Island Railroad, and the New York City Housing Authority).

A large portion of the firm's work consists of placing its employees on projects being developed by clients. In this function, the firm operates as a consultant, rarely as a project leader, with its staff teamed up with the clients own systems division personnel. The firm is working to shift more of its revenue to in-house projects, however. In this respect, the conventional market plays a key role in the firm's strategy.

Most of the firm's consulting work appears to come from the military and aerospace market, where long-established working relationships with a number of the large local contractors generate a staple of regular subcontracts with little sales efforts necessary. While the commercial market is more difficult to enter since contracts often must be won on the basis of competitive bidding, it is the one market where the firm is able to develop complete customized software projects. Recent contracts include software for the New York Mass Transit Authority and software for a point-of-sales terminal system with centralized controllers for the Italian retailer, Benetton.

Finally, the firm is also attempting to enter the packaged software market. Its first product is a school administration system which originally was developed for a group of five proprietary schools. The package handles student registration, financial records, course scheduling, class rosters, and job placement. It is built around a 4GL database package called PROGRESS and operates on the UNIX operating system.

Employment. In addition to a head office in New Jersey, the firm has a small office in Manhattan used by its three executives (all men), who also double as salesmen.

The firm employ 12 people in its main office, mostly working on in-house software development. In addition, it has 58 employees working as consultants on customer premises. Almost all of the 70 staff are full-timers; 15 are women and 55 are men.

Until three or four years ago, all those employed were direct employees of the firm. Around 1986, however, a change in the industry forced the firm to start hiring independent consultants. This is tricky because the firm must guarantee quality with personnel who are not its own employees. The firm tries to overcome the problem through careful screening. Of the 70 staff in the work force, nearly 30 are now operating as independent consultants. In 1988, the firm's independent consultants were paid an average of $100,000. The firm's senior staff, between $50,000 and $75,000; and the firm's junior staff, between $30,000 and $35,000.

Skills Needs. Most of the firm's staff are programmers, systems analysts, or systems engineers. In the assessment of one senior executive, the field has become far more sophisticated and complex than it once was. When there were fewer programming languages and hardware, most computer personnel were trained as generalists and were expected to learn the specifics of a particular operating system or hardware as need materialized. With today's compartmentalized software industry, specialization on different operating systems, different applications software, and different hardware is required. With greater expertise comes less flexibility of personnel. Also, since the life cycle of products keep shortening, specialists are under pressure to continuously retrain. In this respect, the firm has a tuition reimbursement policy for its employees and encourages them to seek training courses.

In terms of hiring, the firm seeks mostly experienced personnel. However, as the firm's work shifts toward more customized or packaged software, the more systems analysts it needs to find. Good systems analysts are hard to find because they constantly need to mix and match two sets of needs and requirements: design needs and client needs. A good systems analyst must be conversant with client requirements, but must also be aware that the user is never clear about his/her requirements.

In addition to programming personnel, the firm relies on its three senior executives for sales. One of the technicians who was involved in the development of the school software package now works as a part-time sales person for that software. At the time of the interview, however, the firm was considering hiring a full-time salesperson for its school software, recognizing that the sales effort associated with that package, if it were to succeed, would require a very different kind of person than those already in place.

Foreign Activity. Separate from the activities of Decision Systems in the United States, some of the founders of Decision Systems are also owners of Defense Software Systems (DSS), a U.S. private company, which is the parent company of a subsidiary located in Israel. The Israeli firm was originally established as a division of Decision Systems in the early 1980s but was converted to a subsidiary when Decision Systems went public later in 1980s. The Israeli firm serves two principal purposes: to develop software projects for the Israeli military and to serve as a subcontractor for projects won by the partners in other countries, at production costs markedly lower than those in other countries. The Israeli company also gives the firm access to pools of educated Israeli labor at a time when the market for software personnel in the United States has tightened up.

Defense Software Systems employs nearly 200 people, including 110 in Israel. The dual U.S.-Israeli set-up gives the firm considerable flexibility. While the United States gives military aid to the Israel, under U.S. law, some of that money must be spent on U.S. suppliers, which DSS is. DSS also has contracts with NATO, Spain, and Germany. Typically, such projects are handled jointly by the United States and Israel: systems design is done in New York, implementation (programming) in Israel, and final assembly and quality control of the software product in the United States.

Challenges for the Future:
A Skill Perspective

Early in this chapter, it was pointed out that growth in many parts of the three industries has been very rapid and that the success of the industries has not been limited to the U.S. market but has extended abroad as well. But past successes may come under question if these industries are unable to meet some of the challenges that their own growth is creating. In this respect, the turmoil that has agitated some of the "Big 8" accounting firms in recent months should not be seen as an idiosyncratic development but rather as a warning.

It is not simply that the large accountancies have had to figure out how to reconcile very different professional cultures within the same organization, but also that they have grown too fast for their own good. They must learn how to manage a large number of people on a worldwide scale and develop a proper balance between managerial centralization and autonomy of local practices. Runaway growth can be costly, as was learned not so long ago by Wall Street, where after years of go-go expansion investment banking suddenly discovered that it did not have in place the systems that were needed to control burgeoning staff.

Rapid growth of these industries has been achieved in part through rapid addition of new personnel. In this respect, one can probably argue that one reason for the remarkably rapid growth of business services in the U.S. economy in recent years lies in the unique, widespread availability of college-educated labor in the U.S. labor market—in many ways so essential to the constitution of those industries. But the U.S. economy is leaving an era of labor surplus and entering one of labor shortage. The ease with which firms in the three industries have been able, in the past, to expand by adding labor, may simply no longer exist. Responding to this new challenge may force firms to pay attention to two issues in a way in which they have not had to in the past: the need to reach out to new labor pools and the need to seek new ways of boosting productivity.

Reaching out to new labor pools will mean strengthening access to female and minority workers, an area in which, relative to other sectors of the U.S. economy, these sectors have been trailing (with the possible exception of the software industry). In addition, it may also mean reaching out to pools of labor located abroad, a realistic option, particularly in the software industry, and also in part of the consulting industry.[13]

Seeking to boost productivity further will also have human resource implications since it will ultimately necessitate reorganizing the division of labor and preparing individuals to contribute to a changing work process. The lack of data makes it difficult to assess the extent to which productivity gains have been achieved in the three sectors during the 1980s. Individual firms do have statistics relevant to their own firm but do not usually share them with outsiders. There are reasons to believe that gains have been achieved, however. The introduction of microcomputers has undoubtedly helped enhanced the productivity of the accounting and audit process, even though one can still find individual accountants and small partnerships where paper, pencils, and calculators remain in use. Paralleling this development, the era when large accountancies used to hire hundreds of recently graduated accountants as part of a pool from which senior staff could choose whenever assistance was required also seems to be coming to an end. Under the old system, large accountancies were staffed in order to meet peak periods in their annual business cycle. The result was tremendous downtime of junior accountants during most of the year, something that firms did not care about as long as costs could be passed along to clients through audit fees.

Likewise, it is clear that the introduction of fourth generation programming language software has boosted the productivity of users, if not that of their producers. However, major productivity gains may not necessarily need to come from the "production" side as is usually thought of, as much as from the "sales" side. This was apparent in several of the firms interviewed.

Finally, as my colleague Olivier Bertrand and I have suggested elsewhere:

In service industries, "products" are procedures which come into being only in the course of a relationship between the firm and its client. "Services" are largely "relationships," and "product knowledge" is in no small way "behavioral knowledge" on the part of both employees and customers. In a world characterized by increasing competition, firms must keep identifying new markets, innovating and introducing new products.

In turn, this implies a never ending need for training in the handling of new products.[14]

In today's world, however, developing and transferring service knowledge is a world-scale project. The evidence uncovered during this research suggests that very few business service firms have begun assessing the importance of this need, let alone putting in place solutions that will assist in the transfer of their technology. The problem is not trivial. First, it assumes that the firm carefully develops its own proprietary technologies—a process that the largest and most sophisticated firms are only beginning to understand (with a few noticeable exceptions). Second, it assumes that training solutions be put in place to support the transfer of these technologies to other locations. However, training solutions that may work in the United States because they are tailored to that country's particular labor market may not work elsewhere if only because of differences in labor market institutions and educational preparation. In the future, however, these issues are critical if U.S. firms are to retain their competitive edge in foreign markets.

This reinforces the notion that in the three industries studied in this chapter the skill formation issue is overwhelmingly a firm-based one, not really one rooted in the educational system. The issue has to do with the development and transfer of firm-specific technologies, which in the case of services is intimately linked to firm-based training. Conversely, most business service firms in the sectors studied here have only a peripheral interest in the travails of the U.S. secondary school system, since their direct exposure to the U.S. educational system is largely at the four-year college or beyond level, where quality is not usually an issue.

Notes

1. See also T. Stanback, P. Bearse, T. Noyelle, and R. Karasek, *Services/The New Economy* (Totowa, NJ: Rowman & Allanheld, 1981).

2. T. Noyelle, P. Peace, and L. Kahane, *Data Processing and Computer Software in New York City* (New York, NY: Conservation of Human Resources, Columbia University, New York, January 1989).

3. T. Noyelle, *The Changing U.S. Software Industry: Can America Keep Its Lead?* (New York, NY: Conservation of Human Resources, Columbia University, March 1989).

4. For example, Coopers & Lybrand, one of the two large accountancies reviewed here, lost the Nabisco account when the firm was taken over by R.J. Reynolds, a Peat Marwick client, resulting in lost work for almost 50 accountants who had worked on the account. On the other hand, the firm did make up

some of the loss when General Foods was taken over by Philip Morris, one of Coopers & Lybrand's long-standing clients.

5. For a review of this period, see T. Noyelle, *The Coming of Age of Management Consulting,* A Report to the New York City Office of Economic Development, April 1984.

6. The Big 8 are soon to become the Big 6. Ernst and Whinney and Arthur Young are about to merge, as are Deloitte, Haskins and Sells and Touche Ross.

7. There are, of course, other reasons to explain the recent inner turmoil in large accountancies: power and money. As consultants have increased their contribution to total revenue, they have wanted to increase their say over the strategic directions of their firm—a responsibility that the accountants, who have traditionally controlled these organizations, have been reluctant to relinquish. Furthermore, to the extent that consultants have produced higher margins than auditors, they have demanded better compensation, something which has not always sat well with the accountants.

8. Note that the firm also relies on outside contractors to do the low-level systems and programming work that may be required to complete a systems integration project.

9. Training costs include the operating and maintenance costs of training facilities, the cost of trainers, the development costs of training materials, and the wages and salaries of employees while being trained.

10. Historically, Arthur Andersen's management information consulting practice developed as a systems integrator. The basic areas of expertise for systems integrators are systems engineering and systems analysis. Traditionally, systems integrators have done very little programming. To the extent that Arthur Andersen needed programming in the past, the firm had it done mostly by entry-level consultants. This is changing, however, and in recent years the firm has felt the need to produce more and more software. To that effect, the firm has now opened programming production offices including several in the United States, one in Paris, and one in the Philippines.

11. "Expertise: The Principal Ingredient," *Industry* (the Official Monthly Magazine of Associated Industries of Massachusetts) (March 1987).

12. Body-shopping differs from independent consulting in several ways. In the case of body-shopping, a firm—sometimes called a "jobber"—recruits and places people on the client's job site, but these people remain employees of the jobber. In comparison, independent consultants are self-employed.

13. See the discussion of the rise of the Indian software industry in T. Noyelle, "Professional/Business Services and the Uruguay Round of Trade Negotiations," A Report to UNCTAD, September 1989.

14. Organization for Economic Cooperation and Development (OECD), *Human Resources and Corporate Strategy: Technological Change in Banks and Insurance Companies* (Paris: OECD, 1988), p. 85.

7

Adult Education
and Training Markets

Nevzer Stacey and Duc-Le To

Adult participation in education and training programs is increasing steadily, and so are the types of providers that offer programs aimed at the adult population. The marketplace where adult education and training are bought and sold is diverse, flexible, unstable, and partly unaccountable. The available statistical information is sketchy at best, and the nature of courses and programs varies greatly. Some even claim that, on the map of contemporary education, adult education now occupies a position at least as significant as that of primary, secondary, and higher education.[1]

In 1984, 23 million adults in the United States indicated that they participated in 11 million adult, continuing education, or noncredit courses. Employers, unions, neighborhood centers, churches, and community groups offered 10 million courses or educational activities.[2] Some of these courses and programs are designed to enrich the lives of individuals, some to provide opportunities for adults to socialize, but most are designed to teach work-related skills. The term "work-related," broadly defined, includes courses in reading, writing, and mathematics as well as courses in interpersonal skills or the art of listening. While the intent of such programs is to increase the skills and productivity of the participants, it is doubtful that the standards are uniform across programs. Moreover, either by design or by accident, many programs have other goals. The providers range from small public vocational schools to multimillion dollar enterprises that operate worldwide.

This chapter describes the education and training providers that serve students after compulsory schooling and identifies the trends that explain their growth during the last two decades. This chapter also reviews research on how important these institutions are in training and educating the work force and how well or poorly they serve different groups of people.

The Providers

Providers of education and training in the United States can be clustered into three groups based on where the education takes place. They are: school-based, work-based, and community-based institutions.

School-Based Providers

This category includes institutions whose primary objective is to educate and train students. These institutions range from adult basic and secondary education programs to two- and four-year colleges and universities. Also included in this category are technical, proprietary, and correspondence schools.

Adult Basic and Secondary Education Programs. In 1984, approximately 2.6 million adults were enrolled in adult basic and secondary education programs. Women and minorities constitute the largest segment of participants in these programs. Funding for these programs is provided by the federal government to the states on a formula basis. States are responsible for designing and administering the programs. In 1984, of the 2.6 million adults who enrolled in such programs, 649,547 were in adult secondary education programs and 1.9 million were in adult basic education programs. While the number of adult basic education participants doubled from 1980 to 1984, the increase in the number of adults in secondary education programs was very small.[3]

Four-Year Colleges and Universities. In academic year 1986–1987, there were 3,406 accredited colleges, community colleges, and universities enrolling approximately 12.5 million students at the undergraduate and graduate levels. Of these institutions, 2,070 offered four years of full-time study leading to the baccalaureate degree.[4] Despite their considerable differences in policies on enrollment, attendance, type of program, and graduation requirements, these institutions usually offer academic and technical programs. In fact, they are the largest school-based providers in training professional and technical workers for both *job qualification* (training needed to acquire current job) and *skill improvement* (training needed to improve current job skills).

According to the 1983 *Current Population Survey*, 69 percent of professionals and 53 percent of technicians acquired their job qualification training from schools (Table 7.1). Among them, approximately 75 percent of the professionals and 84 percent of the technicians were trained in four-year colleges (Table 7.2). These institutions are not only the major

Table 7.1 Number and Percentage Distribution of Occurrences of Training by Type and Source of Training and by Occupation, 1983[a]

	Number of Occurrences (in thousands)	Percent Distribution by Source of Training						
		Total	School	Formal Company Program	Informal On-the-Job Training	Armed Forces	Correspondence Courses	Other
Qualification training								
Executive, administration, and managerial	11,057	100	42	12	38	3	1	3
Professional specialty	15,078	100	69	8	18	2	1	2
Technicians and related support	3,349	100	53	13	29	5	2	1
Sales occupations	6,639	100	25	20	47	1	2	5
Administrative support, including clerical	11,840	100	44	10	42	1	1	2
Private household occupations	106	100	14	9	34	—[b]	—	42
Service workers, except private households	5,321	100	30	21	42	3	0	4
Farming, forestry, and fishing	1,154	100	22	4	44	1	0	29
Precision production, craft, and repair	10,198	100	18	19	46	6	2	9
Machine operators, assemblers, and inspectors	3,201	100	15	15	61	3	1	6
Transportation and material moving occupations	1,708	100	6	18	60	5	0	11
Handlers, equipment cleaners, and laborers	686	100	10	10	68	3	1	8
All occupations	70,381	100	40	13	38	3	1	5

Skill improvement training							
Executive, administration, and managerial	6,324	100	30	30	27	—	—	13
Professional specialty	9,452	100	46	20	19	—	—	15
Technicians and related support	1,901	100	32	29	31	—	—	9
Sales occupations	4,309	100	18	33	38	—	—	11
Administrative support, including clerical	5,927	100	26	26	41	—	—	7
Private household occupations	41	100	24	17	34	—	—	24
Service workers, except private households	3,657	100	22	26	42	—	—	10
Farming, forestry, and fishing	560	100	29	9	36	—	—	25
Precision production, craft, and repair	4,730	100	18	35	39	—	—	7
Machine operators, assemblers, and inspectors	1,743	100	13	16	66	—	—	4
Transportation and material moving occupations	745	100	11	32	50	—	—	7
Handlers, equipment cleaners, and laborers	549	100	10	17	69	—	—	3
All occupations	39,936	100	29	27	34	—	—	11

[a]Occurrence of training is the number of training sources identified by the trainees.
[b]No data reported.

Source: U.S. Department of Labor, Bureau of Labor Statistics, *How Workers Get Their Training* (Washington, DC: GPO, 1985), Tables 2 and 8.

Table 7.2 Number and Percentage Distribution of Occurrences of School Training by Type and Source of Training and by Occupation, 1983

	Number of Occurrences (in thousands)	Percentage Distribution by Source of Training					
		Total	High School Vocational Education	Private Post-High School Vocational Education	Public Post-High School Vocational Education	Junior College or Technical Institute	4-Year or Longer College Program
Qualification training							
Executive, administration, and managerial	4,855	100	7	3	3	12	75
Professional specialty	10,655	100	2	3	2	9	84
Technicians and related support	1,846	100	8	9	10	33	40
Sales occupations	1,735	100	11	9	5	21	54
Administrative support, including clerical	5,790	100	46	9	6	22	17
Private household occupations	15	100	60	13	—a	—	27
Service workers, except private households	1,621	100	13	27	12	28	19
Farming, forestry, and fishing	292	100	26	5	5	20	44
Precision production, craft, and repair	1,929	100	31	10	15	29	15
Machine operators, assemblers, and inspectors	504	100	39	9	16	23	14
Transportation and material moving occupations	95	100	36	24	11	19	11
Handlers, equipment cleaners, and laborers	80	100	38	8	20	26	9
All occupations	29,419	100	16	7	5	16	55

Skill improvement training

Executive, administration, and managerial	1,774	100	1	6	5	30	57
Professional specialty	4,038	100	1	4	3	14	79
Technicians and related support	559	100	1	6	7	43	43
Sales occupations	727	100	4	16	8	39	33
Administrative support, including clerical	1,457	100	9	7	11	47	26
Private household occupations	10	100	40	—	10	30	20
Service workers, except private households	753	100	5	15	11	50	19
Farming, forestry, and fishing	158	100	12	4	23	39	22
Precision production, craft, and repair	816	100	5	16	16	49	13
Machine operators, assemblers, and inspectors	208	100	8	5	26	40	21
Transportation and material moving occupations	75	100	13	19	12	41	15
Handlers, equipment cleaners, and laborers	50	100	22	16	22	40	—
All occupations	10,630	100	3	8	7	31	51

aNo data reported.

Source: U.S. Department of Labor, Bureau of Labor Statistics, How Workers Get Their Training (Washington, DC: GPO, 1985), Tables 2 and 8.

Table 7.3   Number and Percentage Distribution of Adult Education Courses Provided by Educational Institutions and Nonschool Providers by Type and Job-Related Status, 1978 and 1984ª (numbers in thousands)

	1978		1984 Total		Job-Related		Non-Job Related	
	Number	Percent	Number	Percent	Number	Percent	Number	Percent
All providers	26,950	100	40,752	100	26,157	100	14,595	100
School	16,500	61	21,477	53	13,179	50	8,298	57
Elementary/secondary school	2,700	10	2,495	6	853	3	1,642	11
2-year college or technical institute	5,300	20	6,820	17	3,666	14	3,154	22
4-year college or university	5,700	21	6,928	17	4,880	19	2,048	14
Vocational/trade/business school	1,900	7	3,983	10	3,123	12	860	6
Other (correspondence, etc.)	900	3	1,251	3	657	3	594	1
Non-school	10,450	39	17,728	44	12,070	46	6,015	40
Business and industry	3,150	12	6,862	17	6,286	24	576	4
Labor/professional organization	1,100	4	2,294	6	2,157	8	137	1
Government agency	2,450	9	3,223	8	2,315	9	908	6
Community organization	2,400	9	3,617	9	719	3	2,898	20
Tutor/private instructor	1,350	5	1,730	4	600	2	1,130	8
Other, not reported	—ª	—	1,547	4	901	3	646	4

ªData not available.
Source: Susan T. Hill, Trends in Adult Education, 1969–1984 (Washington, DC: U.S. Department of Education, 1987), Tables 2 and 3 and Appendix Tables C, G, and H.

providers of job qualification training but also the key players in upgrading the skills of professional and technical workers. As indicated in Table 7.2, among all school providers of skill improvement training, the market shares of four-year colleges were 57 percent, 79 percent, and 43 percent, respectively, for executives and managers, professionals, and technicians. It is worth mentioning that four-year colleges were also the second largest providers of job-related adult education, accounting for 19 percent of the job-related adult education courses taken in 1984 (Table 7.3).

Some other aspects of four-year colleges are worth noting. First, although approximately 72 percent of the four-year colleges and universities are private and are controlled by independent institutional boards of trustees, they enroll about only one-third of the students. Two-thirds are enrolled in public colleges and universities, which implies that public funding is important in providing training for a high-skilled work force.[5]

Second, programs offered by four-year colleges are becoming more diversified and vocational; the proportion of baccalaureate degrees awarded in professional and applied fields, compared to traditional arts and sciences disciplines, has risen from 53.4 percent in 1975 to 61.5 percent in 1985.[6]

Two-Year Colleges. A major share of postsecondary education is provided by public and independent colleges that award associate degrees after two years of full-time study. These colleges also offer short-term certificate and diploma programs in specific areas. In 1986–1987, approximately 1,336 community colleges were operating, the majority under public control (960 public and 376 private), serving approximately 4.7 million students (Table 7.4). Most public community colleges have open-admission policies. In many states, the law requires these colleges to admit any student holding a diploma from a public high school, but after admission students must take diagnostic placement tests. Some community colleges even give credit for work experience. A wide variety of options in scheduling is offered, and 63 percent of the students are enrolled part-time.[7] One-half of the courses offered in these institutions are noncredit and serve occasional students seeking personal enrichment.

Community colleges awarded about one-half million associate (two-year) degrees in 1985. Although the growth rate of these degrees appears to have slowed somewhat in the 1980s, it remains higher than the growth rate of baccalaureate degrees. An interesting and growing activity for these institutions has been the proliferation of "customized programs" designed to meet employer needs. Many of these programs are developed under formal contracts with employers or labor unions. Indeed, two-year colleges have become more vocational than academic.[8] In 1970–1971, 50 percent of the two-year degrees and other formal awards were in vocational programs, and the remainder in arts, sciences, and general programs; by 1980–1981, the vocational share had increased to 71 percent.[9]

According to a recent survey conducted by the American Association of Community and Junior Colleges, three-fourths of community colleges customize training for private sector employers. The report from the survey also states that

41 percent have campus-based business/industry/labor councils (BICs), 66 percent participate in their local Private Industry Council (PICs), 66 percent have appointed Business/Industry coordinators on campus, 83 percent provide small business support, 90 percent have partnerships with local high schools; and 80 percent work with local and state economic development offices.[10]

For example, the State of Illinois services 39 community colleges through a business center network, which provides job creation and retention, job training, and retraining. With $1.6 million in state industrial training funds, General Foods contracts with North Iowa Area Community College

Table 7.4 Number of Institutions and Participants Engaged in Postsecondary Education, Various Years, 1978–1987

Type of Provider	Number of Institutions	Number of Participants
4-year institutions	2,070 (1)	7,826,036 (2)
2-year institutions	1,336 (2)	4,674,762 (3)
Noncollegiate postsecondary institutions		
Proprietary	6,329 (1)	1,235,667 (4)
Private, nonprofit	1,797 (1)	
Public	830 (1)	451,430 (4)
Correspondence (excluding the military)		500,000 (8)
Private employers		39,000,000 (6)
Apprenticeships		600,000 (7)
Unions		75,000 (8)
Professional assoc. and consulting firms		N/A
Federal government (civilian)		1,238,000 (9)
Military		1,590,000 (10)
Libraries	70,573 (11)	
Religious organizations	338,000 (5)	
Civic and social groups	130,000 (5)	

Sources:
(1) Academic year 1986–1987: U.S. Department of Education, *Digest of Education Statistics, 1988* (Washington, DC: National Center for Education Statistics, 1988), Table 5.
(2) Fall 1986 (preliminary data): U.S. Department of Education, *Digest of Education Statistics, 1988* (Washington, DC: National Center for Education Statistics, 1988), Table 118.
(3) Includes schools accredited by the National Association of Trade and Technical Schools in 1980–1981, part of the noncollegiate proprietary schools.
(4) U.S. Department of Education, *Digest of Education Statistics, 1988* (Washington, DC: National Center for Education Statistics, 1988), Table 254.
(5) M.M. Woods, *What Does the Independent Sector Do for 16–24-Year-Olds?* (Washington, DC: The William T. Grant Foundation, 1988).
(6) "Sixth Annual Industry Report, *Training Magazine,* 1987.
(7) U.S. Department of Labor, *Occupational Projections and Training Data,* Bulletin 2206 (Washington, DC: Bureau of Labor Statistics, 1984).
(8) I. Charner and B.S. Fraser, "Different Strokes for Different Folks: Access and Barriers to Adult Education and Training" (Paper submitted to the Congress of the United States, Office of Technology Assessment, under contract number 433-6020.0., 1986).
(9) U.S. Office of Personnel Management, "Employee Training in the Federal Service: Fiscal Year 1979" (Unpublished report, 1987).
(10) U.S. Department of Defense, *Military Manpower Training Report for FY 1982* (Washington, DC: GPO, 1987).
(11) Fiscal year 1982: U.S. Department of Education, *Digest of Education Statistics, 1988* (Washington, DC: National Center for Education Statistics, 1988), Table 292.

for a staff member to manage the training project for its new high-tech food plant. The variations are too many to list, but the system is robust and growing by leaps and bounds.

The importance of two-year colleges in providing adult education is evident in Table 7.3. In 1978, two-year colleges offered 20 percent of all adult education courses, one percentage point less than the largest provider, the four-year colleges (21 percent). By 1984, four-year colleges, business and industry, and two-year colleges each offered 17 percent of all adult education courses, but two-year colleges still dominated the marketplace in providing non-job-related adult education (22 percent).

With two-year and four-year colleges and universities playing such important roles in providing training, some patterns in postsecondary participation are worth noting. First, more women than men are now taking courses at colleges and universities, especially women aged 35 years and over. In 1985, women's enrollment in institutions of higher education outnumbered that of men by one-half million. The participation rates of men and women appeared to be similar among young cohorts, but in the 35-and-over age category, there were twice as many women as men attending institutions of higher education.[11]

Second, a growing number of older people are participating in postsecondary education. The number of students aged 25 years and over increased 114 percent from 1970 to 1985 compared to 15 percent for students under 25 years. From 1980 to 1985, the number of younger students actually declined 5 percent, while the number of older students continued growing by 12 percent.

Postsecondary Noncollegiate Providers. Postsecondary noncollegiate providers include a wide array of institutions that offer a collage of courses that no one source is able to describe in any detail. Mostly, due to the nature of these institutions, they tend to have short lives, and appear to be constantly adjusting to the needs of the marketplace. This particular characteristic is both an asset, because they can respond quickly to market demands, and a liability, since this flexibility makes it very hard for them to maintain a good and reliable cadre of teachers and offer well-tested and evaluated programs.

In 1986–1987, 8,956 noncollegiate institutions offered postsecondary education in the United States. Only 830 of these were public, and the majority of the remainder operated for profit (they are most commonly referred to as "proprietary schools"). In addition, there are 1,797 nonprofit private technical and vocational institutions. California has the largest number of noncollegiate institutions (1,301), followed by New York (522). Wyoming has the smallest number (14).[12]

Noncollegiate institutions offer postsecondary awards, certificates, or diplomas. They require completion of an organized program of study at the postsecondary level in less than one academic year (two semesters or three-quarters of a year), or less than 900 contact hours by a student enrolled full-time. They also offer programs leading to diplomas, certificates, and awards which require more than one but less than two years.

The mission of proprietary schools is to prepare students with skills that will satisfy employer needs, in the shortest possible time. They often are organizations with a "single purpose." They offer courses of short duration to enable students to acquire skills with a minimum loss of foregone income. Year-round operations and frequent class starts are the norm. Approximately 6,672 proprietary schools, including correspondence schools, are in operation.

There are nine principal types of noncollegiate, noncorrespondence proprietary schools: cosmetology and barber schools, which account for 30.6 percent of the total; schools teaching business and office skills, 17.2 percent; hospital training schools, 10.9 percent; air flight schools, 10.8 percent; vocational technical schools, 10 percent; trade schools, 9.9 percent; allied health schools, 5.1 percent; art design schools, 3.3 percent; and technical institutes, 2.2 percent.[13]

Regardless of their relatively small market share compared to those of colleges and universities, proprietary schools seem to play an important role in training sales and service workers as well as semiskilled workers, such as transportation equipment operators and handlers (Table 7.1). Two problems, however, should be pointed out about proprietary schools. First, transfer from proprietary schools to four-year higher education institutions is minimal, since the proprietary programs are terminal and generally do not include any course work in traditional academic disciplines. Second, the cost of attending these schools is high compared to other kinds of training.

The average cost of a private noncollegiate school program in 1980–1981 was $2,200 for an average of 981 hours of instruction, compared to an average cost of $593 for an average of 1,324 hours of instruction in public noncollegiate programs.[14] For further comparison, a report released by the National Center for Education Statistics indicates that, for academic year 1986–1987, the average annual expense of attending a private, for-profit, less-than-two-year school full time was $7,339, about two-and-half times the expense of attending a public two-year college. However, since most students at private for-profit schools received some form of financial aid, the net cost of attendance dropped by nearly half, to $3,920. The financial aid received by students at public two-year colleges was much lower; on average, students paid 66 percent of the full price.[15]

Even though the tuition for the proprietary schools is high, the quality of the programs appears uneven. As of 1984, only about 45 percent of these schools were accredited by one of the three proprietary school accrediting associations which are supposed to identify minimum standards of quality.[16] This poses a serious problem since proprietary schools are more successful in enrolling female and minority workers who do not receive as much company training as males and whites. Because of their open admission policies, proprietary schools are also one of the few providers that train low-ability and unprepared students. This will be discussed later in the chapter.

Correspondence Schools. Today, more than one-half million Americans are enrolled in home study courses taken through the mail. Correspondence study is accredited or evaluated through three major organizations in the United States:

1. the National Home Study Council (NHSC) which has 90 member schools ranging from small religious institutions to the Armed Forces Correspondence Institute enrolling nearly one-half million servicemen and women, and from private business and industry schools to publicly sponsored schools. NHSC has its own independent accrediting commission. NHSC member schools have course work in 283 categories;
2. the National University Continuing Education Association (NUCEA) which is made up of divisions or departments of regionally accredited colleges and universities. The membership includes 72 accredited colleges and universities offering 12,000 courses at the high school, undergraduate, and graduate levels as well as noncredit courses; and,
3. the Program On Noncollegiate Sponsored Instruction (PONSI), a division of the American Council on Education (ACE), which administers independent evaluations of home study and other courses for college credit. Over 1,500 colleges and universities accept PONSI evaluations for transfer credit toward graduation requirements.

Among the most popular courses taken through correspondence study are business, high school equivalency courses, electronics, engineering (mid-level technician training), other technical and trade courses, and art.[17]

A survey conducted by the NHSC in 1978 found that the average NHSC student is between 25 and 34 years old, that three out of every four students are male, and that courses offered typically require a year to complete.

Work-Based Providers

The primary responsibility of work-based providers, including public and private employers, trade unions, professional associations, consulting firms, and the military is to conduct business, not to educate or train. However, due to technological changes in the workplace, as well as the need to remedy the basic skill deficiencies of entry-level employees, employers (principally private but also public) are integrating employee education and training programs into their business activities.

Employers. While no accurate accounting of expenditures for employer-sponsored educational and training programs is available, what data exist indicate that "corporate learning has become an absolutely essential part of the educational resources of the nation."[18] Estimates of corporate expenditures for education and training range from $32 billion to $100 billion compared with the approximately $130 billion spent annually on public education. Nearly 39 million employees are estimated to be enrolled in corporate-sponsored programs.[19]

According to the 1983 *Current Population Survey,* employer-provided training (formal company training programs and informal on-the-job training combined) accounts for 51 percent of the occurrences of job qualification training and 61 percent of the occurrences of skill improvement training. For training blue-collar, semiskilled workers, such as machine operators and crafts people, employer shares are even larger, mostly exceeding 70 percent (Table 7.1).

Surveys conducted by associations, such as the Conference Board, *Training Magazine,* or Dun & Bradstreet, typically seek to identify the types of programs that are offered, the types of employees that are served by the programs, and the costs to the company.

For example, in 1987, *Training Magazine* mailed questionnaires to 16,277 organizations, a sample culled from Dun & Bradstreet's directory of U.S. businesses and from the magazine's subscribers' list. The sample was limited to organizations with 50 or more employees. A breakdown of the reported $32 billion training budget showed that trainers' salaries accounted for 71 percent of the funds, an increase of 7.2 percent over 1986 figures. This particular survey also showed that $2.3 billion was spent for facilities and overhead, constituting a 7 percent increase in one year. Other categories of expenditure were: off-the shelf materials, custom materials, outside services, hardware, and seminars/conferences.

Employers also categorize training by type of employees. In 1987, according to the same survey, 32.7 percent of all organizations with 50 or more employees provided sales people with training. The total number of sales people trained by all organizations was estimated at 3 million individually, and on the average each received about 43 hours of training a year. On the other hand, production workers constituted the largest group of individuals (8.66 million), but each received, on average, 29 hours of training per year.

In addition to their own educational and training programs mentioned above, employers maintain a myriad of institutional arrangements through which they purchase or provide programs. These are:

1. Education and training facilities, which are separate facilities, often similar to college campuses in appearance, with classrooms, dormitories, and libraries. Examples include the Holiday Inn University, the ARCO campus at Santa Barbara for top executives, the New England Telephone Learning Center, which accommodates 9,000 employees attending classes during the summer, the Xerox Learning Center in Leesburg, Virginia, and even McDonald's Hamburger University for merchandising and retail sales training.
2. Accredited corporate colleges that grant their own degrees. Examples of these degrees include the Northrop University and the Wang and Arthur D. Little Master of Science degrees, to name but a few of the 20 or so such programs.
3. Satellite universities (such as the National Technological University), which beam course work by satellite to corporate classrooms around the country.
4. Cooperative ventures, which include courses held at corporate facilities but staffed by university-based faculty, employee tuition assistance or refund policies for course work taken at traditional colleges, part-time training programs using outside assistance, and cooperative arrangements with local education institutions, particularly community colleges, for training purposes.

Cooperative ventures are most common for corporations with fewer than 500 employees (by far the majority of businesses). At the other end of the spectrum are the Fortune 500 companies and, especially, several high-technology firms such as IBM, Xerox, Boeing, and McDonnell Douglas that spend between 2.5 and 3.3 percent of their sales revenue on education and training.[20]

Apprenticeships and Trade Unions. Approximately 600,000 union members are involved in education training through apprenticeship, union education, labor studies, and negotiated tuition-aid programs. There are over 730 apprenticeable trades in the United States. While an exact accounting is impossible, there appears to be about one-half million participants in apprenticeship programs, which range from three to five years in length.[21] Although apprenticeship training is a very small portion of total training, it is an important component, especially for craft workers. It is also reported that as many as 200 programs may be registered for a variety of reasons.[22] Unions also provide education and training to their members through labor studies programs at educational institutes or through their own facilities. Approximately 75,000 union members participate in courses and institutes made available by union education departments, independent of any school or other outside institution. Such training is primarily to improve understanding of unionism and improve techniques necessary for running unions.

There are 47 institutions of higher education offering a major or concentration in labor studies as well as numerous part-time degree programs that have been developed together with the unions. Recently, unions are engaging in more and more cooperative ventures with community colleges. For example, College of DuPage in Glen Ellyn, Illinois, provided training programs during a one-year period to 87 United Paperworkers, 21 International Meatpackers, 115 United Auto Workers, and 212 United Steel Workers.

Labor studies programs are also provided by the unions through their own facilities. One example is the George Meany AFL-CIO Labor Studies Center, which offers, in cooperation with Antioch College, an external degree program. Another is the College of New Rochelle/District Council 37 program (of the American Federation of State, County, and Municipal Employees) which "represents the first accredited four-year degree program on union premises in the history of America."[23]

Through the collective bargaining process, unions also negotiate for tuition aid so that their members can take courses on their own time in colleges, community colleges, and universities.[24]

Professional Associations and Consulting Firms. This particular category of providers has been one of the least understood providers of education and training, primarily due to the way data have been collected. The National Center for Education Statistics, as well as other data-collecting agencies, have traditionally combined labor organizations and professional associations into one category. Given the different natures of these organizations and the different trends that have affected them, it is quite possible that a decline in programs provided by labor organizations has camouflaged a sizable increase in the professional associations. The number of adult education courses given by labor/professional organizations was 1.1 million in 1972 and 2.3 million in 1984.[25]

Professional associations are known traditionally for providing their members with information about recent developments in their occupations. Recently, there has been an upsurge of activities in the type of services these organizations bring to their members. This change is more noticeable in associations that are not discipline bound, e.g., the

American Management Association (AMA) and the American Banking Association rather than the American Sociological Association or the American Economics Association. For example, the AMA is a major provider of education with its 7,500 lecturers and discussion leaders, and its almost 100,000 courses for management personnel offered in one year.[26]

A study sponsored by the American Bankers Association in 1985 found that 12 percent of all training in the banking industry is done by professional associations.[27] In addition to these well-known professional associations, a growing number of consulting firms develop and sell education and training programs not only in the United States but also worldwide. Among the fastest growing are such firms as Integrated Computer Systems and Telesis, which have become major businesses that export education and training as a major commodity. One of the difficulties of getting information about these firms is that they are not accredited by educational boards and they operate as businesses. Therefore, the only source of information is from surveys where respondents are able to describe the new providers of education and training.

Public Employers. There are approximately 19 million employees in the public sector at the federal, state, and local levels. Civilian federal employees receive education and training to increase their efficiency and to improve their performance on the job. Ninety-nine percent of the training received by these employees was of short duration, averaging 41 hours, 74 percent was performed in-house, and 77 percent of the training provided outside the government was standard academic courses.[28] Participation patterns of federal government employees reinforce the earlier findings that those with less education are less likely to obtain further education or training.

Military. The purpose of training by the military is to prepare incoming personnel to assume specific jobs in military units. A large portion of such training is for indoctrination and initiation, and over half is specialized skill training. The U.S. Department of Defense offers over 7,000 different courses, ranging in length from 5 to 25 weeks. It is estimated that, on any one day of the year, an average of 214,000 people are attending a formal training course.[29] There is also a Voluntary Education Program in the military, where approximately one-half million people take courses on their own time at 1,000 cooperating colleges and universities.

Each branch of the military operates its own programs, and each has three major sections that are open to all four branches. These are: 1) the Defense Activity for Non-Traditional Education Support (DANTES), which administers several credit-by-examination programs through correspondence courses from civilian schools; 2) the Serviceman's Opportunity College (SOC), which is a network comprising some 360 two-year and four-year postsecondary institutions; and 3) the American Council on Education's Office of Educational Credit, which publishes the *Guide to the Evaluation of Education Experience in the Armed Services*. Each branch also offers high school equivalency programs.[30]

Community-Based Providers

If one category had to be singled out as the least known of all the providers, it would be the community-based providers. Yet what little we know indicates that such organizations, regardless of their size and history, may be playing a very important role in educating and training adults. One characteristic of these providers is their availability to the public at little or no cost. This category includes institutions such as: churches and other religious groups; youth organizations (such as YMCAs, YWCAs, etc.) and the Red Cross; civic and social service groups; and cultural and other groups.

One recent development has been the growth of The Association for Community-based Education. The MacArthur Foundation, one of the five largest charitable foundations in the country, has asked the Association to prepare a directory of community-based organizations that operate adult literacy programs. In addition to the literacy programs, some of the Association's members operate education and training programs for economic development. One good example is the Community Women's Education Project (CWEP) in Philadelphia. Since 1980, CWEP has served over 900 people per year through postsecondary programs and support activities. All of its participants are low-income women and nearly one-half are black. CWEP has offered microcomputer training to low-income women through the Software Applications for Neighborhood Enterprise program.

Some of the local and community training programs are funded by the government, but most are targeted for the disadvantaged and unemployed. The number of people who participate in the programs is limited. According to the follow-up survey of the high school class of 1980, only a small proportion of the individuals reported that they had participated in a government community-based training program. For example, from 1980 to 1984, only 2 percent had participated in projects funded by either the Comprehensive Employment and Training Act (CETA) or the Job Training Partnership Act (JTPA), the two largest federal training programs in the 1980s.[31] Furthermore, not all enrollees of these programs received training. Among the 355,000 adult participants of JTPA aged 21 or older, 75,000 received job search assistance, 10,400 received work experience, and 75,000 received other services. Thus, only 239,000 individuals, or 67 percent of the total, received classroom or on-the-job training.

The Trainees

Having a diversified and extensive range of providers does not, however, guarantee everyone access to training. It is also important to know how workers with different backgrounds are trained in the marketplace. A major concern is that people who need training most may have the least chance of receiving it. The remainder of this chapter looks at these issues and seeks to identify how well U.S. training providers reach out to women and minorities.

Who Receives Training?

According to the 1983 *Current Population Survey,* 55 percent of U.S. workers reported that they needed training to qualify for their current jobs.[32] The proportion of workers who received such training was roughly the same for both men and women but varied substantially among different age and race groups. People who were 25 to 44 years old were more likely to receive qualification training (62 percent) compared to the younger and older age groups. The proportions for the age groups, 16–19, 20–24, 45–54, 55–64, and 65 and older were 25 percent, 47 percent, 57 percent, 52 percent, and 41 percent, respectively.[33] Black workers were less likely to get qualification training than their white counterparts. The proportions were 44 percent and 57 percent for blacks and whites, respectively. And, as expected, more educated people were more likely to receive qualification training.[34] Similar results were found in skill improvement training, which is designed to upgrade worker skills in performing current jobs.

The Gender Gap

Previous empirical research has shown that black men and black and white women have flatter experience-earnings profiles than white men, that is, their earnings do not increase with their experience as rapidly as the earnings of white men.[35] One of the speculations for the causes of the flat earnings profiles is that women and minority workers are less likely to get training than their counterparts. However, our findings in the previous section do not fully support this speculation. In fact, the supplementary 1981 and 1983 *Current Population Survey* suggest very consistent results: Both show that female workers receive about the same qualification training as males, but that their chance of getting job skill improvement training is slightly smaller.[36]

To get a clear picture of the male/female differences in training, we calculated a female/male training participation ratio by dividing the proportion of female workers who get training by their male counterparts' proportion. The results are shown in Table 7.5. If male and female workers have the same training participation rate, the ratio equals one. A ratio greater than one indicates that female workers are more likely to receive training; a ratio smaller than one, the opposite.

The results are interesting. The female/male training participation ratios in Table 7.5 suggest that the female/male differences in training tend to be larger for less educated people than for more educated ones. For example, while female college graduates received at least as much qualification training as men, women with fewer than 12 years of schooling had only an 83 percent chance of getting such training as men with the same educational attainment. Similar differences can be found for job skill improvement training.

In terms of occupations, women's chances of getting trained, compared to those of men, are particularly low in traditionally male-dominated semiskilled occupations such as crafts, machine operations, and sales. However, the chance of getting trained among women who are in executive or managerial (administrative), professional, or clerical positions is nearly as great, if not greater, than among men. In fact, the chance of getting skill improvement training is about the same for both genders except for clericals. However, female clerical workers receive more qualification training than men.

Gender differences in training opportunity can also be found by industry. Women seem to do worst in nondurables manufacturing industries and better in the services industries. Indeed, in a number of instances in the services, they do as well, if not, better than men.

In sum, the data suggest that the chances for women to receive qualification training are about the same as they are for men, unless they are less educated or are in male-dominated occupations, such as crafts and machine operation. However, their chances of receiving skill requirement training are low in most occupations, with a few exceptions such as executive and managerial positions.

However, since the duration of training for male-dominated occupations is much longer than it is for female-dominated occupations, women who have the same possibility of receiving training as men might have less training (in terms of time) than their counterparts.[37]

Of course, the concern of policymakers cannot be restricted to the fact that women are less likely to receive training in some occupations and industries than men; it must also address differences in the kind of training they receive as well as where they receive it. Table 7.5 indicates that the gender gap in getting on-the-job training and formal

Table 7.5 Female/Male Training Participation Ratio by Education, Race, Occupation, and Industry, 1981[a]

	Training Needed to Get Current Job		Training to Improve Job Skills	
	Any	Company Training +OJT	Any	Company Training +OJT
Years of schooling				
Less than 12	0.828	0.824	0.915	0.953
12	0.981	0.825	0.977	0.957
13–15	1.077	0.821	0.975	0.93
16	1.031	0.753	0.974	0.855
More than 16	1.002	0.844	1.053	0.859
Race				
White	0.981	0.824	0.951	0.922
Black	1.21	1.046	1.328	1.27
Occupation				
Administrative	0.914	0.92	1.002	1.026
Professional	0.997	0.769	1.034	0.985
Sales	0.715	0.702	0.715	0.746
Clerical	1.373	1.029	0.893	0.713
Services	0.983	0.846	0.808	0.958
Farm operators	0.903	0.994	0.695	0.952
Crafts	0.701	0.676	0.799	0.781
Machine operators	0.683	0.709	0.733	0.822
Transport	1.427	1.51	2.657	2.425
Laborers	1.02	1.173	1.154	1.299
Industry				
Agriculture	1.071	1.135	0.687	0.899
Mining	1.226	0.89	0.627	0.436
Construction	0.976	0.66	0.758	0.476
Manufacturing:				
Durables	0.77	0.739	0.861	0.827
nondurables	0.779	0.716	0.584	0.545
Trans., comm., util.	1.077	1.039	1.154	1.08
Wholesale	1.136	0.916	0.596	0.51
Retail	0.813	0.776	0.768	1.341
Finance, ins.	0.936	0.92	0.866	0.517
Non-prof. service	0.899	0.732	0.983	1.412
Prof. services	0.944	0.99	0.897	0.857
Public adm.	0.935	0.89	0.799	0.729
Total	0.991	0.788	0.966	1.056

[a]Female/male training participation ratio is calculated by dividing the proportion of females who received training by the proportion of males who received training.

Source: Compiled from H. W. Tan, Private Sector Training in the United States: Who Gets It and Why. Draft report (Santa Monica, CA: Rand Corporation, 1988).

npany training is larger than for other kinds of training. Thus, even though women may be getting closer to men in receiving qualification training, they are less likely to receive it directly from employers and more likely to get it from regular schools or other sources.

This is supported by a preliminary compilation of the 1983 *Census of Population Survey* data by Tan.[38] Tan finds that approximately 28 percent of the women received qualification training from regular schools; 26 percent from on-the-job training; and 8 percent from formal company training programs. By comparison, the proportions of men who received qualification training from those three sources were 22 percent, 31 percent, and 12 percent, respectively.[39]

The 1984 *Survey of Adult Education* summarized in Hill corroborates Tan's findings.[40] According to the survey, men took approximately 17.8 million adult education courses in 1984. Of these courses, 23 percent were organized by business and industries and 44 percent were either totally or partly paid by employers. In comparison, 23 million courses were taken by women in the same year. Only 12 percent were organized by business and industries and 30 percent were paid totally or partly by employers. One may argue that employers may not be willing to pay for non-job-related courses in which many women are enrolled, but a closer look at the data shows that men get better financial support from their employers than women in both job-related and non-job-related courses. The data further indicate that employers paid for 59 percent and 9 percent, respectively, for job-related and non-job-related courses taken by men but only for 48 percent and 4 percent for courses taken by women.[41]

Finally, it is worth noting that, unlike white women, black female workers fare quite well in receiving training, including company-provided training. For example, the participation rate of job skill improvement training for black women is 33 percent larger than that for black men (see Table 7.1). The reason for this difference is not clear, but it seems to be consistent with findings by others which show that the education and earnings of black women increased much faster than those of black men during the last two decades. Why some of these differences exist is a complicated issue to which we now turn our attention.

The Racial Gap

Like the gender earnings gap, the wage differentials between white and black workers have been well discussed in the literature. One of the speculations of the causes of these differentials is that black workers are less likely to obtain training in their jobs. This argument is supported by the 1983 *Census of Population Survey*, which indicates that only 44 percent of black workers received qualification training compared with 57 percent of whites.⁴² A similar difference can be found for skill improvement training. The possibility of blacks participating in such training was about 25 percent less than that for whites (27 percent versus 36 percent).

Furthermore, the racial training gap seems to be wider for black men than for black women. The possibility of participating in qualification training for a black man was 29 percent less than that for a white man (41 percent versus 58 percent); but for a black woman, only 15 percent less than that for a white woman (47 percent versus 55 percent). The largest racial gap is found in the opportunity for black men to receive skill improvement training for which their participation rate was only about half of that for white men (21 percent versus 36 percent).⁴³

Possible Causes of the Training Gap

There are various theories to explain the difference in training participation between men and women, but each could benefit from stronger empirical backing. One explanation, shared by many human capital theorists, is that women have fewer economic incentives to invest in on-the-job training than men because they expect to have a less-regular pattern of labor participation and, thus, a shorter work horizon to collect the return from their investment. In addition, employers are less willing to train female workers than men because of the former's relatively weaker commitment to jobs due to their traditional child-rearing responsibilities. While this explanation might be true in theory, it requires additional empirical testing.⁴⁴

One simple test is to observe the training patterns of women over their life cycles. For example, if the above speculation is true, women should receive the least training during child-rearing years. This is indeed what is shown by the data collected in the 1983 supplementary *Census of Population Survey*. A simple breakdown of training participation rates by gender and age shows that women aged 25 to 34 years have the same opportunity to receive training as men of the same age, but that starting at the age of 35, their chance of receiving training becomes significantly less than that of male workers. Since most women get married and raise children between the ages of 25 and 44, the significant reduction of training participation past the age of 34 provides some evidence supporting the speculation.

While the previous discussion may explain part of the gender gap, it offers no hint for racial differences in training opportunity. Alternative models to explain gender and race differences draw on theories of labor market segmentation.⁴⁵ In these models, earnings are largely determined by job and labor market positions rather than the human capital one possesses. An individual acquires training by first getting access to a job that provides training. These jobs are found predominantly in the primary labor market. Women and minority workers are less likely to enter the primary labor market than men, are more likely to be confined to the secondary labor market, and, thus, are less likely to receive training. By showing the disproportionate number of secondary labor market jobs held by women and black workers, the 1983 *Census Population Survey* data seem to lend some truth to the above argument.

Duncan and Hoffman's study lends some support to both the human capital theory and the labor market segmentation models.[46] Based on the 1976 follow-up survey of the *Panel of Income Dynamics*, the authors estimate the probabilities of receiving training for different race-gender groups and the effect of training on their earnings. First, they find some evidence that training decisions are made in an investment context, as the human capital model assumes. For most groups, the potential length of time over which a training investment might yield returns is an important factor in explaining whether or not individuals participate in training. For example, the expectation of having children reduces the chance of training for white women by 6 percent. For black women, past interruptions in their labor force participation leads to fewer training opportunities.

Second, Duncan and Hoffman also find support for the labor market segmentation model. For example, the longer men work, the likelier their chance to receive additional training—especially white men; by comparison, years of work show little or no correlation to women's chances to receive additional training. Coefficients for white men are nearly twice as large as those for black men and about five times as large as those for both black and white women. This does suggest that some institutional forces may intervene in the process by which individuals receive training opportunities.

The Duncan and Hoffman study does show, however, that the effect of on-the-job training on earnings is quite uniform for men and women as well as blacks and whites. In other words, there is no evidence that minority workers had a smaller percentage return for training than white men.

A final, but important, finding is that the overall racial gap in training participation is smaller for the educated than for the less educated. According to Tan, racial differences in training participation was found in all groups of education except among people who had a four-year college degree or a more advanced degree.[47] This seems to suggest that one of the ways to narrow the racial gap and increase training for minority workers is to help them get more education.

Concluding Remarks

The significant finding from the review of education and training providers that serve adults is that, overall, traditional institutions are still the major sources for learning. But this review also suggests that there has been a dramatic increase in the role played by employer-provided education and by a new crop of training firms. As long as new entrants continue to be deficient in basic skills, employers will likely remain heavily involved in the business of schooling the young and not so young workers.

There are several observable changes which beg for careful examination. One such change is the increasing number of training institutions which warrants concern that quality issues need to be addressed. Consumers should be alerted to ask for information about the graduates of these programs and request proof that they are employed in appropriate jobs. In addition, state-wide quality standards should be developed.

Another change is the growing use of community colleges by employers. Community colleges appear to be serving employers in a number of ways. Since such institutions are inexpensive and offer remedial courses to people who need them, the relationship between employers and schools should be supported. Employers should be encouraged to identify their skill needs and work closely with such public institutions.

The review of literature and data on opportunities and patterns of training among different demographic groups reveals substantial differences. To the extent that a firm's size or an individual's race or gender appears to represent significant obstacles to being provided opportunities for training, as suggested by some of the data, then alternative sources of training have to be made available to women and minorities. What is needed at this point is to collect additional information about such issues so that policymakers are in a better position to promote alternative sources of training.

Notes

1. D. Harman, "Adult Education in the United States: Its Scope, Nature, and Future Direction," Occasional Paper No. 105 (Columbus, OH: The National Center for Research in Vocational Education, 1985).

2. S.T. Hill, *Trends in Adult Education, 1969–1984* (Washington, DC: U.S. Department of Education, 1987).

3. U.S. Department of Education, *Digest of Education Statistics, 1988* (Washington, DC: National Center for Education Statistics, 1988), Table 253.

4. U.S. Department of Education (n. 3), Table 163.

5. U.S. Department of Education (n. 3), Table 118.

6. U.S. Department of Education, *Digest of Education Statistics, 1987* (Washington, DC: National Center for Education Statistics, 1987).

7. American Council on Education, *Community College Fact Book* (Washington, DC: Macmillan, 1988).

8. W.N. Grubb, "Vocationalizing Higher Education: The Causes of Enrollment and Completion in Public Two-Year Colleges, 1970–1980," *Economics of Education Review* Vol. 7, No. 3 (1984): 301–319.

9. N. Stacey, N. Alsalam, J. Gilmore, and D.L. To, *Education and Training of 16- to 19-Year-Olds After Compulsory Schooling in the United States* (Washington, DC: U.S. Department of Education, 1988).

10. Association of Community and Junior Colleges, *Technical & Skills Training News* (Winter 1988): 1.

11. U.S. Department of Education (n. 3), Table 119.

12. U.S. Department of Education (n. 3), Table 255.

13. Stacey et al. (n. 9).

14. U.S. Department of Education, *Digest of Education Statistics, 1985–86* (Washington, DC: National Center for Education Statistics, 1986).

15. U.S. Department of Education, *Undergraduate Financing of Postsecondary Education: A Report of the 1987 National Postsecondary Student Aid Study* (Washington, DC: National Center for Education Statistics, 1988), Table 7.3.

16. W.W. Wilms, "Proprietary Schools," *Change* (January/February 1987): 10–22.

17. L. Valore and G.E. Diehl, *The Effectiveness and Acceptance of Home Study* (Washington, DC: National Home Study Council, 1987).

18. N.P. Eurich, *Corporate Classrooms: The Learning Business* (Princeton, NJ: Princeton University Press, 1985), p. ix.

19. A. Carnavale and H. Goldstein, *Employee Training: Its Changing Role and an Analysis of New Data* (Washington, DC: American Society for Training and Development, 1985).

20. Carnavale and Goldstein (n. 19).

21. U.S. Department of Labor, *Occupational Projections and Training Data*, Bulletin 2206 (Washington, DC: Bureau of Labor Statistics, 1984).

22. I. Charner and B.S. Fraser, "Different Strokes for Different Folks: Access and Barriers to Adult Education and Training" (Paper submitted to the Congress of the United States, Office of Technology Assessment, under contract number 433-6020.0., 1986).

23. J. Shore, *The Education Fund of District Council 37: A Case Study* (Washington, DC: National Manpower Institute, 1979).

24. N. Stacey and I. Charner, "Unions and Postsecondary Education," *Education and Urban Society* (1982) 14(3).

25. Hill (n. 2).

26. Anderson et al., *The Costs and Financing of Adult Education and Training* (Lexington, MA: Lexington Books, 1982).

27. American Society for Training and Development, *Training America's Bankers* (Washington, DC: American Bankers Association, 1985).

28. U.S. Office of Personnel Management, "Employee Training in the Federal Service: Fiscal Year 1979" (Unpublished report, 1987).

29. U.S. Department of Defense, *Military Manpower Training Report for FY 1982* (Washington, DC: GPO, 1981).

30. Charner and Fraser (n. 22).

31. U.S. Department of Education, *High School and Beyond 1980 Senior Cohort Third Follow-Up (1986) Data File User's Manual*, Volume I (Washington, DC: Center for Education Statistics, 1987).

32. U.S. Department of Labor, Bureau of Labor Statistics, *How Workers Get Their Training*, Bulletin 2226 (Washington, DC: GPO, 1985).

33. These proportions do not seem to have changed much over the last two decades. See R.B. Freeman, "Occupational Training in Proprietary Schools and Technical Institutes," *Review of Economics and Statistics* (August 1974): 310–318, Table 1.

34. The proportions of college graduates who receive qualification and skill improvement training were 84 percent and 54 percent, respectively; for people with some college education, the proportions were 62 percent and 42 percent; for high school graduates and people with lower education, 42 percent and 26 percent.

35. J. Mincer and S. Polachek, "Family Investment in Human Capital: Earnings of Women," *Journal of Political Economy* (March/April 1974): S76–S108.

36. In their 1979 study, Duncan and Hoffman found a large gap between white men and women. The average number of years for white women to be fully trained and qualified in their current jobs was 0.94 year compared to 2.25 years for white men. For blacks, the gender gap was narrower, with 0.99 year for black men and 0.81 year for black women. Duncan and Hoffman's estimates were based on data from the 1976 Panel Survey of Income Distribution (PSID). G.J. Duncan and S. Hoffman, "On-the-Job Training and Earnings Differences by Race and Sex," *Review of Economics and Statistics* (November 1979): Table 2.

37. U.S. Department of Labor (n. 32), Tables 17 and 41.

38. H.W. Tan, "Private Sector Training in the United States: Who Gets It and Why" (Draft report, Rand Corporation, Santa Monica, CA, 1988), Table 5.

39. This argument is consistent with the fact the majority of students in noncollegiate schools is female. The proportions of female students in proprietary schools, private nonprofit schools, public two-year community and junior colleges, and other less-than-two-year public schools are 70 percent, 75 percent, 54 percent, and 47 percent, respectively. See C.D. Carroll, "Postsecondary Institutions Offering Vocational/Technical Programs: Analysis Findings from High School & Beyond (1980–1986)," *National Center for Education Statistics Analysis Report* (Washington, DC: OERI, September 1988), Table 2.

40. Hill (n. 2).

41. Based on Hill (n. 2), Appendices D–H.

42. U.S. Department of Labor (n. 32), Tables 1, 24, and 28.

43. U.S. Department of Labor (n. 32).

44. Based on the National Longitudinal Survey, Tan found that career women who always worked through the 12-year panel are more likely to receive training than mature men, but the prevalent source of their training is from unspecified

"other" sources. See Tan (n. 38), Table 2.1. The chance of women receiving company training is smaller than both young and mature men. Women who do not work report having received very little training. Women with low labor force attachment reported training patterns that fall somewhere in between.

45. See, for example, P. Doeringer and M. Piore, *Internal Labor Markets and Manpower Analysis* (Lexington, MA: D.C. Heath/Lexington Books, 1971).

46. Duncan and Hoffman (n. 36), pp. 594–603.

47. Tan (n. 38), p. 21.

8

Productivity in Services:
A Valid Measure
of Economic Performance?

Thomas M. Stanback, Jr., and Thierry Noyelle

The postwar era has brought an increasing role of services throughout the member countries of the Organization for Economic Cooperation and Development (OECD) at the same time that the shares of employment and output in the primary and secondary sectors have declined sharply in most nations.[1] The rising importance of services in the developed nations—especially in employment terms since the early 1970s—raises important issues regarding the nature of growth and development under modern capitalism. On the one hand, the shift to the services appears to be a manifestation of fundamental changes in the way we produce—e.g., the increasing role of producer services in the production processes of private sector firms and governmental and nonprofit institutions—and in what we produce—the rise of social (principally, health and educational services), governmental, and consumer services. On the other hand, services as a whole, though not every subsector of the services, has been characterized by lower rates of *measured* productivity growth (Table 8.1).

Several pessimistic interpretations stemming from these observed tendencies have been put forward. One interpretation, prominent in the United States, holds that a process of "de-industrialization" is underway, with losses of well-paying jobs in the declining goods-producing sector (largely manufacturing) being replaced by low-paying jobs in the growing but less productive service sectors. A variant interpretation, more widely held by Europeans, calls attention to the fact that it is in the United States, where measured productivity gains in the services have been the smallest, that the employment record has been the most favorable in recent years, indicating that employment opportunities have come from

Table 8.1   Average Annual Rates of Change in GDP per Worker in Seven OECD Countries: Agriculture, Industry, and Services, 1960–1985, 1979–1985

Country	Agriculture		Industry		Services	
	1960–85	1979–85	1960–85	1979–85	1960–85	1979–85
U.S.	3.4	4.3	1.7	2.2	0.9	0.5
Japan	4.9	3.0	6.4	4.4	4.1	1.3
Germany	5.3	3.5	3.5	1.8	2.3	1.3
France	5.5	—	4.4	—	2.2	—
United Kingdom	4.9	5.5	2.7	3.7	1.8	0.8
Italy	5.8	5.2	3.9	2.2	1.9	−0.7
Canada	3.5	2.1	2.3	1.8	1.4	0.7

Source: Organization for Economic Cooperation and Development (OECD), Historical Statistics, 1960–1985 (Paris: OECD, 1987).

either or both that country's inability to raise service productivity at rates comparable to those achieved in Europe or from inordinate growth of low productivity services.

This chapter addresses two questions relating to productivity in the services. The first concerns its measurement: Are there fundamental difficulties in the measurement of productivity that have led to underestimation of productivity gains in services? The second concerns its conceptual foundation: To what extent does the neglect of quality improvement in productivity measurement lead to a failure in recognizing the improvement of economic performance among the service sectors and the significance of their contribution? To answer these questions, this chapter looks at five issues: (1) the methods utilized in the United States to estimate productivity; (2) the productivity measurement methodologies utilized by selected OECD nations; (3) the findings of William Baumol relating to U.S. productivity trends in services and the usefulness of his model as a paradigm for understanding the role of services in late twentieth century capitalism; (4) the importance of quality improvement (not captured by productivity estimates) as a dimension in evaluating the economic performance of services; and (5) the usefulness of productivity estimates as a welfare measure.

Estimation of Productivity in Goods and Services in the United States

Measurement Methods

In a firm producing a single product of unchanging quality, productivity is readily estimated by dividing physical output by some input measure, typically labor. Preparation of productivity measures for major sectors of the U.S. economy is a much more complex task, however. The principal output series used to measure productivity is the industry deflated Gross Product Originating (GPO) estimates developed for the National Income and Product Accounts by the Bureau of Economic Analysis. They are built up from subindustry data and denominated in terms of constant value monetary units.

Input series may be single factor (typically total hours of employees) or multifactor (typically labor and capital consumption) measures. A total hours input measure is most frequently used. It is also the measure most frequently used in international comparisons. Input series and productivity series are prepared by the Bureau of Labor Statistics.

Deflated or "real" GPO may be estimated by either a process of deflation of gross output or sales (adjustments are usually made for inventory change) of component subindustries using appropriate price indices as deflators or extrapolation from a base year GPO estimate based on an input-output model (or other special studies) using some measure of either output or input as the extrapolator. An important requirement of the estimation process is that GPO be free of all purchased inputs other than factor payments (i.e., it must represent true value added).

In most instances where the deflation approach is utilized, deflated value added is obtained by a process of "double deflation" in which the gross output and total purchased inputs are deflated separately and the latter subtracted from the former. Alternatively, the output or sales figure is sometimes deflated directly (i.e., without double deflation). Where the extrapolation method is used, the extrapolator may be of several types: (1) it may make use of one or more (weighted) physical output series; (2) it may be constructed by deflating one or more (weighted) gross sales or output series; or (3) it may be improvised by use of some labor input measure as an output measure (in practice, in the United States, weighted employment, weighted labor hours, or deflated average labor compensation). This third method is used as a measure of last resort—where no acceptable physical output time series or deflation price series is available. Where such an "input" method of extrapolation is used, measured productivity gains will be zero or minimal since the numerator and denominator of the productivity estimating equation move closely together.[2]

This brief sketch of estimation procedures based on the U.S. experience makes clear that, regardless of method used, the proper measurement requires that outputs must be measurable: units of output must be identifiable and of consistent quality, and, where deflation is carried out, appropriate price information must be available.

Although both marketed goods and services vary in terms of degree of standardization, the variation is much greater for a wide range of services than for goods. For example, the services of the accountant, engineer, architect, consulting firm, and advertising agency vary from customer to customer both as regards the specification of tasks and the quality (skill, time required, etc.) of service performed. While this is true for some manufactured goods (especially custom-built products or products of industries characterized by short product life cycles, e.g., electronics), it is much less likely to be the case among goods than services: manufactured goods tend to be produced repetitively and inventoried as standardized output (although a variety of models or types may be produced); agricultural products are sold according to standard grades in the marketplace.

Accordingly, price indices are much more readily constructed for goods than for services and are likely to be of better quality. In the United States, the Bureau of Labor Statistics prepares more than 60,000 price series but these are largely for goods sold at wholesale or at retail.[3] Series are prepared, however, for selected services, including telephone, electric, insurance, hotels and other lodging, personal services, auto repair services, motion pictures, medical care, and (personal) legal services.[4]

Productivity Measurement in Services and Goods

Tables 8.2 and 8.3 together show methods used by the Bureau of Economic Analysis in estimating constant dollar GPO in the U.S. economy. Table 8.2 simply displays estimation procedures for goods, transportation, communication, electric, gas, and sanitary services along with major data sources. Table 8.3, borrowed from John Kendrick, presents the estimates of 1981 GPO for the remaining service industries and classifies each industry according to method of estimation.

The principal observation is that, for a very substantial part of the service sector—those services listed in Part B of Table 8.3—deflated output was estimated by labor input methods. These services accounted for 36 percent of GPO in the services listed in Table 8.3, and 29 percent of total service GPO (that is, including transportation, communication, and other utilities not shown in Table 8.3). As noted earlier, this method of estimating deflated GPO does not capture productivity increases in any meaningful way. Included in this group are not only the public sector and educational services but also financial services, business services, and legal services, that is, many of the sectors that have experienced the fastest rates of growth during the 1980s.

A second observation is that there is evidence that, for at least a sizable portion of the remaining service sectors shown in Tables 8.2

Table 8.2 Methods for Estimating Constant Dollar Gross Product Originating in Goods-Producing Sectors and Selected Services

Industry	Method	Major Source Data
Agriculture, forestry, and fisheries		
Farms	Double deflation	Department of Agriculture receipts, expenses, and prices
Agricultural services, forestry, and fisheries	Extrapolation	BEA persons engaged in production and Department of Commerce pounds of fish caught
Mining	Extrapolation	Federal Reserve Board index of production
Construction	Double deflation	Census Bureau, receipts, BEA expenses, and privately compiled and BLS prices
Manufacturing, except petroleum and coal products	Double deflation	Census Bureau shipments, BEA input-output composition of consumption, and BLS prices
Petroleum and coal products	Extrapolation	Department of Energy production
Transportation		
Railroad transportation	Double deflation	Privately compiled ton miles and expenses
Local and interurban passenger transit	Extrapolation	Trade association passenger miles
Trucking and warehousing	Direct deflation	Trade association dollars per ton miles
Water transportation	Extrapolation	Census Bureau ton miles
Transportation by air	Extrapolation	Department of Transportation passenger and freight ton miles
Pipelines, except natural gas	Extrapolation	Trade association ton miles
Transportation services	Extrapolation	BEA persons engaged in production
Communication		
Telephone and telegraph	Direct deflation	BLS prices weighted by Federal Communications Commission revenues and BLS average earnings
Radio and television broadcasting	Direct deflation	BLS average earnings
Electric, gas, and sanitary services	Double deflation	Department of Energy receipts and expenses and trade association prices

Source: U.S. Department of Commerce, Bureau of Economic Analysis, "GNP by Industry: Summary of Services and Methods," Survey of Current Business (April 1987): 27.

Table 8.3 Bureau of Economic Analysis Methods of Estimation of Real Gross Product Originating in Service Industries

SIC No.	Industries by Method	1981 GPO (billions of dollars)
A. Independent output estimates		1,057.3
	1. Direct price deflation of GPO:	(703.7)
50-51	Wholesale trade	212.2
65-66	Real estate	324.0
72	Personal services	16.7 B[a]
75	Automotive repairs, services, garages	19.0 B
79	Amusements and recreation, exc. movies	13.5 B
80	Health services	118.3 B
	2. Extrapolation by price-deflated revenues:	(317.9)
52-59	Retail trade	260.5
63	Insurance carriers	36.8 B
70	Hotels and other lodging places	20.6 B
	3. Extrapolation by physical volume indicators:	(35.7)
64	Insurance agents, brokers, and services[b]	15.1 B
	Federal government enterprises[b]	20.6 B
B. Base-period GPO extrapolated by labor indicators		588.2
	1. Weighted employment extrapolators:	(396.1)
	General government	
	federal	92.3 B
	state-local	207.4 B
	State and local government enterprises	16.4 B
73	Business services	71.3
76	Miscellaneous repair services	8.7 B
	2. Weighted labor hour extrapolators:	(90.9)
60	Banking	57.0 B
61	Credit agencies other than banks	3.2 B
62	Security, commodity brokers, and services	12.7 B
67	Holding companies and investment offices	0.6 B
82	Educational services	17.4 B
	3. Deflation by average labor compensation:	(101.2)
78	Motion pictures[b]	6.4 B
81	Legal services	24.1
83,86	Social services and nonprofit membership organizations	27.9 B
88	Private households	7.0 B
89	Miscellaneous professional services	35.8
Total		1,645.5

[a]"B" stands for "Baumol." See footnote 15 in this chapter.

[b]The major portion of the industry real GPO was estimated as indicated.

Source: Table 4 in J. W. Kendrick, "Outputs, Inputs and Productivity in Service Industries," Statistics About Service Industries (Washington, DC: National Academy Press, 1986), p. 69.

and 8.3, productivity measures are less meaningful than for goods. In GPO terms, the largest of these sectors is real estate, where value added includes the estimated value of the services of all buildings and dwellings (including homes) within the economy. Inclusion of value added clearly distorts productivity measurement in this service. The second largest sector is health services, an industry category in which deflation is generally regarded as susceptible to wide margins of error. Together with the services listed in Part B of Table 8.3, real estate and health represented 63 percent of 1981 service GPO as measured by Kendrick. In other words, productivity measurements were distorted (or largely meaningless, as in the case of real estate) for nearly two-thirds of the services shown in Table 8.3!

Some International Comparisons

Methods of Estimating Output

In comparing estimation methods of output among countries, it is useful to group services under two headings: *nonmarket* services, those that are produced either by nonprofit institutions or by government agencies (including public education and health authorities) and *market* services, those that are sold at a profit.[5] In a recent survey of member nations, the OECD secured information indicating methods employed in estimating output for both nonmarket and market services. Below is a comparison of methods among six leading OECD countries: the United States, Germany, France, the United Kingdom, Japan, and Canada.

In all six countries output of *nonmarket* services is estimated by an input method, using some variant of labor as an extrapolator and, accordingly, as was seen above, largely failing to capture productivity gains.[6] Two input methods are used: deflation of compensation of employees and extrapolation of value based on employment. Among the six countries, Canada, Japan, France, and Germany make use of the former method; the United States and the United Kingdom, the latter.[7] The OECD Department of Economics and Statistics does not, however, consider that the two approaches give significantly different results.

As regards *market* services there are differences in methodology which may result in differences in productivity estimates. France, Germany, Japan, and Canada make use of double deflation (an output type method) for all market services; the United States and the United Kingdom in none (Table 8.4). More importantly, the United States and the United Kingdom make use of input methods (deflated wage bill or number employed) for estimating the output of some market services, including, for the United States, financial services, business services, and private

Table 8.4 Methods Used to Obtain Value-Added at Constant Prices for Market Services

	Deflation of Current Value-Added	Double Deflation	Extrapolation of Base Year Value-Added by				
			Volume Measure Obtained by Deflation	Volume Measure Based on Physic. Quant.	Deflated Wage Bill	Numbers Employed	Other
Wholesale, retail	US	Fra Ger Jpn Can	UK	UK			
Restaurants, eating places	US	Can Jpn Fra Ger					
Hotels, other lodging		Can Jpn Fra Ger	US UK				
Transportation:							
Rail, passenger		US Can Jpn Fra Ger		UK			
Rail, freight		Can Jpn Fra Ger US			UK		
Road, passenger		Can Jpn Fra Ger	US	UK			
Road, freight		Can Jpn Fra Ger	UK	US			
Pipeline		Can Fra Ger	UK	US			
Support Services		Can Jpn Fra	UK	US			
Water, passenger		Can Jpn Fra Ger	UK	US			US

Water, freight		Can Jpn Fra Ger	UK	US			
Services, allied		Can Jpn Fra Ger	UK	UK	US		
Communications	US	Can Jpn Fra Ger		US			
Financial institutions		Can Jpn Fra Ger	UK	UK		US	
Insurance		Can Jpn Fra Ger	US UK	US			
Dwellings	US	Can Jpn Fra Ger	UK				
Other property		Can Jpn Fra Ger	US UK				
Business serv.		Can Jpn Fra Ger	US UK		US	US UK[a]	
Sanitary, similar		Ger Fra Jpn				UK	US[b]
Education		Can Jpn Fra Ger	US UK	US UK			

(continues)

Table 8.4 (Continued)

	Deflation of Current Value-Added	Double Deflation	Extrapolation of Base Year Value-Added by				
			Volume Measure Obtained by Deflation	Volume Measure Based on Physic. Quant.	Deflated Wage Bill	Numbers Employed	Other
Research, science		Jpn Ger Fra				US UK	
Medical, etc. Hospitals, clinics		Can Jpn Fra Ger	US			UK	
Doctors, dentists		Jpn Fra Ger Can	US	UK		UK	
Veterinary		Jpn Fra Ger Nor				UK	
Motion picture production, distrib.	US	Can Jpn Fra Ger		UK		US	
Radio, TV broadcasting		Can Jpn Fra Ger	UK	US			
Other recreation, cultural services		Can Jpn Fra Ger	US UK				
Repair service, NEC		Can Fra Ger	US UK			US	
Laundry, cleaning	US	Can Jpn Fra Ger	UK				
Miscellaneous pers.	US	Can Jpn Fra Ger	UK			UK	

[a]Annual adjustment for estimated increase in labor productivity.

[b]Double deflators for gas, electricity.

Source: Organization for Economic Cooperation and Development (OECD), Measurement of Value-Added at Constant Prices in Service Activities (Paris: OECD, 1987).

education and for the United Kingdom, business services and private education.

Of course, we have no way of knowing how well or how poorly the various countries are able to estimate output when output measures are employed, given the problems of collecting and deflating data faced by all. But if it is true that France, Germany, Japan, and Canada use conventional double inflation techniques, then, because of the use of input methods of estimation by the United States and the United Kingdom in some major service sectors, productivity estimates for the market sectors of these two countries are more likely to fail to capture productivity gains (i.e., productivity measures are downwardly biased) than they are in the remaining four nations.[8]

Some Additional Evidence Relating to Productivity

Table 8.5 presents estimates of output per worker, average compensation per worker, and the ratio of capital consumption to total labor compensation for the United States, Germany, and Japan covering the period 1975 to 1985, all computed from OECD data.[9] Computations were based on published deflated series for the first two measures but not the third.[10] Employment data are for full-time labor equivalents. To permit comparability among nations, the measures are presented as index numbers with 1975 set at 100.

Comparison of the 1975 and 1980 data show that growth in output per worker (O/E) was lowest in the United States in services as a whole and in each of the industry groups. Growth in the capital consumption to labor compensation ratios (K_c/L_c) for total services was also lowest in all comparisons for the United States, and K_c/L_c ratios for subgroups were in most comparisons lower than or roughly in line with K_c/L_c ratios in the other countries. Apparently, the United States was, in general, not introducing capital either more or less rapidly than the other countries. As regards the (deflated) labor compensation per worker ratios (Comp./E), gains in real wages were lower than gains in the other countries for total services and lower, or roughly equal to, gains in other countries for each of the subgroups.

To the extent that we might expect increases in the utilization of capital to increase productivity and an upgrading of the work force (reflected in higher wage levels) to increase productivity, there is no evidence in the K_c/L_c and Comp./E measures to contradict the O/E measures. All suggest relatively low growth in productivity in the services in the United States from 1975 to 1980.

Analysis of the period from 1980 to 1985, however, points to a quite different finding. Once again the gains in measured productivity (O/E)

Table 8.5   Selected Indices of Output per Employee (O/E), Compensation per Employee (Comp./E), and Capital Consumption to Labor Compensation (K_c/L_c) in the United States, Japan, and Germany, 1975, 1980, 1985[a]

	U.S.			Germany			Japan		
	1975	1980	1985	1975	1980	1985	1975	1980	1985
Goods									
O/E	100.0	106.4	125.8	100.0	114.8	126.7	100.0	125.6	154.0
Comp./E	100.0	131.0	116.3	100.0	117.6	120.6	100.0	110.3	121.5
K_c/L_c	100.0	86.4	169.4	100.0	85.2	96.5	100.0	106.1	128.3
Services									
O/E	100.0	103.0	106.8	100.0	113.3	121.3	100.0	117.7	129.3
Comp./E	100.0	105.0	110.9	100.0	108.8	106.3	100.0	108.3	115.8
K_c/L_c	100.0	94.3	130.3	100.0	108.0	129.8	100.0	107.2	129.7
Whole, ret., rest.									
O/E	100.0	101.9	109.0	100.0	104.5	114.5	100.0	140.8	149.6
Comp./E	100.0	104.8	104.2	100.0	115.9	117.7	100.0	109.8	111.7
K_c/L_c	100.0	107.7	168.4	100.0	85.1	93.1	100.0	112.9	136.1
Transp., communic.									
O/E	100.0	111.8	119.3	100.0	135.8	152.2	100.0	108.2	129.9
Comp./E	100.0	108.8	109.5	100.0	108.0	105.2	100.0	104.9	120.7
K_c/L_c	100.0	92.2	157.9	100.0	107.4	123.7	100.0	106.3	119.0
Financ., bus. svces									
O/E	100.0	96.5	90.7	100.0	117.4	124.9	100.0	114.6	129.2
Comp./E	100.0	108.5	120.7	100.0	109.6	109.7	100.0	111.4	125.7
K_c/L_c	100.0	79.7	105.3	100.0	108.9	121.8	100.0	107.2	116.5
Communic, soc., pers.									
O/E	100.0	105.8	111.8	100.0	110.7	120.8	100.0	104.4	109.2
Comp./E	100.0	111.8	121.9	100.0	112.5	114.4	100.0	118.6	129.6
K_c/L_c	100.0	99.4	146.3	100.0	137.6	186.3	100.0	68.6	86.4
Financial instit.									
O/E	100.0	103.1	101.0	100.0	125.1	126.0	—[b]	—	—
Comp./E	100.0	108.7	127.9	100.0	108.6	107.6	—	—	—
K_c/L_c	100.0	94.0	174.2	100.0	108.3	133.1	—	—	—
Insurance									
O/E	100.0	94.2	98.7	100.0	114.2	124.8	—	—	—
Comp./E	100.0	104.8	113.4	100.0	112.3	115.6	—	—	—
K_c/L_c	100.0	97.1	240.7	100.0	115.8	152.7	—	—	—
Total									
O/E	100.0		111.2	100.0		124.7	100.0		139.4
Comp./E	100.0		110.9	100.0		112.4	100.0		118.5
K_c/L_c	100.0		138.9	100.0		119.0	100.0		126.1

[a]Ratios have been expressed as index numbers, 1975=100.

[b]Not available.

Source: Compiled from data in Organization for Economic Cooperation and Development (OECD), *National Accounts, Detailed Tables, Volume II, 1973–1985* (Paris: OECD, 1987).

were lowest for the United States in total services, transportation, communication, financial, and business services although they were roughly in line with Germany and Japan in the wholesaling, retailing, and restaurant group, and in the community, social, and personal services group. But increases in K_c/L_c were greater for the United States in every comparison for total services and for all four service subgroups. Furthermore, the increase in Comp./E in total services was greater in the United States than in Germany, though slightly less than in Japan, and greatest in all comparisons in the financial and business service group, and in the community, social, and personal services group. In the wholesaling, retailing, and restaurant group there was little change in Comp./E in any of the three countries, and in the transportation-communications group the United States and Germany fared roughly the same while Japan made sharp gains.

Here, then, is evidence suggesting that at least since 1980 the United States may have led in introducing more capital-intensive technology in many of the services and may have shown a somewhat greater tendency to upgrade its work force. The poor improvement in productivity in the United States, in the face of indications of relatively favorable changes in capital consumption and relative quality of service employment, raises serious doubts as to the reliability of the productivity estimating procedures.

Doubt is particularly strong in the case where data for financial institutions and for insurance are available for analysis (these data are in comparable form only for the United States and Germany).[11] For these two classifications, both K_c/L_c and Comp./E measures moved sharply higher in the United States than in Germany, yet productivity gains were more favorable in the latter.

The Baumol Model: A Paradigm for the Service Economy?

More than two decades ago, William Baumol presented a model that examined the effect of lower rates of productivity growth in the service sector.[12] In this early model, a simplified economy was divided into two sectors, one "stagnant" and one "progressive." The former comprised service activities in which labor was the principal input, opportunities for productivity through applications of capital and technology were limited, and productivity gains, negligible. The latter comprised goods-producing activities in which increased use of capital and the application of new technology brought about continuous increases of output per worker and, accordingly, higher wages. Since higher wages tended to spread out to the "stagnant" sector, costs—and prices—in that sector would rise continuously. Thus, he argued, the service sector was inflicted with a "cost disease" that was essentially incurable. Moreover, he reasoned that the stagnant sector would progressively absorb larger shares of the economy's employment. Baumol concluded finally "that the net result would be a *ceteris paribus* decline in the economy's overall productivity growth rate."[13]

In an article published in the *American Economic Review* in 1985, Baumol and his colleagues put forth a new model with evidence from the U.S. economy to support its validity as a paradigm for modern developed economies.[14]

This new model no longer equates the services with the stagnant sector. Rather, the stagnant sector is a subsector of services, certain of the services being recognized as susceptible to productivity improvements. In addition, a third set of economic activities is introduced, labeled "asymptotically stagnant." In this sector, which makes use of inputs from both the progressive and stagnant sectors, early stages of growth may be characterized by rapid productivity gains and declining costs, but, over time, characteristics of the stagnant sector override and productivity declines set in.

In their empirical analysis, Baumol and his colleagues examine productivity performance in each goods or service classification on both a single factor and multifactor basis and classify those which can be identified as characterized by low productivity as belonging to the stagnant sector. They then compare the percentage of employed persons in the stagnant sector in 1947 with the share in 1976, as well as shares of output produced in each year.

They find that the share of employment rose significantly in the stagnant sector while the share of output did not. A third finding is that prices rose more rapidly in the stagnant sector than in the progressive sector and by a differential roughly equal to average difference in rates of employment growth. All findings are consistent with the expectations based on the model.

Analysis of the asymptotically stagnant sector is based on data relating to two activities, data processing and television broadcasting. In data processing, the progressive component is computer hardware, which has declined dramatically in cost over two decades. The segment with stagnant sector characteristics, because of its labor intensive nature, is software programming, which has increased as a source of system costs from a small percentage in the early 1970s to the dominant cost in the 1980s. In television broadcasting, the components with progressive characteristics relate to transmission, while the stagnant type elements (labor dominated) relate to programming, writing of scripts, etc. Here the findings are that technical expenses in the television industry over 20 years have remained about constant (declined as a share of total costs) while programming costs have soared.

How applicable is this model to the developmental processes of advanced economies? Is it a suitable paradigm for explaining the recent tendency of the U.S. economy with its large service sector to show a greater demand for labor?

The analysis is subject to several criticisms. The first is that a very large proportion of Baumol's stagnant sector—64 percent—is made up of subsectors in which productivity is estimated on the basis of labor inputs and, accordingly, in which productivity estimates fail to capture improved performance.[15] A second criticism relates to the price behavior of the stagnant sector. Baumol does not list the price series that demonstrates disproportionate increases in prices in his stagnant sector. It seems likely, however, that these series are *not* representative of the sector, as defined, for the very reason noted above, that 64 percent of the sector is made up of subsectors for which no representative set of prices is available, i.e., those for which output is estimated using input deflators.

It is difficult to evaluate the significance of the asymptotically stagnant industry case. One criticism, however, is that the analysis neglects the possibility of technical advance in the so-called stagnant segment. Programming is increasingly being done with the assistance of computers, and more powerful computers may well simplify the task significantly in the future. Increasing cost invites substitution of factors and new technology.

Finally, there is a criticism which is more fundamental: Baumol's model relies on conventional concepts and measures of productivity. To the extent that these measures fail to reveal improvements in economic performance due to unmeasured improvements in quality, the model is deficient—as, indeed, is most current analysis of productivity. This issue—the issue of quality—is addressed below.

Basic Weakness in Productivity as a Measure: Quality Considerations

The case for arguing that improvements in economic performance in a number of services may not be fully recognized by productivity measures rests not simply on the evidence that measurement is difficult and subject to error. There is another major weakness: Productivity measures, as conceived, largely fail to reveal the extent of improvement in the *quality* of output and thus do not measure the true contribution to economic welfare. This deficiency may be present in productivity measures for both goods-producing and service-producing industries, but there is considerable evidence that the problem is more serious for the services. Moreover, there are inherent weaknesses in measuring inputs under conditions of changing occupational composition resulting from the evolving division of labor.

A basic axiom among those who prepare official estimates is that changes in productivity measures are not meant to reflect improvements in the quality of output. Rather, they are meant to reflect changes in the output of a properly identified group of products or services per unit of input. Since quality changes are difficult, if not impossible, to measure, this position by official estimators is quite understandable: measure only that which is measurable.

In the United States, the Bureau of Labor Statistics goes to considerable expense to eliminate the quality factor. When there are significant changes in product specifications or when new products appear, the price indices are adjusted: new items are introduced; old ones, eliminated. For example, from July 1967 to January 1975, the Bureau modified 6,400 monthly price observations out of a total of 470,000.[16] As nearly as possible productivity increases represent increased output as represented by those products included in the price index per unit of labor input.

We do not argue that productivity as conventionally defined cannot be a useful measure. Where output is reasonably well standardized, changes in measured productivity indicate improved efficiency. The measure is applicable for many operations in plants and offices and may be useful for a number of aggregated industry classifications—both goods and services. But in a rapidly changing economy the unmeasured quality dimension of economic performance is likely to become increasingly important.

Several aspects of this problem are readily apparent:

1. In today's economy, firms must frequently compete through nonprice competition, and considerable resources are expended to bring about product improvement and develop new products. The productivity measures are not designed to reflect the results of these efforts—and they do not. To the contrary, *ceteris paribus,* increased labor hours devoted to successfully competing through product improvement will decrease productivity as measured since the productivity measures will pick up the increased inputs but not the resulting (quality) outputs.

2. Bringing a wider variety of products into the marketplace and marketing them requires a greater expenditure of resources per dollar of sales. Where wholesalers and retailers distribute an increasingly broad variety of goods, a simple dollar deflation is unlikely to capture the true value of services rendered by these

middlemen. Somewhat differently, where insurance carriers offer a wider variety of new and specially tailored policies to meet customers needs more adequately, sales revenues using simple base period price deflators are unlikely to reveal the true extent of service output increases.

3. The problem of defining units of service output becomes particularly difficult when intermediate services (producer services), the most rapidly growing segment of the service sector, are involved. In contrast to intermediate goods, which are typically sold to specification and thus measurable (e.g., steel sheets, automobile parts), the output of producers services (e.g., legal, engineering, advertising services) is tailored to meet the requirements of the purchasing firm. Moreover, the true productivity of the producer service firm lies often in the enhancement of the profit position of the purchasing firm through finding better, more imaginative ways to solve the customer's problems, not simply in increasing the volume of business per unit of its own resources. As firms turn increasingly to producer services for more specialized and sophisticated services, the true value of the output of supplying service firms will tend to be increasingly understated.

Thus, an important element of economic performance is likely to go unrecognized and there may even be a conflict between improving quality and improving measured productivity. The problem may be a serious one in some manufacturing sectors (e.g., electronics), but it is likely to be even more serious in a number of services.

Recent field studies in the areas of banking, insurance, accounting, universities, hospitals, city government, department stores, and telecommunications have shown this to be the case.[17] An important element in every instance has been the application of computer technology. The effect has been, on the one hand, to bring about sharp increases in productivity (in the conventional sense) where computers have reduced or even eliminated the need for labor in the performance of routine tasks, and, on the other hand, to shift emphasis to more sophisticated tasks of planning, analysis, and the rendering of services more closely tailored to the needs of customers.

Typically, the net result has not been a decline in employment but rather a shift in the nature of work, with emphasis on broader scope of responsibility, greater knowledge of the operation of the firm, and greater emphasis on the need to analyze and diagnose. Concomitantly, there has been a greater insistence on educational credentials in hiring and a greater emphasis on training.

Explaining the Growth of Services
in the United States

As noted earlier, it has been argued by some observers that the growth of services in the United States has been a shift from high productivity to low productivity sectors, and by implication, a turning to less useful activity as a process of deindustrialization takes place.

Such a view is fundamentally erroneous. The reasons for the increasing importance of services in the U.S. economy lie in the needs of its people and firms and the organizational arrangements and dynamic nature inherent in the way its capitalistic system is developing.

Several observations are useful:

1. *The effect of a large adverse trade balance in manufactured goods.* When Japan increases shipments of automobiles to the United States at the expense of U.S. firms two things happen. There is a demand for a host of services to finance, ship, warehouse, and merchandise these cars, but there is also a significant reduction in auto manufacturing in the United States, and the ratio of services to goods production is altered (there may, of course, be a reduction in the demand for services associated with auto manufacturing, but this, we would guess, is relatively small). The point is that the increased importance of imported goods may increase the demand for services relative to goods.

2. *The effect of exporting services.* There is evidence that the export of services is significantly larger than has been recognized.[18] The latest estimates of the Bureau of Economic Analysis predict a $20 billion service trade surplus for the United States in 1989 (exclusive of factor payments). If the United States has a significant comparative advantage in the production of services, then we have a partial explanation of why the U.S. service sector is large and growing.

3. *The rising demand for consumer services.* In *Services/The New Economy*, a point was made of the relatively small size of consumer services (excluding medical and educational services).[19] The case may well have been overstated or, more likely, the generalization may be less true today than in the late 1970s. The finance, insurance, and real estate and transportation sectors provide a very large volume of services to consumers as well as businesses. This is also true of some of the business services (e.g., law). The best data available to us regarding consumer services are consumption expenditure data. They show that consumption of services (deflated) grew somewhat faster (37.9 percent) from 1976 to 1986 than did

total services (35.8 percent) and considerably faster than the national product (31.4 percent).[20]

4. *The advanced development of capitalism in the United States.* Regardless of the importance of the above, it seems highly likely that the growth of services in the United States is largely associated with the fact that the national market is broader and richer and the processes of market segmentation and product differentiation more highly developed. The United States is less bound by tradition and, very probably (in spite of statistics to the contrary) more affluent or at least has a larger *share* of families at the affluent level. We are geared for a greater proliferation of goods and services—a greater array of *choices* to both consumers and businesses. This is true in education, health, charities, apparel, vacations, investment and savings plans, retirement arrangements, third-party health payment plans, and on and on.

In offering this vast array of choices we require a highly complex institutional structure and a very heavy allocation of resources to provide merchandising services, legal services, financial services, not to mention the costs of distribution, training, and institutional housekeeping. At the same time, each generation becomes more attuned to the institutional arrangements and value systems involved, and technology opens up new opportunities to move forward further along this trajectory.

The observation that the rapid growth of producer services reflects in part the way our society achieves a closer "fit" between the output of goods and services and the varied "wants" of consumers by offering them a wider range of choice is helpful in shedding light on the nature of service sector productivity.

The simple model shown in Table 8.6 suggests a possible scenario of what is taking place and points up certain implications. In the model, the United States and Europe are assumed to have identical economies in period 1 with outputs of $100 billion and employment of 10 million. In period 2, measured output (using conventional measurement procedures) has advanced to $110 billion in both economies, but employment has remained the same in Europe and increased to 11 million in the United States. Accordingly, measured output per worker has increased in Europe; remained the same in the United States. Since resource input per unit of output (i.e., labor input in this simplified case) has declined in Europe, real prices per unit of output have declined, and, conversely, real wages have increased.

On the other hand, if the population of both economies is assumed to have increased by the same amount (i.e., by 10 percent) measured

Table 8.6   A Simple Hypothetical Model Comparing U.S. and European Growth

	Period 1	Period 2	
	Europe and America	*America*	*Europe*
GDP	$100 bill.	$110 bill.	$110 bill.
NI	$100 bill.	$110 bill.	$110 bill.
No. of workers	10 mill.	11 mill.	10 mill.
Outcome			
Labor product (index)	1.0	1.0	1.1
Nature of output		increased choice	unchanged
Employment	10 mill.	11 mill.	10 mill.
Unemployment	0	0	1 mill.
Income per worker		unchanged	increased
Income per capita		unchanged	unchanged

output and income *per capita* will remain the same in both economies. The United States will, of course, have a lower level of unemployment.

The model becomes more interesting if we add a special assumption: The additional employment in the U.S. economy is associated with an expansion of producer services made necessary by a changed nature of production in which the economy has shifted to a higher level of product differentiation and the offering of a wider variety of goods (though not a larger output measured conventionally). The United States is now seen as offering a different mix of employment and goods: more "choice" and more employment; Europe, less "choice" and less employment.

It can be argued, of course, that Europe enjoys the option of stimulating its economy through monetary and fiscal policy to enable it to provide higher per capita output (old style) and equally high employment.

But such an answer may be problematic. The United States with its freer and more competitive markets may well be giving greater reign to forces of change in a modern capitalistic system that dictate that producers must increasingly compete through nonprice competition featuring product differentiation and shorter product lives if the economy is to function at high employment levels. Stimulation of the economy, without inflation, may not be an option for Europe, and the conventional measures indicating lower productivity in the United States fail to reflect the enhancement of consumer satisfaction that obtains through provision of a wider range of choice.

Recommendations for Improving Productivity and Other Social Welfare Measures

The principal conclusion from the preceding analysis is that productivity measures computed for the service sectors as a whole on the basis of estimates of GPO are fundamentally flawed, both because of measurement difficulties and conceptual considerations. Estimates for the goods sector appear to be considerably better but suffer to some degree from the same weaknesses. Our position is that in the final analysis the quality element is not measurable and that we must end up using productivity measures conceived in the conventional manner if they are to be used at all. The discussion of quality was important, however, in making clear the fallacy of using productivity measures (as currently prepared) for inter-country comparisons, to indicate limitations that must be placed on the interpretation of all productivity measures, and to provide the basis for several observations relating not only to productivity measures but to the use of social welfare measures generally.

Several observations can be made:

1. Inter-country comparisons of productivity based on a single aggregative measure are unreliable. Inclusion of government services, alone, introduces a major source of error, and there are certain "market" services, such as banking, for which no acceptable single measure can be constructed because of the absence of appropriate price deflators. It is interesting in this connection to observe that the U.S. Bureau of Labor Statistics does not see fit to publish productivity estimates for the public sector: the highest level of aggregation of published productivity measures is for the so-called "business" sector (without government, although including government enterprises). In spite of this, a total U.S. productivity estimate that includes the government sector is regularly used by the OECD for inter-country comparisons.

2. It is important to recognize that what is said regarding the limitations of country-to-country comparisons of overall productivity measures is equally applicable to comparisons of growth of national product (the numerator in the productivity equation). The United States and several other countries with very large service sectors are, of course, the economies for which growth measures are likely to be subject to the most serious underestimate because of conventional measurement practices. Accordingly, inter-country comparisons of growth in real GDP should be made only with full recognition that the measures are subject to considerable margins of error.

3. The major sector productivity estimates based on GPO should be limited to manufacturing and such other goods and service industries as can be shown to be susceptible to reasonably accurate measurement of output as conventionally conceived. A tremendous effort has been made by the United States and certain other countries over many years to develop good measures of output in

the goods sectors and these measures have been the basis for research that has shed considerable light on the role of capital, labor, and technology in increasing productivity. Such efforts should not be discontinued.

4. Greater efforts should be made to standardize measurement techniques throughout the OECD countries. This is, obviously, more easily said than done. Preparation of accurate measures is expensive, and there are budget restrictions. Moreover, the gathering of data in each country is based on well-established arrangements for reporting by companies, requirements of business censuses, and so on. A complete standardization of government statistics among nations would be, at best, a major project requiring a number of years to complete. Nevertheless, such measures as are feasible should be taken. Where lack of comparability continues to be a significant problem the source of difficulty should be flagged, not conveniently glossed over, as currently appears to be the case.

5. Greater use should be made of specially prepared productivity measures for subsectors. The U.S. Bureau of Labor Statistics has been engaged for a number of years in a program in which such productivity measures are prepared, based on total output (not value added) as estimated by carefully weighted physical indices or deflated sales.[21] At present, it publishes annually 140 such productivity estimates for 140 market goods and services, in most cases going back to 1958, and for industries largely at the detailed four-digit SIC level of classification. In addition, the Bureau of Labor Statistics prepares productivity measures for all federal government agencies with 200 or more employees, covering 28 functional areas.

These productivity measures shed considerable light on the inadequacies of the GPO-based measures. They provide impressive evidence of the wide variation of productivity among specific industries. In the manufacturing sector, among 108 industries (predominately at the four-digit level) average annual output rates of change for the period 1980 to 1985 ranged from minus 8.0 percent to 21.0 percent.

As regards the government measures, it is interesting that the overall average for the period 1967–1982 was about 1.5 percent—well above the average for the total "business" sector for the same period, using GPO-based measures (1.2 percent).[22] This indicates that the total economy productivity measure (which uses a labor input method of estimating public sector productivity with resulting measures at or near zero) was, clearly, too low. Moreover, 16 of the 28 functional areas showed productivity gains ranging from

2.0 percent to about 11.6 percent.

These detailed industry measures are based largely on physical quantities but for those industries lacking quantity data, constant value of shipments, sales, or revenue are used to develop output series. Data are carefully benchmarked. Considerable effort is made to develop representative measures in industries where output comprises diverse activities. For example, the Commercial Banking Index includes measures of checks cleared, deposit transactions, loans processed, and trust department activity.[23]

6. The absence of reliable output measures for inter-country comparisons suggests the desirability of looking at alternative measures of economic welfare especially on the input side of the economy. But here too, major problems of comparability arise.

One example is the unemployment rate. Historically, the United States has been characterized by higher labor turnover and higher unemployment rates. The higher U.S. rate, unadjusted, should not always be taken as a measure of poorer performance of its labor market. For example, under the prosperous conditions that obtained among virtually all of the OECD countries during the 1960s, the U.S. rate averaged 5.0 percent (1960–1967) while the EEC countries averaged 2.1 percent—a difference of roughly 3 percent. During the years 1980–1985, however, U.S. average unemployment increased to 8.0 percent; the EEC average to 9.4 percent.[24] Clearly, unemployment in the United States had worsened but not to the same extent as in the EEC nations. A comparison based only on the most recent period would not show this. More importantly, of course, by March 1988 unemployment rates in the United States had dropped to 5.4 percent while it remained in the 8 to 9 percent range in the EEC.

As suggested by our description of the model shown in Table 8.6, another useful comparison might include income per capita. There, too, however, problems of comparability are likely to be daunting.

As regards other measures, the capital consumption to labor compensation and compensation per employee ratios discussed above provide examples that can be usefully analyzed. But these data are available from the OECD in comparable form only for the three countries shown in Table 8.5 and remain subject to considerable debate. Additional coverage would be extremely helpful however.

Notes

1. Organization for Economic Cooperation and Development (OECD), *Historical Statistics. 1960–1985* (Paris: OECD, 1987), pp. 36–37, 58–59.

2. They need not move in lock-step, however, since the extrapolator is often, in practice, a measure of labor other than hours.

3. J.A. Mark, "Productivity Measures Developed by the Federal Government" (Washington, DC: Bureau of Labor Statistics, mimeograph, undated), p. 41.

4. Price series for these services are shown as major data services for estimating constant dollar gross product originating in "GNP by Industry: Summary of Services and Methods," *Survey of Current Business* (April 1988): 27.

5. This classification and the definitions presented are from Organization for Economic Cooperation and Development (OECD), *Measurement of Value Added at Constant Prices in Service Activities* (Paris: OECD, October 1986).

6. The estimating procedures do, however, take account of one potential source of change in labor productivity, "shifts in the skill composition of the labor force as reflected in its grade composition." OECD (n. 5), p. 10.

7. There are several exceptions: France makes use of the extrapolation method for public education; Germany, for medical, dental, other health and veterinary services, and for welfare institutions. In addition, Germany makes a special adjustment that *assumes* an annual increase in labor productivity. OECD (n. 5), p. 11.

8. In discussions with a senior economist from the French Census Bureau (Institut National des Statistiques et Etudes Economiques or INSEE), we learned, however, that while using double deflation in effect INSEE deflates some output and input series using labor deflators for lack of price series (e.g., in the case of business services).

9. All data are from Organization for Economic Cooperation and Development (OECD), *National Accounts. Volume II. 1973–1985* (Paris: OECD, 1987). In spite of efforts by the OECD to bring together comparable estimates of output, employment, and other selected relevant data it is difficult to make more than a limited analysis of the industry data published. In some instances data series are not available; in others, the OECD has found it necessary to group industries with quite different characteristics (e.g., wholesale, retail, restaurants and hotels; community, social and personal services). In one major service group (financial, insurance, real estate and business services), output estimates are badly distorted for productivity estimation by the inclusion of the imputed value of the services of all buildings and dwellings within the economy. Also, there is considerable debate as to the quality of some of these series with the German authorities arguing, for example, that the OECD's capital consumption estimates for their country are way off base.

10. To compute the third ratio, we deflated published capital consumption for a given year by the price index for gross fixed capital formation for the same year. Similarly, employee compensation for a given year was deflated by the price index for private final consumption expenditure. Organization for Economic Cooperation and Development (OECD), *National Accounts: Main Aggregates Volume I. 1960–1985* (Paris: OECD, 1987).

11. Elimination of the real estate classification gets rid of the problem of including imputed services on buildings and dwellings, a source of major distortion of output estimates. See discussion of Tables 8.2 and 8.3 earlier in the chapter.

12. W.J. Baumol, "Macroeconomics of Unbalanced Growth: The Anatomy of Urban Crisis," *American Economic Review* (June 1967).

13. W.J. Baumol et al., "Unbalanced Growth Revisited, Asymptotic Stagnancy and New Evidence," *American Economic Review* (September 1985).

14. Baumol et al. (n. 13), p. 806.

15. The estimate is based on Baumol's list of industries in the stagnant sector and the 1981 GPO estimates for service industries shown in Table 8.3. Baumol's stagnant sectors are shown with a B, like "Baumol," in Table 8.3. Baumol offers several slightly different definitions of the stagnant sector. The one used here is alternative number two based on measures of Gross Domestic Output per unit of labor.

16. Mark (n. 3), p. 41.

17. T. Noyelle, *Beyond Industrial Dualism* (Boulder, CO: Westview Press, 1987); and T.M. Stanback, Jr., *Computerization and the Transformation of Employment: Government, Hospitals and Universities* (Boulder, CO: Westview Press, 1987).

18. Office of Technology Assessment, *Trade in Services: Exports and Foreign Revenues* (Washington, DC: GPO, 1986).

19. T.M. Stanback, Jr., et al., *Services/The New Economy* (Totowa, NJ: Rowman & Allanheld, 1981).

20. J.W. Duncan, "Service Sector Diversity—A Measurement Challenge," *The Service Economy* (Washington, DC: Coalition of Service Industries, March 1988), p. 2.

21. U.S. Department of Labor, Bureau of Labor Statistics, *Productivity Measures for Selected Industries*. 1958–85, Bulletin 2277.

22. U.S. Department of Labor, *Handbook of Labor Statistics*, Bulletin 2217 (June 1985): 269.

23. U.S. Department of Labor, Bureau of Labor Statistics, *Handbook of Methods*, Chapter 14, forthcoming revised edition; and unpublished *Technical Notes* for individual sectors.

24. OECD (n. 1), p. 39.

9

Toward a New
Labor Market Segmentation

Thierry Noyelle

Advanced economies are in the midst of a major structural transformation, a transformation that is linked, in part, to the advent of the
service industries. But there is more to the current transformation than
simply growth of employment and output in the service sectors. Underlying the growth of the services are major changes in the ways in
which production is organized and work is distributed through labor
markets. As the reorganization of production proceeds, earlier labor
market arrangements are being altered, including the very processes of
segmentation specific to the postwar phase of economic development.
Elsewhere, I have dubbed this earlier period the phase of "Industrial
Dualism."[1]

This chapter identifies some of the recent dimensions of labor market
restructuring, based on an analysis of changes in the U.S. economy.
Examples are drawn from recent detailed work on a number of service
industries, including retailing, telecommunications, insurance, banking,
advertising, accounting, and other business services.[2]

The next section reviews some of the factors behind the transformation
in the demand for labor. They include increasing competition and the
introduction of new technology. The latter factors are two of the main
forces that have resulted in the trend towards "vertical disintegration"
and the rise in the demand for "contingent labor." Some of the principal
forces that have transformed the labor supply are then examined, including
growth in the pool of potential part-time workers, the rise in the number
of two wage-earner households, and the increase in educational attainment. How firms have responded to some of these forces—specifically
to the trend towards the dismantling of internal labor markets—is then
discussed. In the final section, the emergence of new labor markets

structured around segments of core and contingent workers is hypothesized. These new segments are shown to differ widely from the so-called primary and secondary labor segments characteristic of the Industrial Dualism of the postwar years.[3]

Changing Labor Demand

Increasing Competition

Of the many factors that have acted to transform the structure of markets in recent years, the most important is the intensification of competition. Growing internationalization and deregulation—two trends that gained momentum during the late 1970s and early 1980s—are usually seen as the principal causes of this renewed competition. In retrospect, however, incipient tendencies often emerged earlier, either in the identification by firms of previously underdeveloped markets or in the response by firms to the saturation of traditional markets. As firms broke away from their old markets, which were often oligopolistic in nature, new competitive situations emerged.

In the department store industry, for example, the revival of competition can be traced back to the late 1950s and early 1960s, once consumer demand had recovered fully from the war and as the trend toward suburbanization gained momentum.[4] In particular, suburbanization, by shifting the locus of demand to new locations, pried open retailing markets to new competition. Department stores—up to that point mostly downtown, local institutions with few competitors—quickly found themselves competing against each other as they saw an opportunity to branch outside their local markets. In addition, discount department stores emerged and vigorously challenged traditional department stores. Thus, even though the concentration of sales in the industry's largest firms increased during the 1960s and 1970s, competition bloomed as new markets, previously protected or largely undeveloped, opened up to competition. During the 1980s, department stores met renewed competition, this time from specialty chains.[5]

In consumer banking, inflation and a tightly regulated price structure helped spur the transformation of an increasingly saturated market in the mid- and late 1970s. As inflation rose and as the gap between the interest charged by banks and the interest paid to depositors widened, consumers began searching for ways to earn better returns on their money, which they found in mutual funds. This, and the attempt by brokerage houses, with Merrill Lynch in the lead, to link brokerage accounts to credit lines and charge cards as a means to add liquidity to individuals' investment funds, resulted in a massive shift of savings away from the banks toward investment banking institutions. Within a few years, a massive process of deregulation was unleashed and a fundamental restructuring of consumer banking markets was set in motion, with an emphasis on product diversification, cross-selling, and customization of services rather than sheer quantitative growth (i.e., finding new customers for the same, traditional banking products).[6]

Similar examples abound in other service areas. An interesting observation is that, in many instances, the resurgence of competition went hand-in-hand with continued market concentration. What disappeared were oligopolistic or regulatory barriers restricting price, product, or geographic service areas, not the need for economies of scale or economies of scope. While in certain sectors, such as air transportation, competition may again be weakening as a result of continued concentration, in most other sectors it seems reasonable to argue that the new-found competition will endure. This is likely to remain true because the increasing integration of markets on a world scale, including in the services, will most likely continue to bring new competitors.

Technological Change

Another important dimension underlying the recent transformation in the demand for labor is the advent of new information technologies, especially the latest generation of computer technologies, characterized by potentially enormous flexibility. In terms of the argument presented in this chapter, the introduction and diffusion of these new technologies have, at the minimum, two important implications. First, they hold tremendous potential not only for altering old products, but for developing new ones and transforming relationships between firms and clients. Second, the new technologies open new opportunities for reorganizing the division of labor, with a direct impact on a firm's skill structure, and, therefore, on its demand for labor.

A banking product such as the credit card could hardly have diffused as widely as it did had it not been for the development of computer technology. It is not that the bookkeeping tasks associated with the product itself could not have been carried out without computers, but simply that no bank could have ever built the clerical support organization necessary to process such a product at a reasonable cost. To a large extent, this is true of many areas of the services whose recent expansion has been built largely around computerized systems, ranging from airline reservation systems to product systems in insurance, ordering and inventory systems in retailing, and parcel tracking systems in the express air courier business. Put another way, this also means that information technologies have helped pave the way for new entrants in a number of sectors and have contributed to altering fundamentally the ways and costs of doing business.

In addition, largely thanks to the new technologies, traditional service production work is being either eliminated, or reintegrated as an adjunct to sales and service assistance work, or simply passed along to customers. Consumers can now use ATMs to process their own cash withdrawals, deposits, and transfers in the same way that merchandise buyers in department stores can process orders directly on-line. In the process, the need for back-office clerks in banks or stockroom clerks in stores is diminishing greatly. In turn, because of the demands of the new competition and because of the potentially enormous flexibility of the new systems, the pressure to expand the scope and complexity of sales and service assistance work is building considerably. In short, production workers are decreasing in number while the remaining labor force is increasingly needed either to sell, to assist customers, or to develop new products, new markets, and new strategies. The upshot is considerable upskilling and a shift toward activities that demand high levels of technical expertise. These skills often are only loosely related to a particular firm or sector (e.g., systems engineering, computer programming, telecommunications engineering, legal expertise, systems accounting, product development, marketing, advertising, and so forth).

Together, growing competition and technological change are playing a major role in bringing about the trend toward "vertical disintegration" and in fostering demand for "contingent labor."

Vertical Disintegration

Disintegration, which in actuality can be either vertical or horizontal, refers to the tendency among firms to externalize (i.e., return to the marketplace) transactions formerly carried out internally (i.e., within the firm). It can involve transactions relating either to service or goods inputs or to labor inputs. To a large extent, disintegration is a by-product of the intensification of competition, as firms find it increasingly difficult to shelter less-than-market-efficient transactions behind monopolistic rents.

While the concept of disintegration was first developed as a way to describe the breakdown of vertically integrated firms in manufacturing,[7] it has remarkable applicability to the case of the services industries. Indeed, as Christopherson and Storper have shown, the U.S. motion picture industry provides perhaps the most extreme example of disintegration.[8] From an industry that once was organized around the studio concept and in which the largest studios "owned" everyone and everything needed to make movies—including writers, producers, and actors under long-term contracts—movie-making by the studios underwent a fundamental transformation during the 1960s and 1970s as a result of growing competition from television networks and independent producers. Today, the largest studios are shadows of their former selves and act mostly as producers. The industry has been reconstructed as a project-oriented sector, with key participants working mainly for small firms or as independent contractors, with producers assembling a combination of writers, actors, technicians, equipment leasers, and other suppliers for a particular project.

Similar tendencies are found in many other service industries. Note that the trend toward disintegration need not contradict the need for scale economies and is not inconsistent with the survival of large firms, as is the case in banking, air transportation, accounting, and retailing. What is happening, however, is that the most successful large firms are increasingly those that are becoming more and more specialized. Furthermore, specialization is increasingly being achieved by focusing on market segments rather than on products, partly in response to the breakdown of the mass market. In banking, for example, the most successful firms often are found among those that have redefined their mission around a few well-defined market segments. Firms like Sears, Roebuck and Co., whose strategies continued to be based on assembling wide-ranging, highly integrated institutions offering everything from shoes and tires to life insurance and brokerage accounts, are finding it more and more difficult to operate profitably. Indeed, in banking Bertrand and Noyelle found an increasing emphasis on running operating units as profit centers, speeding the trend toward disintegration.[9] In perhaps the most extreme case, each profit center of a bank was free to purchase externally anything it needed to conduct its business, ranging from training courses to systems engineering, computer processing services, and even the funds necessary to finance the assets of the business unit. In the airline industry, so far no firm has succeeded in developing so-called synergies among air transportation, hotel accommodation, and other travel-related services. For that matter, United Airlines, the one company that took the synergy strategy farther than anyone else, was forced to divest its hotel and car rental operations after it became evident that such a strategy was a failure. By comparison, large U.S. airlines have been very successful in integrating small regional "feeder" carriers into their larger operations.

The Rise in the Demand for Contingent Labor

As noted earlier, the other dimension of disintegration is the tendency by firms to externalize labor needs, namely the increasing demand for contingent labor. Perhaps the simplest definition of contingent labor is a labor force that employers can use flexibly with respect to fluctuations in product or service demand. Contingent employment can cover situations in which employers either have an extremely weak or a relatively strong contractual attachment to contingent workers—ranging from low wages and no benefits to high wages and high benefits.

In a 1986 paper, Christopherson developed two typologies—one covering some of the principal forms taken by contingent work, the other covering some of the principal models of vertical disintegration by industry groups—which show how the use of different kinds of contingent labor varies depending on how firms in particular industry groups are being disintegrated.[10] In this chapter, it is sufficient to point to Christopherson's four principal forms of contingent labor: seasonal part-time, permanent part-time, temporary, and independent individual contracting. The first form of contingent work is the oldest of all and involves the hiring of labor to cope with levels of high-peak output. Typically, employers resort to such hiring when they have exhausted all possibilities of obtaining extra overtime work from the firm's permanent employees.

The second form of contingent work is associated with jobs that have been designed to be staffed *permanently* on a part-time basis. Peak-shifts in banking or retailing are quintessential examples of such contingent work. Typically, these permanent part-time positions are held by regular employees. In the department store industry, the use of permanent part-time employees became widespread in the early 1960s. In banks, it emerged in the late 1970s.

The third form of contingent work relates to situations in which a given firm turns to another firm to hire trained labor on a short-term basis. Temporary agencies cover the whole gamut, from secretaries to nurses to engineers. Employment via temporary agencies has grown extremely rapidly in recent years. According to the National Association of Temporary Services, approximately 1 million workers are employed as temporary workers at any one time, but more significantly, between 6 and 6.5 million people work as "temps" at some time during a given year.[11] This compares to 20,000 people employed by the temporary agency industry in 1956.

The last form of contingent work covers independent, individual contractors, that is, the growing number of self-employed, mostly professionals or paraprofessionals, who sell their expertise to individual firms, usually on a project basis.

While contingent work finds some of its roots in the transformations described thus far, it would be wrong to fail to see that changes in the labor supply also have fueled its development. In the next section, three such changes are reviewed—the growth in the supply of part-time workers, the rise in the number of two wage-earner households, and the rise in the educational attainment of the labor force—and their impact on the trend toward dismantling internal labor markets.

Changing Labor Supply

The Growing Supply of Part-Time Workers

Even though a substantial proportion of part-time employment in the United States (approximately one-fourth) represents *involuntary* part-time employment and even though a majority of part-time jobs created over the last two years or so qualifies as involuntary part-time (according to the U.S. Bureau of Labor Statistics), it would be wrong not to concede that the growth of part-time employment is partly a result of changes in the labor supply.

First, between 1965 and 1985, female participation in the U.S. labor force rose from 36.7 to 54.5 percent, when measured as a percentage of the total female working age population. This compares to far lesser gains during the previous 20 years as the labor participation rate of women grew from the low to the high 30 percentage points.[12] To a significant extent, this increase in female participation has come in the form of demand for part-time employment during childbearing and childrearing years. Likewise, the lengthening of secondary and post-secondary education has contributed to the increasing demand for part-time employment by youth. Finally, in a society in which life expectancy has risen, demand for part-time employment beyond the early or mid-sixties has grown and has potential to grow considerably in years to come. Together, these and other factors have increased the demand for part-time employment.

Not surprisingly, many instances of firms reorganizing their employment systems by introducing extensive use of permanent part-time employment can be seen as a response to the evolving structure of the labor supply. The extensive introduction of permanent part-time employment by the department store industry when it first moved to the suburbs was dictated largely by the perception that the principal, underused supply of labor in those areas was homebound housewives.[13] Likewise, work in the supermarket sector was reorganized during the 1970s and early 1980s around the introduction of short-hour shifts (four or fewer hours daily) largely to attract school-aged youth as labor.[14]

The Rise in the Number of
Two Wage-Earner Households

As the participation of women in the labor force grew, so did the number of two wage-earner households. Between 1965 and 1985, the proportion of households with two adults and with more than one wage earner grew from roughly 47 to over 70 percent.[15] In a country where social benefits are typically linked to one's job but can be extended to other members of the employee's family, the rise in the proportion of two wage-earner households introduces an important element of flexibility on the labor supply side, as an individual within a given household may be willing to trade medical and other benefits for convenience and/or cash as long as he or she is covered by the benefits of another member of the household.

Rising Educational Attainment

A third major change in the labor supply is the dramatic rise in the educational attainment of the U.S. labor force. This has come as a result of the massive postwar investment in secondary and postsecondary education. In 1985, approximately 45 percent of those between the ages of 25 and 29 had one year or more of college education. Half of those had completed a four-year college education. These numbers must be compared to those for 1965, when less than 20 percent of those in the same age bracket had some college education.

These later developments, perhaps more than any other factor, have had a powerful impact on fueling the trend toward the dismantling of internal labor markets discussed below.

The Dismantling of Internal Labor Markets

By changing the makeup of the labor supply, the rise in educational attainment has put enormous pressure on firms to adjust their hiring and employment opportunity structure to match the new availability of a labor supply increasingly differentiated by levels and types of education. Their response, for the most part, has been an increasing reliance on the external labor market where firms can now find workers at different levels of preparedness. From mostly single-entry point organizations, most firms have evolved towards multiple-entry structures, as they have discovered that they no longer need to shoulder the entire cost of skill formation through internal labor market structures.[16]

At first, this change was felt most strongly at the junior managerial and professional level as firms turned to four-year colleges to hire entry-level candidates while abandoning internal ladders that were once the access routes to these and higher level positions. Under this new arrangement, no longer can a sales clerk expect to become a buyer for a major retailer, a bank teller to become a bank officer, or a messenger to become an insurance executive simply by moving up the ranks.

In *Beyond Industrial Dualism,* I documented the dismantling of traditional internal labor markets in several sectors.[17] While this development was already in the making as far back as the 1960s, it is clear that the 1970s represented a turning point, as the impact of several decades of expansion in the educational system and the coming of age of the babyboomers were felt massively on the labor supply side. In addition, the recent growth in two-year college education provided another way to cut off the lowest skilled jobs from the middle skilled positions of paraprofessionals and technicians, while increases in the number of candidates from graduate university programs (five and six years after high school) have led to further segmentation at the top.

Beyond Industrial Dualism: Toward a New Labor Market Segmentation

The changes described in this chapter suggest a restructuring of labor markets around three major segments: core workers, skilled contingent workers, and low-skilled contingent workers. Some of the contours of these new segments and the principal differences between this emerging segmentation and that which characterized the period of Industrial Dualism are delineated and identified below.

Core Workers

While firms are attempting to minimize the number of workers to whom they are committed by increasing their reliance on contingent workers, they must, nevertheless, continue to rely on a core of workers who can develop, carry out, and communicate to others the strategic message of the organization. Increasingly, this core is shrinking to accommodate only a select group of professional and managerial workers. Alone, this group continues to enjoy mobility opportunities within the firm. Less and less does this core include the growing number of specialized professionals, whose field of expertise, while needed, is often linked only indirectly to the primary mission of the organization. More and more, these specialized professionals are being hired on a contingent basis. In banks, insurance companies, local telephone companies, retailing organizations, and other service firms, core workers are usually recruited carefully to match the special characteristics of the firm and are then placed in restricted trainee programs.[18] Others are integrated into the core on an ad hoc basis, having joined the firm originally under contingent terms.

While the intent is often to remove as many medium- or low-skilled workers as possible from the reach of the internal labor market structure, all such workers are not necessarily excluded. Indeed, in both retailing and insurance, as firms reorganize their internal labor markets, they often find it necessary to preserve a relatively stable, if small, pool of core workers in clerical and low-level supervisory positions. Short of this, high turnover may become counterproductive, with an insufficient number of workers in such positions knowing enough about the firm's way of doing things. One department store, for example, which at first had eliminated many of the low-level supervisory positions that it once used to promote employees from the sales floor to junior and middle management positions, reintroduced a few such positions in order to move a few selected sales clerks through the ranks.[19]

Skilled Contingent Workers

The skilled contingent labor market includes a wide spectrum of individuals with primarily professional or paraprofessional skills, ranging from nurses, accountants, and lawyers to systems analysts, programmers, and other computer specialists. While this segment finds its origins partly in the traditional professions and crafts—teachers, lawyers, accountants—the number and variety of this group of workers have multiplied considerably over the last two or more decades.

Workers in this segment are driven mostly by professional objectives and standards, rather than by firm-based criteria. Mobility among skilled contingent workers is achieved at least as much through lateral job-hopping and additional education and training as through moves within a given firm. This is so partly because the range of experiences that an individual must accumulate in order to develop his or her expertise is likely to be much larger than that which a single firm can offer. Turnover in jobs filled by skilled contingent workers is high, and jobs are usually offered with the understanding that the firm's commitment is short-term. In short, the role of user-firms in organizing this part of the labor market is decreasing, while the role of professional organizations, educational institutions, and professional and personnel networks is growing. Also growing is the importance of organizations whose role it is to structure the supply of such labor and interact with user-firms. Nurse registries, headhunters, and specialized temporary agencies are examples of such organizations.

Bertrand and Noyelle found that for all practical purposes, the labor market for security traders—comprising a few thousand individuals, mostly graduates of U.S. and European business schools—was becoming increasingly organized by a few large head-hunting firms that keep close track of job openings and potential candidates on a global basis.[20] In the most extreme case of job mobility, this might mean that a top-performing trader working, say, for a bank in Paris might receive a phone call from a London-based headhunter one day and find him or herself accepting a job offer in Chicago or Singapore the next day.

Within the United States, networks of skilled immigrants appear to be another means of channeling selected individuals to certain classes of jobs. For example, a growing proportion of engineers employed in the West Coast aerospace industry are East Indian or Pakistani. Likewise, there is a large inflow of Filipino and West Indian professionals in the nursing profession.

In contrast to the segment of low-skilled contingent workers described next, skilled contingent workers usually are able to maintain sufficient control over the supply of their own expertise and shelter themselves from unbridled competition. The implication, of course, is that they can exert some control over wages and benefits. Professional licensing, restricted access to educational programs, and sheer specialization are the traditional ways to enforce such control.

Low-Skilled Contingent Workers

Paralleling the growth of skilled contingent work is the further expansion of low-skilled contingent work. To a large extent, this group of workers has always existed. What is new, however, is that groups of workers which, despite their limited skills, were once part of the internal labor market are increasingly being relegated to a lower tier of the labor market. The inability of unions both to develop a strategy to respond to this weakening of status and to shelter jobs once structured as entry positions on a firm's employment ladder is important in understanding the increasingly tenuous nature of low-skilled jobs.

Consistent with this weakening of status, a growing proportion of low-skilled contingent work is structured to accommodate part-time employment. Youth, women, and low-skilled immigrants provide the bulk of its labor force.

Differences from Earlier Segmentation

The new labor market segmentation hypothesized in this chapter sharply contrasts with the segmentation characteristic of the earlier industrial period.

During the period spanning roughly from the 1920s to the 1960s, there had emerged a structural dichotomy between a core economy comprising mostly large firms and a peripheral economy dominated by small employers. Within the core economy (e.g., manufacturers of steel, automobiles, chemicals, etc.), large firms tended to operate in an oligopolistic environment, where profits and employment were sheltered from the worst possible impacts of the business cycle. By comparison, firms in the peripheral economy faced a far more volatile, competitive environment. They typically bore the brunt of the business cycle. Out of this market-based dichotomy, a particular structure of labor market segmentation had arisen. *Ceteris paribus*, workers employed by large employers in the core economy (the primary labor market) had far better prospects for long-term improvement in earnings and job mobility than those hired by firms from the peripheral economy (the secondary labor market).

The observations presented here suggest the emergence of a new labor market dynamic. Under this new dynamic, the firm's role in structuring labor markets is weakening, except perhaps for a group of core workers, many of whom are employed in professional and managerial echelons. In addition, under the new labor market dynamic, size-of-firm differences are increasingly less important in structuring labor segments. In a market environment where both small and large firms are confronted with far greater competition than in the past, fewer firms can now hide behind oligopolistic arrangements. In contrast, the very nature of skills is increasingly at the basis of segmentation, at least for the segmentation between core and skilled contingent workers. Where skills are somewhat generic and demanded by a broad array of firms, workers who can supply them increasingly are likely to be organized on a contingent basis; where skills remain highly firm-specific, their supply is likely to remain internalized among a group of core workers.

A major issue is how fast these two groups are growing relative to the third group, low-skilled contingent labor. The answer to the question lies partly in one's assessment of how rapidly computerization will eliminate many of the most menial tasks of the economy. Based on the observation that the burden of recent unemployment has fallen more heavily on the least educated, one might argue that the process of elimination of low-skilled jobs is progressing faster than our society can cope with. In other words, we no longer produce enough low-skilled jobs to satisfy large numbers of underprepared, undereducated, and underskilled workers. On the other hand, one can also argue that this mismatch is the result of the inability of our educational and training markets to respond fast enough to the new demands of the economy. Most likely both answers are correct. They both point to the fact that the process of adjustment to the new economy is far from over and is likely to produce additional aches and pains in the years to come.

Notes

1. T. Noyelle, *Beyond Industrial Dualism: Market and Job Segmentation in the New Economy* (Boulder, CO: Westview Press, 1986).

2. S. Christopherson, "The Origins of Contingent Labor Demand in Changing Production Organization" (Geography Department, University of California, Los Angeles, December 1986); S. Christopherson and M. Storper, "The City as Studio; the World as Back Lot: Vertical Disintegration in the Motion Picture Industry," *Society and Space* (September 1986); O. Bertrand and T. Noyelle, *Human Resources and Corporate Strategy: Technological Change in Banks and Insurance Companies in Five OECD Countries* (Paris: OECD Press, 1988); S. Christopherson, T. Noyelle, and B. Redfield, "Retail Sector and Contingent Labor" (Quarterly Report to the Employment and Training Administration, U.S. Department of Labor, Washington, DC, February 1989); T. Noyelle and A. Dutka, *International Trade in Business Services: Accounting, Advertising, Law and Management Consulting* (Cambridge, MA: Ballinger, 1988); Noyelle (n. 1); and T. Stanback, Chapter 6 of this volume.

3. P. Doeringer and M.J. Piore, *Internal Labor Markets and Manpower Analysis* (Lexington, MA: D.C. Health/Lexington Books, 1971).

4. B. Bluestone, P. Hanna, S. Kuhn, and L. Moore, *The Retail Revolution* (Boston, MA: Auburn House, 1981); and Noyelle (n. 1).

5. Stanback, Chapter 6 of this volume.

6. Bertrand and Noyelle (n. 2).

7. M. Piore and C. Sabel, *The Second Industrial Divide* (New York, NY: Basic Books, 1984).

8. Christopherson and Storper (n. 2); Christopherson (n. 2).

9. Bertrand and Noyelle (n. 2).

10. Christopherson (n. 2).

11. National Association of Temporary Services, *The Temporary Help Industry: Annual Update* (Washington, DC: 1989).

12. U.S. Department of Labor, Bureau of Labor Statistics, *Employment and Earnings*, various years.

13. Noyelle (n. 1).

14. T. Bailey and R. Waldinger, "The Youth Employment Problem in the World City," *Social Policy* (Summer 1985).

15. Department of Labor (n. 12), various years.

16. Noyelle (n. 1), especially Chapter 3.

17. Noyelle (n. 1).

18. Noyelle (n. 1).

19. Noyelle (n. 1), Chapter 3.

20. Bertrand and Noyelle (n. 2).

10

Conclusion

Thierry Noyelle

Current studies of growth and change in service industries remain rife with conceptual controversies, conflicting interpretations, and unexplained issues. The chapters in this book do not escape this fate, even though most, I believe, push the discussion of service-related issues at least as far as it has been pushed up to this point. In this concluding chapter, I try to review what we know about recent service growth and what remains ill-understood. Admittedly, my closing assessment remains clouded by a certain lack of conclusiveness. This may frustrate a few readers, but the fact is that the current shift to the services remains symptomatic of a much larger transformation of the postwar economic order, a transformation to a new economic order that remains too incomplete and too unsettled for many new "truths" to have had a chance to take hold.

Employment Growth and Service Productivity

The fact that the U.S. economy, like the economies of nearly every other advanced nation, has experienced a dramatic employment shift from goods to services in recent years is a largely uncontroversial fact. What remains controversial, however, is how different analysts explain this recent development.

In Chapter 8, Stanback and I explain that there are, fundamentally, two schools of thought on the issue: one that emphasizes the relationship between low productivity growth in the services and rapid employment expansion in the sector; the other that links employment growth in the sector to the growth and transformation of the demand for services, particularly as they come to play a new and far more critical role in the production process.

In Chapter 3, Appelbaum and Albin seem to espouse the low-productivity growth theory. In fairness to the authors, however, they do not investigate the issue directly themselves but rather base their determination on the work of others. While Stanback and I would agree with many of Appelbaum and Albin's findings, we indicate, in Chapter 8, that the conceptual and empirical foundation of the low-productivity growth theory of employment expansion in the services remains rather weak. This is why we put the emphasis on the second school of thought, which we view as providing a more powerful explanatory model of employment growth in the services.

Having seriously questioned the validity of service productivity measures and concepts as they are currently used, it is true that Stanback and I leave the reader with minimal leads as to how to address the issue of efficiency in the services. If I were to try and summarize our current view on this issue, I would have to state that we think the issue can only be addressed sector by sector.

The usefulness of measured productivity—assuming that issues of price deflation have been addressed either with the assistance of reliable price series or by using non-price-based measures of output—is in direct relationship to the degree of standardization and uniformity of the output of a service sector. Conversely, the greater the degree of uniqueness and customization of the output, the less useful measured productivity will be. For example, measured productivity maybe a useful concept with which to assess efficiency gains in the airline industry because of the limited scope for product differentiation and product changes both among airlines and over time, but it is proving to be a largely unworkable concept when attempting to measure efficiency gains in the health care sector. For sectors in between these two extremes, our assessment of the validity of measured productivity would lie somewhere in between: It is helpful only in so far as we are clear as to what it measures and what it fails to take into account.

One example, drawn from the preliminary findings of research currently carried out by Stanback, myself, and our French colleague Jean Gadrey may help illustrate the level at which the analysis needs to be carried out.[1] Similar conventional measures of productivity in the French and U.S. retailing industry suggest that productivity gains in that sector were roughly the same in the two countries for the period of 1978–1986 (+1.6 percent average annual gain in the United States; +2.5 percent average annual gain in France). Yet employment declined slightly in the French sector (−0.2 percent average annual loss) but grew in the United States (+2.2 percent average annual gain). Clearly, then, the growth differential in retail employment between the two countries could not be attributed to a productivity differential. What our preliminary studies suggest is that, while U.S. retailers were busy differentiating their service (adding quality to their service by deploying more employees in their stores) in order to fend off competition, French retailers were still at the stage of developing mass retailing—emphasizing scale economies and standardization of service. Consistent with this interpretation, a major share of recent productivity gains in the French retailing sector could be attributed simply to the continuing shift from traditional to modern forms of retailing (from mom-and-pop stores to multistore chains), while in the United States it had to be explained by the introduction of new computer systems, just-in-time delivery systems, and other organizational changes aimed not simply at further refining the U.S. mass merchandising system already dominant in this country but at providing the tools for greater store differentiation and deeper customer service.

One tentative conclusion then is that we must reject current, flat-footed assertions about U.S. (or other country) service productivity, and concentrate on deeper studies of this difficult issue before any new, useful formulation regarding trends can be ventured.

Wage Trends and Skill Trends

Another area of the study of services that is rife with conflict is that which relates to skill trends and wage trends. There are, actually, two dimensions along which conflicting views are expressed, but these are often combined into a single debate. The first dimension deals with the extent to which the rise of service employment has contributed to a polarization of the wage distribution in the United States; the second, with the extent to which this new wage polarization reflects an underlying skill polarization.

The debate about wage polarization is one that has occupied U.S. economists for a good part of the 1980s. Without wanting to get deeply involved with this issue here, I would have to agree with Appelbaum and Albin and conclude that, despite evidence on both sides of the debate, the weight of it leans heavily on the side of those who argue that recent employment transformations have led to a wage polarization in the United States. However, I would also contend that this development is not only the result of inordinate growth in low-paying service industries or service occupations, but also the result of a sharp intensification of labor market competition during the 1980s (weakening of unions, breaking down of traditional labor market shelters, and so on), a phenomenon that has affected both manufacturing and services and has allowed a bidding-down of wages by U.S. employers. It may be useful to note here that other advanced countries that have experienced a similarly rapid shift to the services have not necessarily experienced the same wage polarizing effect. For example, recent empirical work on wage distribution in France shows no evidence of a similar polarization in that country.[2]

The fact that wage distribution in different countries may or may not have been affected by the shift to service employment, while each may have been undergoing relatively similar skill transformation, is important in reminding us that wages are not a very good surrogate measure for skill content. This is not surprising, after all, if one considers that wages are determined by many factors, including not only skill levels, but also the degree of labor market competition, the extent of unionization and credentialing, the degree of internationalization of a sector, and yet other factors. By the same token, neither are low or high wages conclusive evidence of low or high productivity gains in a given sector.

While productivity gains are the only sound economic basis for wage increases, the existence of productivity gains does not guarantee wage increases, and wage increases can easily take place in the absence of productivity gains. The case of the U.S. airline industry during the 1980s is a classic example of a sector that experienced large productivity gains while real wages declined, a reflection of employers' ability to bid down wages during the period. Conversely, the field of nursing has seen the explosion of wages, for reasons having to do principally with labor shortages. (In fairness, no one knows for sure what has happened to productivity in nursing.) Of course, when firms raise wages in the absence of productivity gains, they must usually pass the additional costs along to consumers.

Looking beyond wages, the reality is that there is no valid, direct, quantifiable measurement index of skill content. Furthermore, occupational rankings, educational requirements, and other measures are equally as imperfect in measuring skill content as wages are. At this point, perhaps the only true measures of skill transformation are those derived from the largely qualitative and descriptive findings from industry case study research, in which researchers identify clusters of emerging new skills and clusters of disappearing old skills for various sectors of the economy to assess the requirements for training and skill preparation. Findings from most such work go in the direction of those reported for the two sector studies presented in Chapters 5 and 6 and suggest a relentless, across-the-board transformation toward new and more demanding skills.

In the end, such assessment of skill transformation need not conflict with researchers' assessment of wage trends: these two issues are largely unrelated to each other.

Skill Trends and Training Trends

Another major area of controversy involving services is the extent to which findings from case studies of firms can be generalized for an entire sector. The answer, in my opinion, is a rather simple one.

Typically firms selected for case studies tend to be "lead" firms: They are often more progressive in the introduction of new technology than their competitors, are often gaining market shares over their competitors, and, not unlikely, are performing better financially. Not surprisingly then, they often precede others in organizational innovation, new uses of human resources, new skills, and new training.

But the way in which lead firms are changing usually points to changes that other firms in the sector will likely need to undergo if they are to survive in a transforming market environment. In that sense, case studies of lead firms are extremely useful as long as we remember the limitations of their findings.

While case study work may be the most appropriate investigative tool we have to understand skill transformations, there are other means to get at the issue of training changes and training trends, particularly large-scale surveys of employers or employees. In this respect, the 1983 Department of Labor survey, *How Workers Get Their Training*,[3] on which Stacey and To report in Chapter 7, has proven to be an extremely valuable tool and deserves being repeated, despite its principal limitation: It measures only what it can measure, namely, formal training and not on-the-job training.

One critical finding from the 1985 survey, carefully noted by Stacey and To in Chapter 7, is that women and minority workers did not receive as much firm-based training as white men, at the time the survey was conducted. We are thus confronted with a twofold question: Why was it so, and is it changing for better or for worse. The answer to the "why" is usually that training investment of firms tends to focus on workers who are high on the occupational ladder, and that this discriminates against women and minority workers who tend to be concentrated at the bottom of the occupational hierarchy. Also, the argument is often heard that firms are increasingly unwilling to invest in the training of the growing numbers of contingent workers—mostly women and minority workers—further fueling this training differential. While the aggregate data may indeed support these analyses, they do conflict somewhat with what is suggested by the case studies presented in this book. Chapters 5 and 6 indicate that lead firms are expending considerable resources on the training of workers at the bottom of the occupational ladder and that they often do not differentiate their training effort between "core" and "contingent" workers. If these findings hold true, is it because "lead" firms behave differently than other firms or is it because the training practices of U.S. employers have changed during the 1980s? Clearly, more work is warranted to clarify these questions and their ramifications, for if it is the case that women and minority workers are being discriminated against in term of access to firm-based training, then there is a major EEO issue that warrants attention.

The 1990s and Beyond

A final, largely unresolved, issue is the extent of the applicability of some of the findings of this research to the 1990s and beyond. In Chapter 2, Christopherson is careful in noting a fundamental change in the underlying forces shaping U.S. labor markets, namely, the shift from an era of labor surpluses to one of labor shortages. But she is also careful in noting that the environment of intensified competition and the resulting need for greater firm flexibility are developments that are here to stay. Her conclusion: The new focus on "contingent work" is here to stay, although, in the 1990s, it may take on new forms adapted to the new labor shortage environment.

To this fundamental observation by Christopherson, I would add that the environment of labor shortages will likely put a new premium on more intensive firm-based training of all workers, since firms will no longer have the easy option of simply dipping into the labor markets to adjust their labor force anytime the need might be felt. Of course, labor shortages will give firms a special incentive to introduce additional technology as a substitute for labor. But this is unlikely to get firms off the hook since, as was suggested by the case studies, in a world of increasingly segmented markets, shorter product cycles, and growing customization, technology rarely is used purely as a substitute for labor but rather as a means to redeploy labor to handle new, more demanding and more complex tasks.

A possible overall conclusion then is that service productivity did increase in the 1980s, but that the intensification of competition made it possible for employers to hold down wages for a large number of workers. One issue for the 1990s is whether this or a different scenario might take hold. What seems sure, however, is that upward pressure on skills will remain a dominant feature of work transformation in the services during the 1990s.

Notes

1. J. Gadrey, "La Productivite du Travail dans le Commerce de Detail Français et Americain," mimeograph, 1990.

2. J. Gadrey, "Sur l'Effet d'Eponge et le Nouveau Dualisme des Services," *Cahiers Lillois d' Economie et de Sociologie*, Numero 9, 1er semestre, 1987.

3. U.S. Department of Labor, Bureau of Labor Statistics, *How Workers Get Their Training*, Bulletin 2226 (Washington, DC: GPO, 1985).

About the Contributors

Peter Albin is Professor of Economics and Director of the Center for the Study of System Structure at John Jay College, City University of New York, New York.

Eileen Appelbaum is Professor of Economics at the School of Business Administration, Temple University, Philadelphia.

Robert Bednarzik is Senior Economist in the Division of Foreign Economic Research, U.S. Department of Labor, Washington, D.C.

Susan Christopherson is Assistant Professor of City and Regional Planning, Department of City and Regional Planning, Cornell University, Ithaca, New York, and Adjunct Research Scholar, Conservation of Human Resources, Columbia University, New York.

Thierry Noyelle is Senior Research Scholar and Associate Director, Conservation of Human Resources, Columbia University, New York.

Nevzer Stacey is Senior Education Research Analyst in the Office of Research, U.S. Department of Education, Washington, D.C.

Thomas M. Stanback, Jr., is Professor Emeritus of Economics, New York University, and Senior Research Scholar, Conservation of Human Resources, Columbia University, New York.

Duc-Le To is Economist in the Office of Research, U.S. Department of Education, Washington, D.C.

Index

A&P supermarkets, 85
Abraham & Strauss, 89
  and employment of blacks, 119
  profile of, 93–97
  women in managerial positions at, 117,
    118
Accountancies
  inner turmoil in, 159(n7)
Accounting, 6–7, 122–123
  future challenges, 156–158
  labor markets in, 130, 132, 133–134
  large firms in, 129
  and other business service sectors, 128
  revenues of, 128(table)
  transformations of, 125–126
Accounting firms
  Arthur Andersen & Co., 142–146
  Coopers & Lybrand, 137–142
  eight largest, 129(table)
ACE. See American Council on Education
Adult education, 8, 160–186. See also
    Education; Educational attainment;
    Educational markets; Educational
    programs
Agricultural workers, 28(n11)
Agriculture
  self-employed in, 19
Airline industry
  and synergy strategy, 216
Albertson's, 107
Allied Stores Corporation, 94
Allstate Insurance, 146
Alumni network
  in business services, 136
American Council on Education (ACE),
    171, 176
American Telephone and Telegraph
    (AT&T), 72
Apparel specialty chains, 84. See also
    Specialty apparel stores
Apprenticeships

and educational training, 173–174
Armed Forces Correspondence Institute,
    171
Arthur Andersen & Co., 142-146, 159(n9)
  varied specializations of, 128–129
Associated Dry Goods, 97
Association for Community-Based
    Education, 176
AT&T. See American Telephone and
    Telegraph
Audit industry, 125–126

Bain, 127, 148
Banking
  consumer, 213–214
  and disintegration, 216
Baumol model
  for the service economy, 199–201
Benefit(s)
  at High's, 115, 116–117
  in retail firms, 91-92
  at Rose's Stores, 106
Blacks
  college-educated, 58
  and the racial gap in training, 180–183
  and retailing, 118, 119
  and the self-employed, 20
  in the temporary work force, 17
  in the work force, 44, 51–52
  See also Minorities; Minority workers
Body-shopping
  in computer software, 159(n12)
Boston Consulting Group, 127, 148
Britain
  and young people entering the work
    force, 25
  See also United Kingdom
Bureau of Labor Statistics
  and productivity measures, 202, 207,
    208
Business services, 5, 6–7, 122–159, 204

annual receipts of, 124(table)
college-educated labor force in, 122, 123
distribution of jobs in, 73(table)
employment growth in, 38, 124(table), 125
future challenges, 156–158
government's reporting on, 125
growth of, 122, 123
industry specializations in, 134, 135, 136
job growth in, 67, 72–74
jobs in, 75(table)
labor markets, 130, 132–134
and salesmanship, 134, 135–136
and skills, 134–136
Buyers
at Lord & Taylor, 100, 101
Buying
in the Federated Department Stores, 94
at Rose's Stores, 103, 104

Campeau organization, 94
Canada
and methods of estimating output, 193–197
Capital consumption
in the service sector, 9
Capitalism
and services, 187, 205
Case studies
of lead firms, 229
Cash 'n Carry, 107
CETA. *See* Comprehensive Employment
and Training Act
Circle K Corporation, 86
Clerical workers
in the temporary work force, 17
College campuses
retail management trainees recruited on, 96, 100, 101, 105, 115
See also Colleges
College degree
in accounting, 132, 139
and employment at Lord & Taylor, 101
and Publix Super Markets, 109
College-educated labor
in business services, 122, 123
in the U.S. labor market, 156
College-educated workers
in the information and knowledge sectors, 44–45, 64

at Information Builders, 151, 152
College education, 219
and the computer software industry, 133
and the labor force, 59
College graduates
and Coopers & Lybrand, 138, 140–141
increase in employment of, 61(table)
and retail management trainees, 91
in the services sector, 59–63
Colleges
accredited corporate, 173
four-year, 161, 164–165(table), 166–167, 169
two-year, 167, 169
See also College campuses; Community colleges
College tuition assistance
and Abraham & Strauss, 97
for management-bound retail employees, 91
for managers at Publix Super Markets, 109
at Rose's Stores, 105
Communications skills
in business services, 136
Communication training
and business services, 135
Community colleges, 167, 169
and employers, 183
Community Women's Education Project (CWEP), 176
Competition
Abraham & Strauss' view of, 94–95
in the audit market, 126
High's view of, 114
increasing, 212, 213–214
Lord & Taylor's view of, 99
Rose's Stores view of, 103
Comprehensive Employment and Training Act (CETA), 176
Computers
Decision Systems' mainframe, 154
IBM's first mainframe, 127
mainframe, 149
See also Microcomputer(s)
Computer service companies
top fifteen, 131(table)
Computer software, 6–7, 122–123, 127–128
employment held by women in, 5

estimates of employment and output in, 125
future challenges, 156–158
labor markets in, 133
large firms in, 129
revenues of, 128(table)
top fifteen companies, 131(table)
Computer software companies
Decision Systems, 153–156
Information Builders, 148–153
Computer system(s)
at Eckerd's Drug Stores, 111
in Federated Department Stores, 94
at High's, 115
and Lord & Taylor, 98, 120–121(n15)
in retail firms, 87–88, 89, 90, 93
at Rose's Stores, 104
Computer technologies
and the demand for labor, 214–215
Computer technology
and the services, 203
Consumer demand
changes in, 87
Consumer services
rising demand for, 204–205
Contingent employment
patterns of, 3–4
Contingent labor
increasing demand for, 212, 216–218
Contingent work
in the 1990s, 230
Contingent workers
and labor markets, 9–10
and labor market segmentation, 220, 221–222, 223
in the service sector, 2
and training, 229–230
Contingent work force, 11
Convenience store chain(s), 86, 114
Coopers & Lybrand accounting firm, 137–142, 158(n4)
Cornell University correspondence course(s), 105, 109
Correspondence schools, 171
Costco, 86
Cross-selling
in business services, 136
at Coopers & Lybrand, 141
Customer service
at Abraham & Strauss, 95, 97
in business services, 134–135

at Eckerd's Drug Stores, 110
at Lord & Taylor, 102
new emphasis on, 6, 90
at Publix Super Markets, 106–107, 108, 109
in retailing, 92
at Rose's Stores, 104, 105–106
CWEP. *See* Community Women's Education Project

DANTES. *See* Defense Activity for Non-Traditional Education Support
Data processing, 127, 128
and the Baumol model, 200
employment held by women in, 5
large firms in, 129
official estimates of employment and output in, 125
Dayton-Hudson Corporation, 83
Decision Systems, 153–156
Defense Activity for Non-Traditional Education Support (DANTES), 175
Defense Software Systems (DSS), 155–156
Department stores
and competition, 213
discount chains, 80–81, 83
permanent part-time employment in, 218
and specialty chains, 84
traditional, 80–81, 83
Disintegration
vertical, 212, 215–216, 217
Drug chains, 86
DSS. *See* Defense Software Systems

Earnings
in the information and knowledge sectors, 45
See also Wages
Economy
and the Baumol model, 199–201
Education, 7
community-based providers of, 176–177
employer-provided, 183
facilities, 173
institutions and participants in postsecondary, 169(table)
school-based providers of, 161–171
and training, 182
work-based providers, 172
See also Adult education

Educational attainment
in the information and knowledge
sectors, 44–45
and occupations, 54, 56
rising, 219
trends in, 56, 58–59
Educational markets
and demands of the economy, 223
Educational preparation
in computer software industry, 133
and the services, 1
Educational programs, 7–8
Educational requirements
in accounting, 132
in management consulting, 133
Educational system
and business service firms, 158
EEO. *See* Equal employment opportunity
Employee leasing, 17–18
Employees
more careful selection of, 90
See also Personnel
Employment
and the Baumol model, 200
and producer services, 206
in the services, 187–188
trends in, 34–36, 37(table), 38–41
Employment growth
in business services and retail trade,
67–79
economic and social costs of, 33–34
and income inequality, 64
and income inequity, 5
toward non-information and knowledge
service sectors, 4
in the services, 8, 9, 63, 225–227
and unions, 50
in the United States, 31
Employment security system, 26
Equal employment opportunity (EEO)
old and new policy, 2–3
Europe
employment growth in the services in,
8
employment in, 206
unemployment in, 63

Federated Allied Stores Corporation, 83
Federated Department Stores, 94
Female students
in noncollegiate schools, 185(n39)

Female workers
and business services, 157
and proprietary schools, 171
See also Women
Flexibility
of the U.S. labor market, 63
of the U.S. work force, 25–27
Flexible work, 20
and labor supply conditions, 24–25
FOCUS database software, 149, 150
Food Lion, 89, 107
Food retailing, 84–86
France
methods of estimating output, 193–197
wage distribution in, 228
French retailing sector, 226–227

Germany
methods of estimating output, 193–197
Giant Food supermarkets, 85
Government
contracts, 137
and Harbridge House, 147
temporary workers in, 16
See also Public employers
GPO. *See* Gross Product Originating
estimates
Gross domestic product, 35
distribution of, 35(table)
rates of growth of, 36(table)
Gross Product Originating (GPO)
estimates, 189, 190, 191(table), 207,
208

Harbridge House, 146–148
Health insurance, 28, 50
Health services, 41
and college graduates, 60
employment in, 22
High's, 89
and minority employment, 118
profile of, 114–117
women in managerial positions at, 117,
118
High school dropouts, 58, 59
High school graduates
and retail management trainees, 91
Hospital services
part-time jobs in, 46–47
Human resource management, 7

Human resources
  and customer service, 90
Human resources department(s)
  at Abraham & Strauss, 96
  at Eckerd's Drug Stores, 112, 113
  at Lord & Taylor, 101, 102
  in retailing, 91, 93
Hypermarkets, 85

Imported goods
  and demand for services, 204
Independent consulting
  in programming, 153
Independent consultants
  in computer software, 159(n12)
  at Decision Systems, 154–155
Independent contractors, 217
  self-employed, 11, 18–20
  in the service industry, 23
Industrialized countries
  women workers in, 27
  and work force flexibility, 25–26
Information and knowledge industry, 32
  and college graduates, 59–60
Information and knowledge
    manufacturing, 32, 34
  and employment growth, 36, 37(table),
    38, 41
  output growth rates in, 36
Information and knowledge sector(s), 5
  and labor force characteristics, 42–
    43(table), 44–52
  and occupational composition, 52–56
Information and knowledge services, 4,
    32, 33, 34, 63–64
  employment growth in, 36, 37(table), 38
  output growth rates in, 36
Information Builders, 148–153
Information technology services
  and accounting firms, 126, 128
  at Coopers & Lybrand, 137, 140, 141
Israel
  Defense Software Systems in, 155–156

Jack Eckerd's Drug Stores, 89, 91
  profile of, 110–114
Japan
  methods of estimating output, 193–197
J.C. Penney, 81, 83
Job qualification training, 161, 166
Job Training Partnership Act (JTPA), 176

JTPA. See Job Training Partnership Act

K mart
  opening hypermarkets, 85
  Rose's competition, 103
  spectacular growth of, 81
Kroger supermarket, 107

Labor costs
  non-wage, 26
  and temporary workers, 16
Labor demand
  changing, 213–218
  in services, 26–27
  structural change in, 11
Labor force
  characteristics, 41–53
  characteristics by industry, 47(table)
  characteristics by sector, 42–43(table)
  educational attainment of, 56, 58–59
  quality of, 28
  up-skilling, 1
  See also Work force
Labor market(s)
  in accounting, 130, 132
  at Arthur Andersen & Co., 143–144
  and business services, 7, 158
  college-educated, in the U.S., 156
  competition, 227, 228
  in computer software, 133
  at Coopers & Lybrand, 138–139
  dismantling of internal, 212, 219–220
  flexibility of the U.S., 63
  future transformations, 10
  groups, 3
  and large firms, 129
  of management consultancies, 138
  in management consulting, 132–133
  restructuring of, 9
Labor market segmentation, 212–223
  and contingent workers, 220, 221–222,
    223
  and core workers, 220–221
  new and earlier, 222–223
  and training, 181–182
Labor pools
  and business services, 157
Labor relations contracts, 27
Labor shortage(s), 5, 25
  and business services, 156

in the 1990s, 3, 230
and part-time workers, 14, 15
Labor supply
changing, 218–219
conditions, 24–25
in the service industry, 23
transformation of, 3
trends in, 12
LEVEL 5 database software, 149
Literacy programs, 176
Lord & Taylor, 89
and computer systems, 120–121(n15)
friendliness program, 121(n16)
profile of, 97–103
and specialty stores, 120(n13)

MacArthur Foundation, 176
Macy's, 95
Male workers
in information and knowledge sectors, 45
See also Men; White males
Management
minorities in retail, 119
Publix's record of women and minorities in, 118–119
recruitment and training of High's, 115–116
recruitment and training of Publix Super Markets', 108–109
in the retailing sector, 6
training and recruitment of Lord & Taylor's, 100–101
women in retail, 117–118
Management advisory services (MAS)
at Coopers & Lybrand, 137, 140, 141
Management consulting, 6–7, 122–123
and accountancies, 128
at Arthur Andersen & Co., 142–143
at Coopers & Lybrand, 137–138, 140
demand for, 126
future challenges, 156–158
labor markets in, 132–133
large firms in, 129
major changes in, 126–127
and MBAs, 148
revenues of, 128(table)
twenty largest firms, 130(table)
See also Managers
Management skills
at Arthur Andersen & Co., 145

and Coopers & Lybrand, 139
Management training
at Abraham & Strauss, 96–97
at Rose's Stores, 105
Managers
at Abraham & Strauss, 95–96
at Eckerd's Drug Stores, 111–113
at High's, 115
at Lord & Taylor, 99–100
"people" skills in retail, 92
at Publix Super Markets, 108
retail, 88, 91, 92–93
at Rose's Stores, 104, 105, 106
See also Management
Manufacturing
and annual output rates, 208
and business services, 21, 73
declining, 187
and employment growth, 38, 41
and information and knowledge intensity, 32
and information and knowledge sectors, 33
and information and knowledge services, 4
job growth in, 69, 70
and part-time workers, 15
and productivity estimates, 207
self-employed in, 19
and service firms, 22
shift back to, 34
MAS. *See* Management advisory services
May Department Stores Co., 83, 97, 99
Men
in institutions of higher education, 169
real mean earnings for, 24
in the self-employed work force, 19–20
in the service sector, 2
in the temporary work force, 17
and training, 185–186(n44)
in the work force, 12, 72
See also Male workers; White males
Merchandising
at Eckerd's Drug Stores, 111
at High's, 114–115
at Publix Super Markets, 107
in the retailing sector, 6
at Rose's Stores, 103, 104
in specialty chains, 84
Microcomputer(s)
advent of, 127

at Arthur Andersen & Co., 145
and Information Builders, 149, 150
and productivity, 157
Military
    training programs of, 175–176
    See also Navy
Military aerospace contractors
    and Decision Systems, 153, 154
Military consulting division
    at Harbridge House, 147
Minicomputer(s)
    advent of, 127
    and Information Builders, 149
Minorities
    in flexible work, 20
    retail employment of, 118–119, 120
    and the self-employed, 20
    and training, 8
    See also Blacks
Minority workers
    and business services, 157
    and firm-based training, 229
    and proprietary schools, 171
    in the service sector, 2
    and training, 182
    See also Blacks
Montgomery Ward, 81
Motion picture industry
    and disintegration, 215–216

National Home Study Council (NHSC),
    171
National Technological University, 173
National University Continuing Education
    Association (NUCEA), 171
Navy
    and Harbridge House, 147
    See also Military
NHSC. *See* National Home Study Council

Noncollegiate institutions
    postsecondary, 169–171
Nordstrom
    customer service, 95, 111
North Iowa Area Community College,
    167, 169
NUCEA. *See* National University
    Continuing Education Association

Occupational characteristics, 55(table)
Occupational composition, 52–56

Occupational distribution
    of employment by sector, 53(table)
OECD. *See* Organization for Economic
    Cooperation and Development
"Old boys" network
    in business services, 136, 141
Organization for Economic Cooperation
    and Development (OECD)
    and methods of estimating output, 193–
    197

Part-time employees
    at Abraham & Strauss, 96
    permanent, 217
    at Publix Super Markets, 108
Part-time employment
    at Rose's Stores, 104
    in services, 46–50
Part-time jobs, 12, 13–15
    in service industries, 44
Part-time personnel
    at Eckerd's Drug Stores, 112, 114
    turnover of retail, 90
Part-time workers, 11
    growing supply of, 212, 218
    at Lord & Taylor, 100
    in retail firms, 91
    in the service sector, 23, 46
    in the United States, 26
Part-time work force, 28(n11)
Penney's. *See* J.C. Penney
Personnel
    Abraham & Strauss' training for, 97
    recruitment and training of Lord &
        Taylor's, 101–102
    recruitment of Eckerd's Drug Stores',
        113
    recruitment of retail, 90–91, 96
    training of High's, 116
    training of Rose's Stores', 105
    See also Employees
Pharmacists
    at Eckerd's Drug Stores, 112
Pharmacy, 86
    at Eckerd's Drug Stores, 110, 111
PONSI. *See* Program on Noncollegiate
    Sponsored Instruction
Poor people
    in the United States, 33
Price's Club, 86

Production organization
in the service industry, 21–24
Productivity
and business services, 157
growth, 63
inter-country comparisons of, 207
measurement in services and goods,
190–193
measurement methods of, 188–190
and methods of estimating output, 193–
197
and the quality of output, 201–203
at Rose's Stores, 106
in services, 1, 8, 187–211, 225–227, 230
and wages, 228
Product knowledge
in apparel specialty stores, 84
and business services, 157
at Publix Super Markets, 109
in retailing, 92
training in, 6
and vendor-store cooperation, 102–103
Product training
at Abraham & Strauss, 97
at Eckerd's Drug Stores, 113
Professional associations
and education and training programs,
174–175
Programmers
and Information Builders, 151
Programming language(s), 149, 157
Program on Noncollegiate Sponsored
Instruction (PONSI), 171
Public employers
and education and training programs,
175
See also Government
Publix Super Markets, Inc., 89, 91
profile of, 106–110
and women and minority employment,
118–119

Racial mix
of the work force, 12
Ralph's Grocery Company, 85, 89
Retail firms
employment at, 22
Retail industry
employment and productivity in, 226–
227
jobs in, 77–78(table)

Retailing, 5, 80–121
Retail sector
and part-time workers, 14, 15
skills in, 6
Retail trade
and college graduates, 61
distribution of jobs in, 76(table)
job growth in, 67, 74, 76–79
jobs in, 69
part-time employment in, 46, 47, 48
Robinson Patman Act, 88
Rose's Stores, Inc., 89
and minority employment, 118
profile of, 103–106
and women in management, 117, 118

St. Charles Center for Professional
Education, 144, 145
Salesmanship
and business services, 134, 135–136
at Coopers & Lybrand, 141
and Harbridge House, 148
Sam's warehouse club, 86
Scale economies
in retailing, 83, 87, 88–89, 90, 94, 119
Scanning, 81
at Eckerd's Drug Stores, 111
at Publix Super Markets, 107
in retail stores, 88
Schnuck's Markets, 89, 91
Schools
proprietary, 169–171
See also Colleges
Sears, Roebuck, 81, 83, 216
Sears World Trade Corporation, 146
Security traders, 221–222
Self-employment
in the information and knowledge
sectors, 45–46
Self-service
in the service industry, 23, 25
Service bureaus
and Information Builders, 149–150
Service industries, 21–24, 225–231
diverse, 31
employment growth in, 63
growth of, 212
and information and knowledge
intensity, 32
and information and knowledge
services, 4

part-time workers in, 15
women in, 41, 42–43(table), 44
See also Services; Service sector(s)
Serviceman's Opportunity College (SOC),
175–176
Service-producing industries, 34
job growth in, 68, 69, 70–71(table), 72
Services
and disintegration, 215–216
export of, 204
and information and knowledge
intensive sectors, 33
inter-country comparisons of, 207
labor demand in, 26–27
and methods of estimating output, 193–
197
part-time employment in, 46–50
productivity in, 187–211
productivity measurement in, 190,
191(table), 193
See also Service industries; Service
sector(s)
Service sector(s)
capital consumption in, 9
employment, 31
transformation of, 10
See also Service industries; Services
SGV. *See* Sycip, Gorres, Velayo & Co.
Skill improvement training, 161, 166
Skill needs
of business services, 130
Skills
in business services, 134–136
and Coopers & Lybrand, 139
and Decision Systems, 155
and Harbridge House, 148
and the 1990s, 231
required by service industries, 22
in the retailing sector, 6
work-related, 160
Skill trends
in the services, 227–230
SOC. *See* Serviceman's Opportunity
College
Southland Company, 86
and High's, 114, 115, 116–117
Specialty apparel stores, 95. *See also*
Apparel specialty chains
Specialty stores, 99
and Lord & Taylor, 120(n13)
Supermarket chains, 84–85

Sycip, Gorres, Velayo & Co. (SGV), 142,
143
Systems analysts, 155
Systems integration, 127–128
at Coopers & Lybrand, 140
and outside contractors, 159(n8)
Systems integrators
and Arthur Andersen & Co., 159(n10)

Target discount department store, 81
Technologies
and the demand for labor, 214
firm-specific, 123
Technology
and business services, 158
and labor shortages, 230
transfer, 150
Teenagers
in the work force, 24, 25
See also Young workers; Youth
Telephone monopoly
breakup of, 69, 72
Television broadcasting
and the Baumol model, 200–201
Temporary help industry, 15–17, 18(table),
74
Temporary workers, 217
in the service industry, 23
Tipped occupations, 67
Trade unions
and educational training, 173–174
See also Unionization
Training
in accounting firms, 130, 132
at Arthur Andersen & Co., 144–145
community-based providers of, 176–177
and contingent workers, 229–230
at Coopers & Lybrand, 139–140
costs, 159(n9)
of employees in business service firms,
134
expertise at Harbridge House, 146, 148
female/male participation ratio,
179(table)
firm-based, 2, 7, 10, 135, 158, 229, 230
gender gap in, 177–180, 181–182
at Information Builders, 152
lifelong, 1
at Lord & Taylor, 100
qualifications, 8
racial gap in, 180–183

in the retailing sector, 6
school-based providers of, 161–171
skill-improvement, 8
by type and source and occupation,
162–163(table), 164–165(table)
work-based providers, 172
Training facilities, 173
Training markets, 160–186
and demands of the economy, 223
the trainees, 177–182
Training program(s), 7–8
at Eckerd's Drug Stores, 113
at High's, 115, 116
at Lord & Taylor, 101
new emphasis on retail, 92
at Publix Super Markets, 108, 109
in retailing, 93
at Rose's Stores, 105
Transportation
self-employment in, 19
Turnover rates, 25
at Abraham & Strauss, 96
in accounting and management
consulting, 136
at Arthur Andersen & Co., 143
at Coopers & Lybrand, 139, 141
at Eckerd's Drug Stores, 114
at Information Builders, 152
at Lord & Taylor, 100
at Publix Super Markets, 108
at Rose's Stores, 104
in skilled contingent workers, 221

Unemployment
in Europe, 63
European solutions to, 27
by sector, 45
U.S., 12, 67
worsened, 209
Unionization
in the United States, 50
See also Trade unions
United Kingdom
methods of estimating output, 193–197
See also Britain
Universities, 161, 164–165(table), 166–167
providing training, 169
satellite, 173
University of Florida School of Retailing,
113

Vendor representatives
in retail stores, 102–103
Voluntary Education Program
in the military, 175

Wages
at Abraham & Strauss, 96
in business services, 67, 75(table)
and employment growth in services,
38–39
at Lord & Taylor, 102
low-wage jobs, 34
in part-time employment, 49, 50
in the retail trade, 67, 74, 76, 77–
78(table), 79
in the service sector, 46, 64, 227–229
See also Earnings
Walgreen drug chain, 110
Wall Street
and MBAs, 148
and programmers, 151
and runaway growth, 156
Wal-Mart, 22, 88–89, 105
competitor of Eckerd's Drug Stores, 110
fastest growing retail organization, 81
opening hypermarkets, 85
Rose's competitor, 103
Warehouse clubs, 86
West Germany
and young people entering the work
force, 25
White-collar work
rising importance of, 87
White males
in flexible work, 20
in the work force, 1
See also Male workers; Men
Winn Dixie supermarket, 107
Women
in business service jobs, 74
college-educated, 58
employed at Lord & Taylor, 98
and firm-based training, 229
in flexible work, 20
and the gender gap in training, 177–
180, 181–182, 185(n36)
increased employment of, 114
in information and knowledge sectors,
45, 56
in institutions of higher education, 169
in the labor force, 3, 12, 218, 219

in the part-time work force, 14
in the retail sector, 5, 79, 117–118, 119
in the self-employed work force, 19–20
in the service industries, 41, 42–
  43(table), 44
in the service sector, 2
in the temporary work force, 17
and training, 8, 185–186(n44)
workers in the U.S. vs. other
  industrialized countries, 27
in the work force, 21, 24, 51, 72, 87
See also Female workers
Work
emerging patterns of, 11–28
flexible forms of, 20
Workers
discouraged, 12
Work force
companies trying to upgrade their, 119–
  120
costs of a flexible, 27–28
flexibility of the U.S., 25–27
leased employee, 17–18
men in, 12, 72

part-time, 11, 13–15, 28(n11)
self-employed, 18–20
strategies for an effective, 90–91
temporary, 15–17, 18(table)
white male workers in, 1
women in, 21, 24, 51, 72, 87
See also Labor force
Work hours
year-to-year variation in, 13
Work time
distribution of, 13
redistribution of, 11
Workweeks
longer and shorter, 13

Young workers
in service industries, 44
See also Teenagers
Youth
in flexible work, 20
labor supply, 3
in the part-time work force, 14, 218
in retailing, 80, 120(n1)
See also Teenagers

SKILLS, WAGES, AND PRODUCTIVITY IN THE SERVICE SECTOR

edited by Thierry Noyelle

Increasing competition, the rapid diffusion of new technologies, and the rise of the services have all contributed to profound changes in the nature of work, the demand for skills, and the structure of U.S. labor markets over the past decade or more. In this book, eight labor market economists and educational analysts take an in-depth look at the ongoing transformation of work in the service sector and the implications this transformation has for the education and training of U.S. workers.

Analyzing both macro-level labor market and educational data and case studies of firms in retail and business services, the contributors argue that despite the disproportionate growth of low-wage employment in the services, considerable evidence exists that skills, including those of many low-paid workers, are being upgraded throughout the sector.

The contributors also argue that current evidence contradicts the view that the U.S. service sector fell behind in productivity during the 1980s. A possible overall conclusion is that while productivity and skills rose steadily throughout the 1980s, increasing competition was used by companies—with substantial success—as a reason to hold wages down. The issue for the 1990s is whether this or a different scenario will take hold; what seems sure, however, is that emphasis on improving skills will remain a dominant feature of work transformation in the services during the 1990s.

Thierry Noyelle is senior research scholar at Conservation of Human Resources, Columbia University. He is editor of *New York's Financial Markets: The Challenges of Globalization* (Westview, 1988) and *Beyond Industrial Dualism: Market and Job Segmentation in the New Economy* (Westview, 1987) and coeditor, with Eli Ginzberg and Thomas M. Stanback, Jr., of *Technology and Employment: Concepts and Clarifications* (Westview, 1986).

For order and other information, please write to:

e • Boulder, Colorado 80301

ISBN 0-8133-1078-4